THE BOOK OF SURVIVAL TO THRIVAL

CREATED BY

MULTI #1 INTERNATIONAL BESTSELLING AUTHOR & AWARD WINNING SPEAKER

ERIK SWANSON

.

THE BOOK OF

SURVIVAL
TO THRIVAL

FORGIVENESS

ERIK SWANSON

50 AMAZING STORIES OF TRIUMPH

ALSO FEATURING CELEBRITIES

COLT REID, GREG S. REID,
REX SIKES, & JON KOVACH JR.

Orders by U.S. trade bookstores and wholesalers.

Email: *Team@IntegrityPub.com*

Manufactured and printed in the United States of America and distributed globally by Integrity Publishing International.

Paperback ISBN: 978-1-964330-39-6

Hardback ISBN: 978-1-964330-40-2

www.IntegrityPub.com

Global Speakers Mastermind & Habitude Warrior Masterminds

Join us and become a member of our tribe! Our Global Speakers Mastermind is a virtual group of amazing thinkers and leaders who meet twice a month. Sessions are designed to be 'to the point' and focused while sharing fantastic techniques to grow your mindset as well as your pocketbooks. We also include famous guest speaker spots for our private Masterclasses. We also designate certain sessions for our members to mastermind with each other & and counsel on the topics discussed in our previous Masterclasses. It's time for you to join a tribe who truly cares about **YOU** and your future and start surrounding yourself with the famous leaders and mentors of our time. It is time for you to up-level your life, businesses, and relationships.

For more information to check out our Masterminds:
Team@HabitudeWarrior.com
www.DecideToBeAwesome.com

BECOME AN INTERNATIONAL
#1 BESTSELLING AUTHOR & SPEAKER

Habitude Warrior International has been highlighting award-winning Speakers and #1 Bestselling Authors for over 25 years. They know what it takes to become #1 in your field and how to get the best exposure around the world. If you have ever considered giving yourself the GIFT of becoming a well-known Speaker and a fantastically well known #1 Best-Selling Author, then you should email their team right away to find out more information in how you can become involved. They have the best of the best when it comes to resources in achieving the bestselling status in your particular field. Start surrounding yourself with the N.Y. Times Bestsellers of our time and start seeing your dreams become reality!

For more information to become a #1 Bestselling Author & Speaker on our Habitude Warrior Conferences Please text the word AUTHORS to 619-304-6268 And also go to: www.DecideToBeAwesome.com

FORGIVENESS

CONTENTS

FORGIVENESS

INTRODUCTION

THE BOOK OF SURVIVAL TO THRIVAL

A TRANSFORMATIONAL SERIES ON
RISING ABOVE & THRIVING

The Book of Survival to Thrival is a transformative book series designed to help you achieve personal breakthroughs and empower the human spirit through real stories of grit, growth, and grace.

Each of us may experience trials in life. Some come suddenly and shake our world, while others may quietly wear some of us down over time. But there is a defining choice in every challenge: we can merely survive—or we can rise and thrive.

This series was created by Erik Swanson and was born from that choice to thrive. Through the voices of courageous contributing co-authors in each volume, *The Book of Survival to Thrival* invites you into the most personal moments of pain, truth, resilience, and victory. These are not just stories—they are blueprints for transformation. You'll learn how people just like you made the decision to grow instead of break, to forgive instead of stay bitter, and to persevere instead of give up.

With each volume, we explore a core human quality required to go from surviving life… to thriving in it.

VOLUME 1 ~ COURAGE

Courage is the first step in the journey from survival to thrival. It's a steady resolve to rise, even when fear, pain, or uncertainty threatens to hold us down. In this powerful first volume, **courage** sets the tone for everything that follows. The authors in this book didn't wait for fear to disappear. They stepped into their battles while still trembling. They moved forward while still doubting. They showed us that real courage isn't reserved for heroes—**it's a choice that everyday people make in extraordinary moments.**

This collection of stories invites you into the deeply personal turning points of people who dared to face what tried to break them. These stories are not just inspiration—they are activation. You'll discover how courage looks different for everyone:

- For some, it was choosing forgiveness over resentment.
- For others, it was starting over with nothing but faith.
- For many, it was showing up for others when they could barely show up for themselves.

You'll also uncover patterns: that courage is a habit, built one small brave step at a time. It grows stronger through adversity. Let this volume be your reminder: You don't have to be fearless to be brave. You don't have to have it all together to take the next step. You just have to **decide**—to try, to rise, to keep going.

VOLUME 2 ~ FORGIVENESS

Forgiveness is highly misunderstood, yet the most transformative force in the human experience. Many believe it's about excusing wrongdoing, forgetting betrayal, or minimizing the damage done. But in reality, **forgiveness is not about the past—it's about your future**. It's about releasing yourself from the chains of bitterness, resentment, guilt, or shame that keep you stuck in survival mode.

In this second volume, our authors pull back the curtain on what it really means to forgive—and how that decision can radically change your life. Through real-life stories of heartbreak, betrayal, self-blame, and deep emotional wounds, you'll witness the rawness of the human spirit and the courage it takes to move forward. These stories are deeply personal accounts of people who had every reason to stay angry, to hold on, to let their pain define them. And yet, they chose healing, growth, and **freedom**.

Our authors reveal that **forgiveness is not a one-time event** but a process—a practice—a path to reclaiming peace and restoring personal power. **Forgiveness is one of the boldest acts of strength you will ever make**. It is the turning point where survival ends and thriving begins. It's how you stop carrying what was never meant to define you and start living in alignment with who you're becoming. You don't need permission to forgive. You don't need the apology. You just need the willingness to take one step toward healing. Allow our authors to help guide you in the blissfulness of forgiveness.

VOLUME 3 ~ PERSEVERANCE

Getting started is brave. Finishing is bold. But the space in between—the messy, painful, uncertain middle—that's where **perseverance** lives. And that's where most people give up.

In this third volume, we explore what it truly takes to **keep going**. This volume is a tribute to the quiet, relentless spirit that refuses to quit.

Our co-authors know what it's like to feel stuck, exhausted, or even defeated. But they also know what it's like to keep showing up, one small step at a time, until breakthroughs happen. Perseverance is not just for athletes or entrepreneurs or the "strong-willed." It's a human skill we all need to develop to thrive in today's world. And it's more available than you think.

This volume isn't about pushing through blindly. It's about pressing forward **with clarity, compassion, and conviction**— even when no one sees you trying. It's about staying true to your values when shortcuts are tempting. It's about embracing the process, not just the outcome. Let these stories renew your strength. Let them remind you that you are not alone, and that even in the silence of your struggle, something powerful is being built inside you.

You don't have to have it all figured out. You just have to keep going. Because perseverance is how thrival becomes your reality.

A NOTE FROM OUR SERIES CREATOR
ERIK SWANSON

This series is more than a collection of stories. It's a movement.

I created *The Book of Survival to Thrival* to share with the world that our hardest moments can become our greatest turning points. Whether you're in the middle of a storm or reflecting on past pains, these stories will meet you where you are and walk with you to where you want to be. Shoutout to Eric D. Jackson for the conversations that sparked the creation of the stories you are about to embark on.

Let these stories lift you. Let them heal you. Let them remind you that thriving is your birthright—and the journey starts with one courageous step.

"NDSO!"

No Drama, Serve Others!
With strength, grace, and perseverance,
~ Erik Swanson, Integrity Publishing International

ERIK SWANSON

THE POWER OF FORGIVENESS AS YOUR FREEDOM CODE

There's a moment in every human life when the world seems to pause... sometimes violently. A moment when everything you thought you knew gets challenged. A moment when life walks up, taps you on the shoulder, and says, "Hey, you—it's time." Time for what? Time to evolve. Time to rise. Time to transition from merely surviving... to fully thriving.

This book and series are about that moment. And that moment can change your life forever!

It's about the bridge—the emotional, spiritual, vibrational bridge—between the version of you who claws through life just to get by... and the version of you who steps boldly, confidently, awesomely into a world of purpose, power, and peace.

And the key to that bridge?

Forgiveness!

Forgiveness isn't weakness. Forgiveness isn't letting someone "off the hook." Forgiveness is an energetic technology—one of the most powerful forms of personal liberation ever engineered. It's what frees you from carrying the experiences that wounded your past into the destiny you are meant to walk into.

Forgiveness is the upgrade.

Forgiveness is the shift.

Forgiveness is the frequency.

Let's walk through this frequency together—from Survival to Thrival—and unlock the real power that has been waiting inside you.

THE SURVIVAL STATE: WHERE MOST PEOPLE LIVE WITHOUT KNOWING IT

I've met thousands of people in my career—entrepreneurs, leaders, parents, students, CEOs, New York Times #1 bestsellers, retirees—and there's one universal truth:

Most people live in survival mode longer than they need to.

Now, survival mode isn't always a dramatic battle for life. Sometimes, survival mode is subtle. It's the quiet fear that keeps you from taking a step. It's the memory of a past hurt that influences your present decisions. It's the voice inside that whispers, "Be careful. Don't get hurt again. Play small. Don't risk it. Don't speak up. Don't trust. Don't believe."

Survival mode is energy-conserving. It's protective. It's a biological gift in times of danger—but a spiritual prison when carried into your everyday life.

Think of it like this:

If your internal operating system runs on fear, shame, resentment, or anger, then no matter how hard you hustle or how many goals you write down, you're trying to build a masterpiece on a shaky foundation. That's why so many people feel stuck even when they're doing "all the right things."

Survival mode isn't your fault. It's a learned pattern. A conditioned response. A leftover emotional reflex from moments in your past that left a mark.

But here's the truth:

You don't break free from survival mode through force.

You break free through forgiveness. I want to say that again because it's one of my Habitude Warrior foundational truths…

You break free through *FORGIVENESS*!

THE WEIGHT YOU DIDN'T REALIZE YOU WERE CARRYING

Over the past few years, I've gotten into hiking and love it! There's a story I've shared from our Habitude Warrior Speaker Hearts stages around the world—a story about a hiker who decides to climb a mountain. Halfway up, he notices his backpack feels heavier. Then heavier. Then impossibly heavy. When he finally drops the pack and opens it, he discovers that every time he experienced a negative thought, memory, or emotion... he subconsciously picked up a rock and put it inside the bag.

Anger? Rock.

Resentment? Rock.

Betrayal? Rock.

Regret? Boulder.

And forgiveness?

Forgiveness is the moment he realizes:

"I don't have to carry this anymore."

The astonishing thing about life is how cleverly we learn to function while carrying emotional weight. We adapt. We compensate. We get used to it. Until one day, something breaks down—our health, relationships, joy, creativity, drive—and we wonder what went wrong.

What went wrong is simple:

We were never meant to carry what forgiveness was designed to release.

The moment you let go, you reclaim energy that has been tied up in the past… and redirect it into your future.

HABITUDE WARRIOR FREQUENCY SHIFT: WHY FORGIVENESS IS MORE THAN AN EMOTIONAL ACT

Let me share a truth that every high achiever eventually learns:

Energy is your real currency.

Not time. Not money. Not opportunity.

Energy.

You can have all the time in the world, but no energy? You're stuck.

You can have all the money in the world, but no energy? You're lost.

You can have massive opportunity, but no energy? You're overwhelmed.

Forgiveness is one of the highest-energy-generating tools known to the human nervous system.

When you forgive, here's what happens on a vibrational level:

- Your emotional frequency rises from constrained to expansive.

- Your mind shifts from threat-detection to possibility-creation.

- Your spirit detaches from old patterns and opens to new timelines.

- Your physiology transitions from cortisol-driven survival to serotonin-rich thriving.

Forgiveness is energetic alchemy.

It transforms the frequency of your past so it no longer sabotages your future.

This is why, in the world of personal development, every breakthrough—whether in confidence, leadership, relationships, or purpose—includes some form of forgiveness work.

Because you can't pour new wine into an old vessel.

You can't play a symphony on an instrument that's out of tune.

You can't build a skyscraper on a shaky emotional foundation…

And you can't become a true Habitude Warrior unless you accept and adopt the act of forgiveness in your life!

Forgiveness tunes you.

Forgiveness strengthens you. Forgiveness frees you.

MY "AIRPORT LESSON" THE MOMENT THAT CHANGED EVERYTHING

Years ago, I was in an airport, racing to a flight to a speaking engagement to share the stage again with my mentor, Brian Tracy—a flight that I was definitely, absolutely, 100% not going to make. You know that moment—when you're running with one shoe untied, your coffee is sloshing like a storm at sea, and the gate agent is already shaking her head before you even reach the counter?

Yep. That moment.

Well, I missed the flight. And in that same moment, a man next to me lost his calm and started yelling at the gate agent. I mean, full crazy-mode meltdown. And this poor agent was standing there, doing her best, dealing with the storm.

Now here's the twist.

As I'm watching this unfold, I feel my own frustration rising. My stories start shouting in my head:

"That's the last flight today."

"This ruins the whole event."

"Why didn't they delay the plane?"

"This is going to cost money, time, everything!"

But then—like a quiet whisper from the universe—something inside me says:

"Erik, breathe. Forgive the moment. Forgive yourself. Forgive the situation."

That's it. Nothing fancy. Just a shift.

So, I do it. Right there. In front of Gate 27B. I take one deep breath and decide:

I forgive the situation.

I forgive the inconvenience.

I forgive myself for not being perfect. I forgive the universe for the detour.

And I swear to you—instantly—my energy changed.

And here's the wild part:

The moment my energy shifted, my perspective shifted. And when my perspective shifted, opportunities appeared.

Within minutes, the gate agent— the same one who had just been yelled at—looked at me with relief in her eyes because I wasn't adding to the chaos. She said, "Sir... give me a moment... I think I can help you."

And she did.

She put me on a different connecting flight, and I arrived at my event only ten minutes later than I would have.

Now, was this all because forgiveness magically changes airport schedules?

No.

It was because forgiveness changes **you**, and when *you* change, the world responds differently.

Forgiveness is not just an emotional gift—it's a strategic advantage.

MY THREE LEVELS OF FORGIVENESS—AND WHY MOST PEOPLE ONLY DO LEVEL ONE

Most people think forgiveness is a simple "I forgive you."

Nope. That's like thinking climbing Mount Everest means taking one step.

Forgiveness works in three levels:

Level One: Forgiving Others

This is the one everyone talks about.

Forgiving the friend who hurt you, the boss who overlooked you, the partner who disappointed you, the stranger who wronged you.

This level is powerful—but incomplete in my eyes.

Level Two: Forgiving Yourself

This is the level most people avoid because it requires facing your past decisions with compassion rather than criticism.

It means forgiving yourself for:

* Staying too long.
* Leaving too soon.
* Not knowing what you didn't know.
* Believing someone else's opinion of you.
* Silencing your voice.
* Accepting less than you deserved.

- Hurting others when you were in pain.

Self-forgiveness is emotional medicine. It removes the hidden debris inside your heart so you can breathe again.

Level Three: Forgiving The Circumstance Itself

This is the frequency most people never reach—and yet it's the one that changes everything.

It's the moment you say:

"I forgive the circumstance for not being what I expected."

"I forgive the timing, the setbacks, the detours."

"I forgive the circumstance for the lessons that hurt."

"I forgive this particular circumstance."

This level is where survivors become thrivers.

Because once you stop resisting life… you start co-creating with it.

THRIVAL:
THE STATE WHERE YOUR NEW IDENTITY IS BORN

Thrival isn't a place you visit.

Thrival is a frequency you become.

Thrival is when your energy no longer reacts—it leads.
When your past no longer defines you—it refines you.

When your heart no longer protects itself, it expands itself.
When your vision no longer hides, it ignites.

Thrival is where your true identity emerges—your aligned, powerful, authentic identity.

And here's the real gold:

Thrival is not the opposite of struggle.

Thrival is the mastery of struggle.

When you thrive, challenges become classrooms.

Obstacles become opportunities.

Triggers become teachers. Setbacks become setups.

Forgiveness is what clears the runway.

Thrival is what allows you to take flight.

MY THRIVAL FORMULA—A DAILY PRACTICE

To move from survival to thrival, here's a simple but powerful practice you can use every day.

1. Center — 60 Seconds

Close your eyes. Breathe deep.

Tell your nervous system: "We're safe. We're here. We've got this."

2. Identify — 60 Seconds

Ask yourself:

"What memory, person, or emotion am I still carrying?"

Don't judge. Just notice.

3. Release — 90 Seconds

Say the words:

"I forgive you."

"I forgive me."

"I forgive this moment." "I release it."

This is energetic alchemy.

Your frequency recalibrates instantly.

4. Reframe — 60 Seconds

Ask:

"What lesson did this experience give me that I can now use to thrive?"

This transforms pain into wisdom.

5. Activate — 60 Seconds

Declare:

"I am stepping into my next level of awesomeness today."

This sets your entire system—mind, heart, energy—into thrival mode.

Five minutes a day.

And your life changes.

YOUR FUTURE SELF IS ALREADY THANKING YOU

Imagine your highest, most awesome, most empowered future self standing across from you right now.

Imagine them looking at you with pride. Imagine them saying:

"Thank you.

Thank you for letting go.

Thank you for choosing peace.

Thank you for releasing the weight.

Thank you for forgiving what happened.

Thank you for healing the wounds you didn't cause. Thank you for stepping into the life we were meant to live."

Forgiveness isn't for the person who hurt you.

Forgiveness is for the person you're becoming.

Forgiveness is for the future you.

THE FINAL TRUTH: SURVIVAL CREATED YOU; THRIVAL UNLEASHED YOU

Here's the final truth I want you to take to heart!

You didn't go through what you went through to break.

You went through it to awaken.

Survival shaped your strength.

Survival sharpened your instincts. Survival sculpted your resilience.
But thrival...

Thrival awakens your purpose.

Thrival unlocks your gifts.

Thrival elevates your frequency.

Thrival allows you to serve, inspire, lead, and transform.

Forgiveness is the bridge.

Forgiveness is the code.

Forgiveness is the permission you've been waiting to give yourself.

And when you give yourself that permission?

You become unstoppable.

You become unshakable.

You become **AWESOME**—not because of what you've been through, but because of what you've chosen after everything you've been through.

You are not here to survive.

You are here to shine.
To serve.

To elevate.

To embody your highest frequency.

You are here to **THRIVE!**

And it all begins with the courage—the power—the decision—
to forgive.

Let's go.

Let's rise.

Let's step boldly and beautifully into your next level of
awesomeness.

"NDSO!" No Drama - Serve Others!

~ Erik Mr Awesome Swanson ~

ERIK SWANSON

As an Award-Winning International Keynote Speaker and Multi-Time #1 International Bestselling Author, Erik Swanson is in great demand around the world! He speaks to an average of more than one million people per year. Mr. Swanson has the honor of having been invited to speak to many schools around the world, including the prestigious Harvard University. He is also a recurring faculty member of CEO Space International and an alumnus keynote speaker at Vistage Executive Coaching.

Mr. Swanson is also the recipient of the 2024 International Book Impact Award and the United States Presidential Lifetime Achievement Award presented by the White House in 2024 for his ongoing community service and philanthropy work. Erik's speeches can be found on Amazon Prime TV, as well as on TED Talks, where he has contributed his speeches titled, "A Dose of Awesome" and "NDSO ~ No Drama, Serve Others."

Erik got his start in the self-development world by mentoring directly under Brian Tracy. Quickly climbing to become the top trainer around the world from a group of over 250 handpicked coaches, Erik started to surround himself with the best of the best and very quickly started to be invited to speak on stages alongside such greats as Jim Rohn, Bob Proctor, Les Brown, Sharon Lechter, Jack Canfield, Lisa Nichols, and Joe Dispenza —just to name a few.

Erik has created and developed the super-popular Habitude Warrior Conferences and Speaker Hearts Mastermind & Retreats, which have a two-year waiting list and feature thirty-three top-named speakers from around the world. They are "TED Talk" style events which have quickly climbed to the top ten events not to miss in the United States! He is the creator, founder, and CEO of the Habitude Warrior Mastermind, Global Speakers Mastermind, and Cafe Mastermind. He is also the creator and publisher of many book series, such as *The 13 Steps To Riches* book series, as well as *The Principles of David & Goliath* book series. His motto is clear: "NDSO!" No Drama – Serve Others!

www.SpeakerErikSwanson.com

COLT REID & GREG S. REID

LIFE'S BLESSINGS & RESETS

- -

A beautiful conversation of realizations, struggles, and lessons learned by a teen and his father, Colt and Greg Reid.

~ COLT'S PERSPECTIVE ~

BEFORE THE STORM

Basically, I wake up around 1 PM. I sleep in a lot.

I grab my phone and text a few of my buddies to come over. We all just ride bikes, do wheelies down the road. It's so fun.

Then we invite like forty kids over to my house. We order Cane's, Handel's ice cream, all that. Forty kids with forty bikes —rolling around my neighborhood.

That was normal for us.

My days consisted of riding bikes, hanging out with friends, and being happy. Life was amazing. I had that same kind of day a hundred times. Nothing could go wrong because nothing ever had.

THE ACCIDENT THAT "I REMEMBERED"

When I first came out of the hospital, I had this whole image—like a video—of the crash in my head.

In my mind, I was at a stoplight, waiting for it to turn green. A car came from behind me and hit me. I went into a coma. I thought I remembered it all. I can still see that image today.

But that's not actually what happened.

They told me I'd been on my motorized dirt bike, heading back to my house. A black Ford Explorer was making a left turn into a neighborhood, following another vehicle. That driver thought the way was clear. I was there, and I went right into the car.

It was a one-in-a-million accident. Even with a high-end full-face helmet, the impact was severe enough to crack it. I was airlifted to Rady Children's Hospital and put into an induced coma.

The version in my head and the version in real life were two different stories. The doctors and my parents had to keep reminding me: This is what actually happened!

The truth is, I don't remember the day of the crash at all. It's just blank.

~ GREG'S PERSPECTIVE ~

A FATHER'S FEELING

I was sitting at home in the living room, talking to a friend, when I got *that* feeling—something only a parent can really understand.

I started to have a strange feeling about where my son, Colt, was and whether he was okay. I checked Colt's GPS location on my phone. He wasn't moving.

I called him. No answer. Called again. No answer. A third time. Still nothing. That wasn't like him.

A couple of minutes later, I refreshed the GPS location tracker, and he was suddenly on the freeway traveling about eighty miles an hour.

I turned to my friend and said, "Let's go!"

No socks. No shoes. No wallet. I just jumped in the car and started driving, following that little GPS dot to find my son.

I pulled up to a park, and there were more police cars and fire trucks than I could count.

"Are you Colt's dad?" they asked.

"Yes!"

They told me he'd hit the side of a car on his E-bike and had been airlifted. He was so close to the fire station—one block away—that the paramedics were on the scene almost immediately. A doctor out walking his dog got there about thirty seconds after the crash. A nurse from the biggest ER in the area pulled up ninety seconds after that.

Together, they stabilized my son. When the paramedics arrived, those two professionals told them exactly what to do. The paramedics followed their lead.

If they hadn't gotten there when they did to assist, Colt probably wouldn't have made it.

I don't believe that's a coincidence. That's synergy. That's relationship capital and divine timing all colliding at one intersection, one block from a fire station, with a doctor and a nurse walking right into our lives at the exact moment we needed them.

THE CRITICAL DAYS

At the hospital, they told us the truth straight away. Colt had suffered a traumatic brain injury. He was put into an induced coma.

They didn't have a bright prognosis. Stating, the best case was that it might be two years before he could speak, and it was extremely unlikely that he would live a life without caretaking assistance.

I sold my stocks. I sold my Rolls-Royce. I traded in my sports car and bought a soccer-mom car I could lift my kid into. We got a giant dumpster, and I threw everything away. I had no idea what my life was going to look like, but I knew one thing: my son was going to get every ounce of my focus.

My former wife, Allyn—Colt's mom—never left his side. Twenty-four hours a day, she was there. She wouldn't leave to take a shower. She watched every doctor, every nurse, every time they touched our son. She studied what they were doing.

For clarity, I want to say this: **the hospital saved our son's life.**

Then we added something else.

Through our friends and community, we brought in extra modalities—red light therapy, alternative approaches, and ideas we were connected to through years of relationships. One of our Habitude Warrior connections sent us a red-light cap. We put it on Colt's head in the hospital. Other people shared methods and treatments. Some we used, some we didn't.

Allyn became the orchestrator. I'd say, "Colt's got this." She'd say, "Let's do it." Someone else would offer something, and she'd say, "Let's not." She was the conductor of this whole healing symphony.

The hospital saved our son's life. The extra modalities we applied brought him back to life.

~ COLT'S PERSPECTIVE ~

NEUROSTORMING & COMING BACK

After the coma, I went into what they called a vegetative state.

The part nobody planned for was what came next— neurostorming. My brain was rebooting and refiring. I screamed at the top of my lungs. I kicked. I thrashed. I could have hurt myself.

They had to lock me into a medical bed that looked like a cage, just so I wouldn't injure myself.

My mom stayed there and learned the language of my screams. She figured out which yell meant I needed the bathroom, which shout meant I was in pain, and which one meant something else. For my mom, it was like having an infant again, but this time the infant was a full-sized teenager.

Meanwhile, a friend posted online asking people to rally around us. He wrote that I'd been "involved in a serious accident while returning from a dirt bike ride on the back trails of Carlsbad," that I'd suffered "a traumatic brain injury after colliding with a vehicle," and that the next eighteen months would be crucial for my rehabilitation and healing.

He was right.

People started sharing my story. They shared pictures of me in the ICU, my cracked helmet, and old photos from before the crash. They said things like, "Colt is a fighter," and they were right about that, too.

FORGIVENESS IS THE WAY

One of life's beautiful lessons is forgiveness. We all have people and things we can forgive. I chose to forgive the SUV with which I had an accident. I chose to forgive the driver of the SUV. I chose to forgive the universe for allowing this to happen. I chose not to complain, but to forgive.

CONFIDENCE IS THE SECRET

At the hospital and rehab, everyone kept reminding me of something I'd said before all this ever happened:

"Confidence is the secret."

I believed that as a kid, riding with my friends every weekend. After the accident, I had to believe it on a whole new level.

My mantra became:

My name is Colt
I am powerful
I am brave
I am worthy
I am wise

I am successful
I help people
My name is Colt

Those words were on repeat in my head. People prayed. They sent messages. They showed up. All that confidence and belief around me—and in me—helped pull me forward when I couldn't remember the day that changed everything.

~ GREG'S PERSPECTIVE ~

A COMMUNITY OF MIRACLES

The miracles kept stacking.

Colt was at Rady Children's Hospital in San Diego, and later we learned that the rehab center on his floor—the place he walked into every day to relearn how to walk and talk—had a name on the wall:

Donated by John and Maria Assaraf.

John and Maria have been friends of ours for years. We had no idea until the day we were checking out of the hospital and took a picture. My son received his healing at a center created by people we love.

Another dear friend wrote about our journey and thanked Dr. Chris Giza, the pediatric neurologist from UCLA, who joined Colt's case. He discussed our "unified loving community," spiritually enlightened, consistent, applied effort, and how that kind of collective courage and focus is exactly what our world needs.

He was right, too.

From Secret Knock to Habitude Warrior to long-time friends from San Diego, people prayed as one community. They sent messages, meals, and money. They reminded us of our own philosophies when we were too tired to remember them ourselves.

Sometimes in life, you never know when your relationship capital is going to pay a dividend you can't measure. This was one of those times.

~ COLT'S PERSPECTIVE ~

GOING FOR MY GOALS

Before the accident, I wanted this ebike more than anything.

The one I crashed on was worth around $5,000. I was eleven years old.

My parents didn't just hand it to me. They said, "What are you good at?"

I told them I was connected. I could make social media videos. I knew people.

They introduced me to Garth, the guy who runs America Hat Makers—the number one hat-selling business in the United States. We made a deal: if I brought him twenty models to do photo shoots with his hats, he'd give me $2,500. My dad agreed to cover the other half of the cost of the bike.

So, I went to work. I found the models, set up the shoots, and completed the work.

That's why you'd see me at events in San Diego with a bunch of kids all wearing hats. Now you know the backstory.

Working for that bike taught me something big: **work for what you want** and be grateful when you get it. I used to have everything kind of given to me. My parents had to teach me gratitude. That lesson helped me a lot with everything that came later.

~ GREG'S PERSPECTIVE ~

WORK YOUR STRENGTHS, HIRE YOUR WEAKNESSES

I learned a lesson about parenting and money right around that time.

I was on a podcast and mentioned that I paid Colt to do tasks around the house—mow the lawn and make his bed. The host stopped me. She said, "You're training your child that the only way to make money is to do something he doesn't like."

I'm a student first, so I listened.

I sat Colt down and asked, "What are you good at? What are your strong suits?"

He said, "I'm connected. I can make videos. I know people. You've opened a bunch of doors. How can I benefit from that?"

That's how we got to the hat company deal. He got paid to work on his strengths, not his weaknesses.

Later, after the 2020 pandemic, we held our first party back at the house. I said, "Go upstairs. Do me a favor. Make your bed, clean your room. We call that contribution back to the family for living this lifestyle."

Twenty minutes later, one of his friends came downstairs with a handful of money and asked his dad to put it in the bank.

"Where'd you get that?" I asked.

"From your son, Colt," he said. "He paid me to make his bed and clean his room."

I yelled, "Colt, get down here! Why would you give him money to do the stuff I asked you to do?"

And Colt said, "Dad, you taught me—and I've heard you say it from the stage—you work your strengths, and you hire your weaknesses. I had other things to be doing."

That's when it really hit me: our kids are listening to every single thing we say. They're not just hearing the speeches; they're watching whether our actions line up with our words.

~ COLT'S PERSPECTIVE ~

CONTROLLING MY EMOTIONS

People keep asking me what it felt like to wake up and realize the story in my head wasn't what actually happened.

I'm actually really good at controlling my emotions. I'm good at accepting what happened and just stepping into it and just living with it.

Some of that comes from my parents, and some of it comes from what I'd already been through. I'd been through breakups. I'd already felt heartbreak, disappointment, and getting back up again.

When I woke up from the coma and started understanding, "You got hit by a car. You've been in a coma. You've been in a vegetative state," I didn't spend a lot of time on "Why me?"

I focused on, *Okay. This happened. What now?*

~ GREG'S PERSPECTIVE ~

RESPECT YOUR KIDS

We've always treated Colt like a person, not just "the kid." Colt is Colt.

You hear clichés like, "You learn more about life from your kids." For us, that's not a cliché. It's real. We pay attention to our words and our actions because we know he's watching to see whether they match.

During this whole journey, we kept our family promise: if the Reid boys say something and give our word, we do it. It doesn't matter what it is. If we commit, we have to do it. The end.

That promise kept me going when the prognosis was brutal. It kept Colt going as he relearned how to walk and talk. It kept his mother, Allyn, by his side when he was screaming through neurostorming, and she was the only one who could translate what he needed.

~ COLT'S PERSPECTIVE ~

FINDING PURPOSE AFTER THE RESET

I've been through a pandemic. I've been through a brain injury. I've been through all these injuries at thirteen—at twelve.

If I can do it, anyone can.

Ever since I've been back out in the world, my philosophy is simple: **give it your all.** I'd give anything just to give everything my all.

I've noticed something big: living life without a purpose is pretty boring, honestly.

Before, I loved riding bikes with my friends. I still do. I've started riding dirt again, carefully, getting my sea legs back. But we're not going on the streets any time soon. I'm a good rider. It's the cars you've got to watch out for, and my reaction time has to be one hundred percent.

Now I also think differently about my influence. I've had videos get crazy views online. I've had attention. But after everything I've been through, it's not just about bikes anymore.

I want to help people.

My mantra says it: *I help people. My name is Colt.*

If telling my story helps someone else find their purpose, control their emotions, or get back up after their own accident —whatever that looks like—then this reset I was given at twelve is going to mean something bigger than a crash on a bike. In fact, the crash on the bike could be a vehicle for my success in helping people around the world.

~ GREG'S PERSPECTIVE ~

THRIVING, NOT JUST SURVIVING

One of our annual events, Secret Knock, was scheduled to take place while Colt was still in critical condition. People asked if I was going to cancel.

But remember our rule: when the Reid boys give our word, we keep it.

So, I kept moving forward with the event while living at the hospital and near Allyn's place, so we could take care of Colt as a family. That decision put me in rooms with people who had ideas, connections, and modalities that helped my son. If I'd shut it all down, we might never have met some of them.

That's the thing about thriving. Surviving is doing whatever it takes to make it through the night. Thriving is looking for purpose in the middle of it.

Sixty days after doctors gave us a worst-case scenario with no precedent, Colt walked out of the hospital shaking everyone's hands.

He laughs spontaneously now. He rides again. He's back to having friends over and eating all my food. The difference is, now he knows life can turn in a second—and he's choosing to live with purpose.

OUR MESSAGE TO YOU

Sometimes in life, we're given a reset. **Mine just happened to come at age twelve.**

We wouldn't wish what our family went through on anyone. But we love the person it's helped Colt become and the community it revealed around us.

If you're reading this as a teenager or young adult, here's what we want you to know:

You are more powerful and brave than you think.

You can learn to control your emotions and accept what happened without letting it define you.

You can find a purpose that makes life more than just video games or scrolling.

If you're reading this as a parent:

- Your kids are listening. Every word. Every story. Every talk in the car.

- They're watching whether your actions match what you say.

- The relationship capital you build today may become the miracle you need tomorrow.

From a cracked helmet on the back trails of Carlsbad to walking out of the hospital sixty days later, our story is simple:

Don't just survive your hardest moments. Use them as your reset. Find your purpose. Give it your all, and remember to always give yourself grace and forgive yourself and others through the process.

COLT REID

Colt Reid is an award-winning young actor, model, musician, and speaker based in California. A rising star on screen and online, he is best known to his 70,000+ Instagram followers and growing TikTok audience as **@coltareid**, where he shares his day-to-day life, behind-the-scenes moments, and his journey from Survival to Thrival. He is also an Amazon bestselling spoken-word contributor.

Colt's film and television credits include the series *Purple Case* (as Johnny), *Secret of Happiness*—for which he received a Best Actor award—*Wake Up and Crush It*, *Wish Man*, and appearances on *Teens Wanna Know*, commercials, and online projects. A former student at The Treehouse Academy, Colt loves both drama and comedy and continues to train his craft while working steadily in front of the camera.

Away from set, Colt is a true multi-hyphenate. He plays piano and drums, enjoys soccer, football, and tennis, and has training in archery and Filipino martial arts (Kali/Eskrima). An avid electric dirt-bike rider, Colt survived a life-altering accident in 2023 that resulted in a traumatic brain injury and sparked the global **#PrayForColt** movement. Thanks to his medical team, alternative healing modalities, and an outpouring of community support, he made an unprecedented recovery—going from hospital bed back to the classroom in just six months.

Today, Colt shares his story and his mantra—"My name is Colt. I am powerful. I am brave. I am worthy. I am wise. I am successful. I help people"—from stages such as **Secret Knock**, on podcasts including **Millionaires to Billionaires** and **Hustle & Flowchart**, and across his social platforms. A "boy with many hobbies" and an even bigger heart, Colt continues to build his career in film, television, and digital media while inspiring other young people to find their purpose and give life their all.

www.ColtAReid.com

GREG S. REID

For over twenty-five years, Greg has inspired millions of people to take personal responsibility and step into their potential. As such, his life of contribution has been recognized by government leaders, a foreign Princess, and luminaries in education, business, and industry.

Mr. Reid has been published in over 100 books, including 33 bestsellers in 45 languages. Titles include *Stickability: The Power of Perseverance, The Millionaire Mentor,* and *Three Feet from Gold: Turn Your Obstacles into Opportunities,* which have inspired countless readers to understand that the most valuable lessons we learn are also the easiest ones to apply.

Greg Reid is known best for being Founder of Secret Knock, a *Forbes* and *Inc.* magazine top-rated event focused on partnership, networking, and business development.

He is the producer of the Oscar-qualified film, *Wish Man*, based on the creator of the Make A Wish Foundation, which streamed globally on Netflix.

For his work mentoring youth in his hometown of San Diego, Mr. Reid was honored by the White House, where a former President commended Greg for his positive work with youth through a local mentorship program.

And if that is not enough, recently, Greg was honored with the star of the infamous Las Vegas Walk of Stars.

www.GregReid.com

REX SIKES

THE GREATEST FREEDOM

· ·

HOW TO TRULY FORGIVE, LET GO, & CHOOSE TO BE HAPPY

You're carrying around a forty-pound rock. You didn't mean to pick it up. You never wanted it. But you've been dragging it around for years, maybe for decades, telling yourself, "I've forgiven them, but I'll never forget."

Sound familiar? That rock is resentment. That weight is your past. And you carry it because no one ever taught you how to truly release it. It's not your fault, but it is your choice to set it down.

Forgiveness is misunderstood. We tend to think of it as something noble but optional, something we *should* do, but often don't know *how*. Worse, we think it's something we do for someone else, as if offering forgiveness somehow lets them off the hook. That's where we go wrong. Forgiveness isn't about letting them off the hook. It's about taking ourselves off it.

Forgiveness is freedom. And freedom is the path to happiness. Let me tell you what changed my life.

I used to live under the weight of grudges. I know what it's like to wake up with heaviness in your chest because of what someone did, or what you think they did. I've had friends betray me. Family members wound me. Strangers cause harm without a second thought. I've replayed those moments in my mind like a broken record, hoping that if I thought about it enough, it would make sense. Or hurt less. Or maybe give me some control.

But it never did. All it did was prolong my suffering. Then something shifted. I began to look at forgiveness differently, not as an act of moral superiority, but as a practical, powerful tool for healing.

I thought about Jesus.

Now, whether you believe in the historical Jesus or see him as a symbol of compassion and transcendence doesn't matter. This is not about religion. It's about liberation.

Jesus, in the most excruciating moment of his life, nailed to a cross, mocked, betrayed, and dying, said, "Father, forgive them, for they know not what they do."

He didn't demand justice. He didn't seek revenge. He didn't say, "Forgive them, but don't let them off easy." He didn't carry a grudge into the afterlife. He let go. Completely. Why?

Because forgiveness is not about them. It's about you.

That realization wrecked me in the best possible way. I saw that holding onto pain is like drinking poison and expecting the other person to die. Forgiveness, then, is the antidote. It is the release valve for the pressure cooker of pain. And it's something we must choose, repeatedly.

So, I began to practice. Not just once. Not just when it was easy. But daily. Hourly. With strangers. With my past. With myself. I whispered it in traffic: "Forgive them." I said it after tense phone calls: "Forgive me." I thought it during moments of self-doubt: "I release this."

Little by little, the weight lifted. It didn't happen all at once. It was more like sunrise than lightning, soft, gradual, but undeniable.

And that's when I realized the truth: **happiness isn't something you find. It's something you choose.** Forgiveness isn't weakness. It's the strongest thing you can do. And letting go doesn't mean forgetting; it means freeing yourself to live fully.

Letting go gave me my life back. This is the work I do now. In my trainings, workshops, and coaching programs for more than 4 decades.

I don't just teach theory. I guide people through the actual process of transformation. I help people release their pain and gently, lovingly become free.

You don't need to suffer any longer. You don't need to be at the mercy of your past. I've seen people heal decades of pain in just a few hours. I've watched people reclaim joy, rebuild relationships, and discover new purpose. Not because someone else changed, but because *they* did. They made the courageous choice to release the rock.

Here's the secret: You don't need an apology to forgive. You don't need justice, closure, or explanation. You just need willingness. Willingness to feel. Willingness to let go. Willingness to be free.

I've worked with people from every walk of life: high-powered executives, trauma survivors, spiritual seekers, skeptics, veterans, stay-at-home parents, and teenagers. I've seen people come in hardened, cynical, shut down, and leave glowing, laughing, at peace. Not because I gave them anything, but because I showed them how to unlock what was already inside them.

You don't have to change your whole life to start this work. You just must change your next thought. What would your life look like if you forgave?

Imagine waking up tomorrow without bitterness. Imagine looking in the mirror and seeing someone you respect. Imagine starting your day with calm rather than chaos. What would it feel like to be free?

That's what's possible. That's what's waiting for you.

Now let me be clear: forgiveness is not about pretending that bad things didn't happen. It's not about denying injustice or tolerating abuse. It's not a get-out-of-jail-free card for toxic behavior. Rather, it's about reclaiming your power. When you forgive, you say: "You may have hurt me, but you don't get to control me anymore. I'm taking my peace back."

You choose happiness, not because life is perfect, but because you are worthy of joy.

One of the most profound things Jesus said on the cross was, *"Why have you forsaken me?"* In that moment, he wasn't speaking as some divine, all-powerful figure. He was human. He was alone in pain, stripped of power, abandoned by friends and followers. And yet, he forgave. That, my friend, is power. That is strength. He forgave not because he was divine but because he was completely human.

He accepted his fate. *"Not my will, but yours."* No struggle. No resistance. Just acceptance. He didn't fight what was. He surrendered to it. Think about that. He didn't beg to escape. He didn't retaliate. He didn't blame. He chose love. He chose peace. He chose to forgive. That's the ultimate model for us.

Now contrast that with how we tend to operate. We resist. We fight. We hope someone or something will swoop in and fix it for us. But here's the very powerful truth: circumstances don't have to change for you to be free. *You* must change. Your power isn't in controlling the outer world. It's in mastering your inner one.

You may want someone to leave your life. You may wish a situation would go away. But they don't. And wishing, hoping, even begging doesn't always change a thing. So, what's the smarter move? Resist and suffer, or release and soar?

Acceptance isn't weakness. It's freedom. It's realizing that if things won't change, then *you* can. You don't have to let anything steal your peace. You can smile anyway. You can move on anyway. You can thrive anyway.

Is that easy? Perhaps not. Is it possible? Absolutely. Forgiveness, letting go, choosing happiness, these aren't magical gifts handed out to the lucky few. They're decisions. Disciplines. Practices. And the more you do them, the stronger and freer you become. The more you do them, the easier they become. The easier they become, the more you are inclined to do them. You create momentum, and your life changes.

Look around. Some people live in the worst conditions and still manage to smile, laugh, love, and inspire. Others have fame, wealth, and luxury, and they're miserable. Why? Because happiness isn't out there. It's inside. It's a mindset. A choice. A commitment.

I can hope, pray, fight, and resist forever that a particular person leave me alone, and I may never get what I seek. That may never happen. That person or unwanted circumstance may persist.

Things are as they are. The people around us may never change no matter how we hope and pray. The circumstances may never get any better. So, what can you do? Fight forever. Live with the stress. Be dismayed, unhappy, and miserable, or you can accept that's how it is, it will never change, so why let it affect your happiness? If it is going to go on, no matter what, why be unhappy about it? Why not accept it, allow it, and go about your life anyway, choosing to be happy rather than distressed? It is YOUR choice, after all.

If you never begin to take charge of yourself and make your life what you want it to be, it will always be as it has been. If others and circumstances dictate how you think, feel, and behave, and what you possess, you will be a victim, not a victor.

There are people from everyday walks of life who have learned how to be happy. These people manage to inspire themselves and others. We should choose these as examples to emulate, if we choose any examples at all to follow.

Every day, every moment, you're presented with a decision: repeat the past or release it. Dwell in bitterness or rise in joy. Blame others or empower yourself. You decide whether you live from your wounds or from your wisdom.

Don't wait for perfect circumstances to be happy. Choose happiness now. Don't wait to be forgiven. *Forgive yourself first.* Then extend that forgiveness to others. Not for their sake, but for yours. Let it go. Drop the burden. Free yourself. Learn the lesson and forget the experience.

You may think it's impossible, but it's not. I speak from experience. I began to think better thoughts. I chose gratitude. I focused on what I wanted more of, not what I lacked. I started looking for the silver linings and stopped feeding the storm.

And guess what? Life changed. Not because the world around me changed, but because *I did.*

This is your life. You get to write the story. So why not write a good one? Why not flood it with love, light, forgiveness, and joy? If you persistently practice loving-kindness, forgiveness, and celebration, especially when it's hardest, you create a reserve of power you can draw from when you need it most.

The moment you choose forgiveness, you set yourself free. The moment you choose happiness, you begin to truly live. Choose to thrive. Choose to rise. Choose to love anyway.

Happiness comes from within us. It is how we think and respond to what happens around us. There are people suffering while held in captivity who give up. Then there are those who remain hopeful and optimistic.

Don't judge anyone, not even yourself. The point is, some thrive in chaos, others buckle. If it is possible for some, even one person, it is possible for all the rest of us.

We have a choice. We have a decision to make. Either we keep doing what we are doing and things remain the same, or we change what we are doing to achieve the changes we want. If you always think as you have always thought, you get nothing new.

When you change your thinking, you can begin to entertain and find new things to explore. When you let go, drop resistance, learn to forgive, AND forget, you become free. The circumstances may not change, BUT YOU HAVE!

I have experienced a freedom and wonderful opportunities when I began practicing deliberate control of my thoughts and feelings. When I decided to think the best of the situations, the people, and myself, everything changed, even when it didn't, because I changed how I viewed it.

If you persistently practice loving-kindness, happiness, forgiveness, and celebration, you get it back when you need it. If you are never challenged, you don't learn how to have it in those trying times. Every moment becomes an opportunity to learn and better enjoy life.

I determined to make it wonderful. Now it is! Even when the circumstances are not good, life can still be wonderful. This is the point I became aware of and that I have been trying to make.

When we learn to do as Jesus did, our lives improve. Give it a try and then stick with it. You will discover many marvelous benefits. If Jesus could do it at the very worst in his life, I ought to be able to do it in as many circumstances as possible. For me, it has made an incredible difference. It will for you to.

So, how do we actually forgive?

Step 1: Acknowledge the Pain

You can't heal what you don't feel. Name the hurt. Write it down. Speak it aloud. Let yourself be honest. It's okay to feel angry, betrayed, and sad. These are human emotions. They're not weaknesses. They're guideposts.

Step 2: Shift the Story

The mind is a meaning-making machine. Often, what hurts us isn't what happened, but the story we tell ourselves about what happened. "They disrespected me." "They abandoned me." "I'm not lovable." What if you looked at it differently? What if you said, "They were acting out of their own wounds"? What if you said, "This taught me strength"? The story we choose determines the freedom we feel.

Step 3: Choose Compassion

Compassion doesn't excuse bad behavior, it transcends it. It says, "I see your pain behind your action." I don't condone it, but I also don't let it define me. Compassion is the bridge between justice and peace.

Step 4: Practice Release

Don't wait to "feel ready." Start now. Imagine cutting a cord. Imagine setting down the rock. Say it aloud: "I forgive." Even if it feels awkward. Even if it feels fake. You're building the muscle. One day, it won't feel forced; it will feel like flying.

Step 5: Rinse & Repeat

Forgiveness is not one-and-done. It's a cycle. You may forgive someone today and feel resentment rise again tomorrow. That's normal. That's okay. Keep practicing. It gets easier. And remember to forgive yourself.

You are not your past. You are not your pain; you are the power that can change it. When you forgive yourself, you stop punishing the person you've become for the choices of the person you were.

You are worthy of your own compassion. So, what do you choose?

You could choose to keep carrying the weight. To stay angry. To replay the story. That's one option. But it comes at a cost. Or you could choose something new. Something brave. Something better.

You could choose peace. You could choose joy. You could choose freedom. You can begin today.

Don't wait for life to get easier. Don't wait for the world to say sorry. Say yes to yourself. Say yes to healing. Say yes to the life you've been longing for. This is your invitation. Let go of what hurts. Embrace what heals. Forgive. Love. Rise. It's your time. If you'd like help, reach out to me at rexsikes.com.

With love and blessings,
Rex Sikes

REX SIKES

Rex Steven Sikes is known as "The Mindset Master" & "The Attitude Doctor" in his industry. He's been called a dynamic force of nature. He can be unassuming or powerfully charismatic. He's helped countless thousands transform their minds, lives, and pocketbooks for over five decades.

His innovations include Mind Design™, Directed Questions™, The Attitude Activator™, and The Mastery Loop™. He's the author of *Life on Your Terms*. Sikes conducts online programs on transformation, Mind Design™, Manifesting, and the Law of Attraction, and NLP at public events.

His life experiences make him a riveting professional keynote and endnote speaker, offering exciting, life-changing topics, and a life and business mentor, consultant, educator, and corporate presenter. He's an actor, filmmaker, and entertainment industry consultant. He writes a blog at gratitudeactivator.com.

Rex presents live and online seminars, public and corporate programs, full workshops, and training events. He mentors professionals and newcomers in their fields. He's appeared before millions on television and radio, providing commentary and interviews.

Some of his topics include, the power of your mind to create your dream life, how to increase your bottom line, conditioning and nutrition for the mind and body, why affirmations don't work and how to make them work, creativity and intuition, making a great impression, how to create trust and rapport, and how to understand and utilize body language to become an incredible expert communicator.

His captivating message inspires audiences and will remain with you! To learn more and to book Rex today visit: *www.rexsikes.com & rexsikestv.com*

www.RexSikes.com

JON KOVACH JR.

THE GIFT OF FORGIVENESS

· ·

UNDERSTANDING FORGIVENESS: FOR • GIFT • NESS

The moment I learned the true meaning of forgiveness, I was not kneeling in prayer or reading a sacred text. I was standing in a crowded hallway, heart pounding, as whispers spread like wildfire and I realized my world had shifted. Forgiveness, I discovered, isn't a gentle act—it's a radical, life-altering decision.

Forgiveness, I have come to believe, is the bridge that carries us from mere survival to genuine thrival. It is not about forgetting or excusing, but about freeing ourselves to cross into a life of peace and possibility.

To truly forgive, you must be willing to let go of several deep-seated attachments and expectations.

- Offer genuine acceptance and acknowledgment of what occurred.
- Grant yourself and others permission to move forward.

- Seek restitution or justice where possible, while accepting that some wounds may never be fully healed.

"Turn the other cheek" is a phrase often cited in religious and philosophical teachings, yet true forgiveness extends far beyond passivity.

THE EMOTIONAL ARC OF FORGIVENESS

Throughout my life, I have encountered religious persecution, faith-based polarity, and discrimination within Christian communities. I never considered myself a victim; I was raised to understand that misunderstanding often breeds mistreatment. My mother frequently reminded me of Jesus's teaching to "turn the other cheek," instilling in me the idea that compassion and humility are at the core of forgiveness.

As I entered professional environments, I encountered additional maxims such as "kill them with kindness" and "be the bigger person." These phrases suggest ways to respond to wrongdoing with grace, but I began to sense their limitations. These sayings felt like fragments of true forgiveness, often tinged with subtle arrogance, revenge, or a sense of moral superiority—none of which resonated with my core beliefs. Forgiveness, I realized, is far more profound, requiring genuine effort, introspection, and time. Most people struggle to forgive because it demands deep emotional labor and unwavering commitment.

Seeking healing for lingering wounds, I explored the true meaning of forgiveness. Simple words like "Sorry" or "It's okay" often fall short. Forgiveness, at its core, involves a profound sense of connection and trust. While responses such as "Thank you. I trust you won't do it again," or "I'm grateful for your apology. I believe we can move forward," are closer, they can still feel superficial. Words matter, but forgiveness is ultimately an ongoing, lived experience rather than a single utterance.

I recall a pivotal experience from my high school years. One day, the intercom summoned me to the principal's office. As my classmates reacted with the usual chorus of "ooooos" and "aaaaaahs," I felt a wave of anxiety and uncertainty. With apprehension, I made my way to the office, unsure of what awaited me.

I wracked my brain for any potential wrongdoing, my mind racing through every possible misstep or secret. The anxiety of being called out in such a public way caused me to spiral internally, even though I genuinely had no idea why I was being summoned.

Upon arriving, I found one of my football teammates in tears, his head in his hands. He looked up, his face streaked with emotion, and blurted out, "I AM SORRY!"

THE BACKSTORY

I was deeply involved in competitive sports throughout high school, both at school and in my church's sports league. The Young Men's Activities (YMA) basketball league was infamous for its intensity, often likened to a full-contact sport because of the lack of paid referees and the volunteer-driven nature of the games. This environment bred a highly competitive, physical atmosphere where boundaries were frequently tested.

On occasion, teams would invite their school friends to play as substitutes. One weekend, we held an eight-team season-ending playoff. This brought out everyone's most competitive sides. My team was undefeated for four years, and in the championship game, we faced a team that had recruited some of my teammates from the football team. The game was fiercely competitive, but we dominated on the court. After our victory, the other team's anger and disdain didn't end with the final whistle.

Following that intense game, my football teammate (opponent in the championship)—wounded by defeat—resorted to spreading rumors and engaging in bullying, specifically targeting my church and faith. Overnight, gossip and religious shaming swept through the school. Unaware at first, I became the subject of unwanted attention. Thankfully, a perceptive counselor recognized what was happening and promptly intervened, ensuring the responsible student was held accountable. The swift support from school leadership was both surprising and reassuring.

I was astonished at how quickly and seriously the situation escalated, all without my initial awareness. When my teammate offered a tearful apology, I forgave him almost instinctively. In hindsight, I realized that it was easier to forgive because I hadn't fully grasped the extent of the damage done. Sometimes, forgiveness comes easily when we are shielded from the actual impact of another's actions.

However, when we are confronted with the full magnitude of harm—whether it's the loss of trust, property, or even life— true forgiveness becomes exponentially more challenging. In cases of deep betrayal or irreversible loss, the process of acceptance, moving forward, and seeking justice can feel insurmountable.

This story may not be the most dramatic example of forgiveness, but it illustrates an essential truth: forgiveness is not simply given; it is a deliberate act of generosity. By choosing to coexist and rebuild trust with my teammate—even after a public betrayal—I learned that forgiveness is a gift extended not only to others but also to ourselves. The process involved public acknowledgment, uncomfortable conversations, and lingering social consequences, yet it also allowed healing to begin for all involved. As a coach and counselor, I've seen that these moments—however uncomfortable—are opportunities to foster true resilience and growth.

At first, I felt nothing—a numbness that masqueraded as strength. But as the days passed, anger and confusion tangled inside me. I wanted justice, even revenge. Letting go felt unfair. Only when I allowed myself to feel the full weight of betrayal did I begin to glimpse the freedom forgiveness could offer.

THE COST OF NOT FORGIVING

The cost of withholding forgiveness is steep. Resentment festers, poisoning our capacity for joy. Our bodies carry the burden—higher blood pressure, restless sleep, a heart that never fully unclenches. Unforgiveness can trap us in the very past we long to escape, blocking the path to thriving.

THE ANATOMY OF FORGIVENESS:
A FRAMEWORK FOR GROWTH

After working with individuals and teams over the years, I've distilled forgiveness into a practical process that anyone can follow, no matter how deep the wound or how difficult the situation. Consider these five stages:

1. **Acknowledgment:** Name the hurt honestly. Don't minimize what happened or its impact on you. Real healing begins with truth.

2. **Understanding:** Strive to see the situation from every angle. Understanding does not excuse the harm, but it can

soften the burden of resentment and help you see the humanity in others—and in yourself.

3. **Release:** Consciously let go of the anger, bitterness, or urge for revenge. This is often the hardest step, but it is essential for your own peace of mind.

4. **Redefinition:** Decide what boundaries are needed moving forward. Forgiveness does not always mean reconciliation, but it does mean you are choosing your freedom over your pain.

5. **Growth:** Reflect on how this experience can serve your growth. What wisdom or compassion can you carry forward?

Modern science echoes what spiritual traditions have taught for centuries. Psychologist Dr. Frederic Luskin, director of the Stanford Forgiveness Project, found that people who practice forgiveness experience lower stress, better relationships, and even improved physical health. Across faiths and philosophies, forgiveness is universally recognized as a cornerstone of healing.

As Desmond Tutu wrote, "Forgiveness says you are given another chance to make a new beginning."

COMMON MISCONCEPTIONS ABOUT FORGIVENESS

As you walk the forgiveness journey, remember:

- Forgiveness does **not** mean approving of or excusing what happened.

- Forgiveness does **not** require forgetting or erasing the past.

- Forgiveness does **not** equate to weakness; it is a courageous reclaiming of your well-being.

- Forgiveness does **not** always mean reconciliation. Sometimes, it is an internal process that leads to healthy boundaries.

REFLECTION

Pause for a moment. Bring to mind a time when someone hurt you deeply. How has holding onto that pain shaped your days, your relationships, your sense of self? What might become possible if you chose to cross the bridge to forgiveness?

EXERCISES FOR GIFTING FORGIVENESS

Here are some techniques I've used personally and with those I counsel:

- **Journaling Prompt:** Write about what you are still holding onto and how it affects your daily life. Ask yourself, "What would it feel like to let this go?"

- **Letter Writing:** Compose a letter to the person you need to forgive (you do not need to send it). Express your feelings honestly. Sometimes, just writing the words is enough to begin the release.

- **Guided Visualization:** Imagine placing your hurt in a box, then setting it down and walking forward—lighter and freer. Repeat as needed until you feel a shift.

ENCOURAGEMENT FOR YOUR THRIVAL JOURNEY

Forgiveness is rarely easy and almost never linear. If it feels easy, you might find yourself in the same position I was in, where the effects didn't sink in immediately. You may revisit old wounds or feel stuck at times. That is normal. Progress is measured not by perfection, but by persistence and openness to growth. Remember, the act of forgiving is one of the greatest gifts you can give—to yourself, to others, and to the world around you.

As you embrace forgiveness, you move from mere survival to true thrival, embodying the resilience and hope that this journey offers. Forgiveness is not the higher state of being—I believe it is after true forgiveness that you then walk the higher road.

Forgiveness is the most courageous bridge you will ever cross. Step onto it, again and again, until you find yourself not just surviving your story, but thriving within it. This is the journey, and the gift, of true forgiveness.

JON KOVACH JR.

Jon Kovach Jr. is an award-winning and international motivational speaker and global mastermind leader. In his work as an accountability coach and mastermind facilitator, Jon has helped and coached thousands of professionals achieve their goals with his Irrefutable Laws of High Performance. Jon is the Founder of Champion Circle Professional Development Association. He is also the featured Mastermind Facilitator and Team Leader of the Habitude Warrior Mastermind and the Global Speakers Mastermind & Masterclass series.

Jon is a 28x National #1 Bestselling Author. He is a featured keynote speaker on *SpeakUp TV*, an *Amazon Prime TV* series, and a TEDx speaker, delivering his signature speech, "Getting

Unstuck." Jon's motivational messages have been viewed by over 1 million people, and his voice has trended and been used by global brands on TikTok, YouTube, and Instagram, including Red Bull, Michael Bublé, Powell Books, GoDaddy Studio, Canada's Wonderland Amusement Park, the LSU Cheer Team, and the NHL.

www.SpeakerJonKovachJr.com

ANGÈLE LAMOTHE

FORGIVENESS: ULTIMATE FREEDOM & POWER

In life, we sometimes see challenges as roadblocks and unplanned detours that take us away from the path we had carefully laid out. We question, resist, and sometimes obsess as to why things didn't unfold the way we had expected, at least I have anyway. But what if those very same obstacles weren't accidents at all? What if they were carefully placed along our path to guide and to align us with something even greater than we could ever have imagined?

Truthfully, difficult moments in life often become our most defining ones. They push us beyond our perceived limitations and challenge who we think we really are. In those challenges, we discover extraordinary strength we never knew we had. These experiences don't break us, they magnify our courage, power, and compassion. They shape us into powerful, resilient, and extraordinary humans. This is what I want to share with you today, not a polished version of life, but a deeply personal story of growth, of resilience, of power, and of forgiveness through my most challenging hardship. Because within that pain came true purpose, even if I couldn't see it at the time.

And within those struggles came the most unexpected, beautiful gifts: the gifts of insight, clarity, power, and limitlessness. And one thing I know to be undeniably true is that you have that same power inside of you. It lives in you, it always has, no matter your circumstances, no matter how heavy the burden you're carrying, or how unclear the path ahead may seem.

But it's there, waiting for you to begin again. You may not be able to control what happens to you, but you always have the power to choose how you'll respond. And in that conscious decision, you reclaim your inner power. I have journeyed down that path, witnessing my child go through such hardship and not being able to fix it or make it go away. Three years plus, spent in and out of hospitals, is one of the most painful moments I've had to endure as a parent. And yet, this journey has transformed me in ways I could never have possibly imagined. I'm a better mother, sister, daughter, and friend, a better human, capable of facing life head-on and anything that comes my way.

These life obstacles are not punishments; they are purposeful. They serve as stepping stones. And while they may feel impossible and unbearable in the moment, they are the very experiences that shape us into better and stronger versions of ourselves.

Throughout my journey, I watched my child endure deep hardship and pain, feeling helpless in the face of suffering I could not fix or erase. As a parent, there is no greater pain than seeing your child struggle and not being able to make it better. Yet, through that deep heartache, something unfolded, strengthened, and reshaped my life forever. The pain didn't destroy me, it revealed parts of me I didn't even know existed. It called me into a better version of myself; I learned to forgive myself for not having all the answers and for making mistakes. I learned that I didn't need to be perfect, just present.

And in that presence, I discovered the grace of beginning again. Every moment became a new invitation to choose differently, to show up with more intention, and to grow into the next best version of who I was becoming. In that shift in perspective, rooted not in control, but in surrender and clarity, I found the power and freedom that I wish for all of you.

What if life isn't really about right or wrong, or good versus bad—or even about forgiving others in the traditional sense? What if it's not about fitting our experiences into black-and-white or little boxes of judgment? What's "right" for one person may be "wrong" for another. And maybe that's okay. Maybe the only truth that really matters is your truth—your lived experiences, your values, your growth. For a long time during his illness, I carried guilt and shame, layers of it, inherited through generations, and believing that, somehow, bearing that weight made me a more responsible, stronger, and loving mother. I would lie awake at night wondering: If I had made different choices, could my son's path have been different?

But in retrospect, I've come to see that guilt and shame are not signs of love or strength. They are anchors that paralyze us and keep us stuck in old ways. They keep us locked in patterns of blame and regret. And when we stay stuck in those patterns, we miss the profound opportunity that exists in the present, that chance to grow, to evolve, and to forgive, not just others, but mostly ourselves.

That's the real gift of forgiveness. It's not transactional; it's an act of true freedom that ignites exponential growth and the permission we give ourselves to finally move forward. So, instead of asking, "Why is my child so ill?" "Whose fault is this?" I began asking, "How can I grow from this experience?" "How can I become a better mother?" "What can I do differently"? "How can I grow in closer connection to him?" That shift in perspectives propelled me forward in ways that brought me closer to my son—closer than we had ever been, or perhaps will ever be, through this beautiful journey of healing.

I chose to let go of shame and to choose responsibility, not because I was guilty of what was happening, but because taking responsibility gave me the power to create change and to forgive myself. When I stepped into ownership, something changed within me. I began to notice what was working and what wasn't. I stopped blaming myself for what I didn't know and started opening up space for growth, healing, and change. I stopped hiding from the pain and instead met it with presence, honesty, and grace. In that space, I was quietly and powerfully forgiving myself—for not having all the answers, for not being perfect, for simply being human. Because the truth is, no parent wakes up thinking, "Today I'm going to mess up my child."

If you love with everything that you have and from a place of unconditionality, even when we get it "wrong," it's never wrong if you are doing the best you can with what you know in the moment. And the beauty of life—and of parenting—is that every single moment offers a new invitation to begin again. A new chance to show up with more awareness, more compassion, more intention, and more love. Parenting, like all relationships, is not a fixed destination. It is a living, breathing, evolving journey that continues to teach us who we truly are and can become, if we open our hearts and minds to it.

When you take responsibility and don't blame yourself or others, you take ownership of our choices and shift from powerlessness to empowerment. This is about claiming your ability to influence your inner world, which in turn, transforms your outer experiences. Instead of waiting for circumstances to change or for others to validate your worth, you generate that change from within. This is the heart of transformation—the moment we stop living by default and start living by design. It is how we move from being passive victims of life to conscious creators of it. And in this space, there is nothing to forgive or to be forgiven for. When you live authentically, with integrity and awareness, you begin to see that mistakes are not flaws—they are gifts and a portal to true freedom, and the opportunity to begin again.

You may not be able to change what has already unfolded, but your story is still being written, moment by moment, choice by choice.

Let me be very clear, forgiveness is not the absence of accountability. It is not about excusing harm or bypassing pain. True forgiveness is the presence of something much deeper—a radical commitment to taking responsibility for your life, to heal and grow exponentially from it. It's the brave and conscious decision to no longer allow the past to dictate the future. It's the choice to break generational cycles of pain, to stop trauma, and to become the author and creator of your reality.

Forgiveness honors and acknowledges the work required and then refuses to be controlled by it. In choosing forgiveness, you are choosing freedom. You are declaring that your life will not be defined by your circumstances. That is ultimate freedom and power. It means you always have the ability to reinvent, reimagine, and rise above any challenge.

This is one of the greatest gifts I received from this hardship: the ability to transform these painful moments into wisdom, power, resilience, freedom, and to accelerate growth. The ability to trust and surrender into knowing that all is always happening for me in this universal magic of abundance and oneness.

Forgiveness transcends what we give to others; it's something we gift ourselves. And through that conscious choice, we release healing energies: higher frequencies of love, compassion, and gratitude for the lessons and growth. And the Universe has no choice but to respond with the same energies.

Forgiveness is not a sign of weakness; to truly forgive with integrity and intention is one of the boldest, most powerful acts of strength you can choose to engage in. It may come with some uncomfortable moments, because as you shine that spotlight on parts of you you may not wish to see or have been hiding from, it stirs a sea of suppressed emotions within you. But each time you take that brave step, you let go and create space for expansion, and the key to leading an extraordinary life—the secret to self-mastery and manifestation of your desired reality.

True healing doesn't come from pretending that everything is perfect; it comes from honoring your pain and refusing to let it define you, while meeting it with forgiveness, grace, and power. It's about seeing it with purpose as you shift your energy and return to the essence of who you always have been: A powerful, loving, and incredible human capable of surmounting anything the universe intentionally places along your path—twists and turns along the road that provide the map to an extraordinary life, and so sit back and enjoy the ride that has already been chosen for you.

ANGÈLE LAMOTHE

Angèle Lamothe is a high-vibrational leader who lives a heart-centered life and whose mission is to help raise the consciousness of our planet and transform the world. She is a mom of three, a triathlete, an author, and an empowerment coach who works with high-performing leaders to help them create abundance and develop their intuition, enabling them to live their richest life.

Angèle works in an acute care hospital and is obsessed with people's transformational journeys and how the power of the mind, when aligned with purpose and action, can create miracles.

Angèle leads a high-performance lifestyle and has the joy, energy, and time to do things she deeply enjoys. She can support you in developing tools to help you connect with your intuition and unleash your full power within so that you can lead a balanced and abundant life that is full of gratitude! To find all my links, visit: *www.linktr.ee/AngeleLamothe*.

Author's Website: *www.AngeleLamotheCoaching.com*

Charity Awareness: *www.DareToBeVulnerable.com*

BILL GOOD

FREEING THE PRISONER

. . . .

"To err is human, to forgive, divine."
~ Alexander Pope

"Forgiveness is the fragrance that the violet sheds on the heel that has crushed it."
~ Mark Twain

Disclaimer: Before we dig in here, I feel compelled to confess that I am a Christian and I have no choice but to write from a Christian worldview, drawing on Christian examples. However, it is my fondest hope that what you will find here has applicability to your life and beliefs, no matter how different they might be. The importance of forgiveness is by no means limited to any single social or religious perspective. For instance, how different might the situation in the Middle East be had *all* the cultures and faiths involved (including Christianity) embraced forgiveness over the past 3,000 years?

What spiritual practice do you think presents the greatest challenge—even amongst those most committed to the Divine will? The list is long. Would you say: Chastity? Charity? Prayer? Sacrifice? Surrender?

As someone who spent a significant portion of my adult life ministering to God's people of various faiths, I can tell you that the answer is Forgiveness... Hands down!

- Forgiveness is challenging because it demands more of us than any of the other biblical virtues.

- Forgiveness is challenging because the world often sees it as a weakness, when in fact it requires the greatest of strengths.

But—like it or not—it's right *there* in the Scriptures.

Not only is it there, it's there in abundance. Consider this— throughout the Old and New Testaments, the faithful are called to "repent" *forty-five times*. That's a lot and speaks clearly to the signal importance of the practice. However, a similar search of those texts reveals that we are instructed to "forgive" a total of *seventy-two times*—which speaks to God's deepest desire for God's people.

And when Jesus' disciples ask him to teach them to pray, *what does he say?*

- First, he calls them to acknowledge and worship God's "otherness"—the Divine character and will for creation.

- Next, he instructs them to ask that God provide for their most basic physical needs—food being key among them.

- Then—and before anything else—he charges them to pray: "Forgive us our sins as we forgive those who sin against us."

Now, Jesus' right-hand man, Peter, has been paying attention. He's absorbed enough to understand the frightening significance of his teacher's instruction. Retaliation is in no way God's way. So, the disciple asks for some specifics on behalf of all of us who would follow behind.

"So... How many times must I forgive? *As many as seven?*"

Now, seven is a pretty ambitious answer, and Peter must have been quietly feeling like the brightest boy in the class. After all, the old Rabbinic Law under which they've all been raised only calls for three. Peter more than doubles it. Surely, he's anticipating a gold star on his theology report card.

But then Jesus answers: "Seven! Hardly! *Try seventy times seven!*"

490 times! Peter is floored. And so are we.

But here's the heart of the matter—Jesus understands Peter's question better than Peter does. Because Peter's question (and ours as well) isn't really, *"How many times must I forgive?"* It's really, *"When can I STOP forgiving?"*

Jesus' answer is, *"Never!"*

Ouch! I'm reminded of a friend who once dryly remarked: "You know, if it weren't for Jesus, this being a Christian would be a heck of a lot easier." Amen!

The Divine priorities are as clear as they are challenging. As CS Lewis insightfully observes: *"There is no slightest suggestion that we are offered forgiveness on any other terms.*

It is made perfectly clear that if we don't forgive, we shall not be forgiven. There are no two ways about it."

Forgiveness, you see, is to be our way of life. And it marks a defining characteristic separating life as mere survival and life as full-blown thrival.

The problem is our hearts are so often hard, and this work is so often alien to us.

Our very human sense of fairness tells us that people should pay for what they do. The normal calculus of human interaction mimics the familiar Laws of Nature, which declare that for every action there is an equal and opposite reaction. This kind of thinking normalizes lashing out in anger and withdrawing in sorrow. And in this light, forgiveness seems almost unnatural.

But forgiving is love's power to break Nature's ruthless Rule. Forgiveness ushers us into a universe beyond such mechanical genius into a new, unimagined, and altogether marvelous world where the tyrannical economics of cause and effect, tit-for-tat, cease to govern.

But what exactly is forgiveness? What are its hallmarks in human relationships?

Few commentators have brought more clarity to this conversation than the late Lewis Smedes, former professor at Fuller Theological Seminary, who said: "Forgiveness is God's invention for coming to terms with a world in which, despite their best intentions, people are unfair to each other and hurt each other deeply."

Contrary to volumes of overly simplistic teaching, forgiveness doesn't seek to deny a hurt. Rather, it releases the one who hurt us. From this perspective, to forgive is not to gloss over injury and injustice. In fact, it does something quite opposite (and considerably greater): it acknowledges the magnitude of a wrong... and then says, *"But I'm not going to let that continue to matter."*

Here's the important part: *We need to forgive precisely because we can't forget!*

Let's talk first about some things that *forgiveness IS—it's:*

- A refusal to accept the imprisonment of isolation that is the byproduct of broken relationships.

- A miracle of grace whereby a particular offense no longer separates God's people from one another.

- A recognition that the power of love that *binds* us as children of God is greater than the power of anger that *divides* us as enemies.

Now some things forgiveness ISN'T—*it's:*

- Not the end of pain—it doesn't mean that we will immediately cease to hurt—only that hurt now has a creative avenue toward healing.

- Not pretending nothing has happened or that an offense didn't matter—rather intentionally willing that it no longer **controls** our future.

- Not denying that relationships may be irrevocably changed, but creating emotional space so that things *may become*, with grace and time, *better.*

- Not necessarily forgetting—but instead choosing not to use memory as a weapon against others.

And how does it work?

By surrendering our perceived "right" to judgment to the sovereign desires of our Creator.

As a conscious decision—an act of choice and will made possible through the awareness of the grace that we ourselves have received.

Slowly—as *a process,* not an *event.* Sometimes, we may not even be aware of exactly when it occurs.

In confusion and with the understanding that the end is not always a rehabilitated relationship—sometimes, the ability to be in the same room with our "offender" at the same time is enough.

At the end of all this, perhaps the greatest surprise of this entire discussion is that the real beneficiary of our efforts toward forgiveness isn't necessarily who we might expect—the one forgiven.

Therapeutically, it has been widely published and commonly recognized that retained anger and feelings of malice toward others are unhealthy, even to the point of making us sick. That being the case, it's indisputably in our own best interest to divest ourselves of these life-crushing emotional straightjackets. The fact is, we are never so free as when we reach back into our past and forgive the person who caused us pain.

In the memorable words of Lewis Smedes: "When we choose to forgive, we set a prisoner free... then we discover the prisoner was us."

Forgiveness defines our world—as either fair or merciful. As survival or thrival.

How many times must we forgive? Well, it depends upon which of those worlds you choose to inhabit. But we do well to remember the words of another student of the subject, Philip Yancey, who points out: "The only thing harder than forgiveness is the alternative."

Survival or thrival? The choice is yours.

References

Luke 11:2-4 echoing Matthew 6:9-12
This story is recounted in Matthew's Gospel beginning at 18:21ff
From Lewis' unfortunately titled book, *Forgive and Forget*
Forgive and Forget
Philip Yancy, *What's So Amazing About Grace?*

BILL GOOD

Bill Good is a Speaker, Teacher, Bestselling Author, and Counselor. Bill Good is passionate about implementing world change through personal transformation and relationship recovery. He is dedicated to creating a pathway to healing and leading beyond the ordinary to living a life without limits. Bill holds a Master's of Divinity from Fuller Seminary and is retired from Pastoral Ministry. He currently teaches at Grand Canyon University. He also received advanced certifications in Christian Reconciliation and Peacemaking, is a Graduate of Transformational Leadership Training, and holds a Master's in Leadership. He is also the CEO and senior counselor of Path to Peace, which provides conciliation services to organizations and individuals seeking to overcome trauma. But Bill's first love is encouraging hope through his writing and speaking. A four-time Amazon Bestselling Author as well as a Speaker Hearts and TedX speaker, he is presently preparing a trilogy of books for publication: *Between Sundays*: *A Practical Study of Jesus' Reconciliation Ministry; From Here to There: A Collection of Autobiographical Reflections on Spiritual Development; The Good Factor: A Functional and Life-Giving Perspective on Manifesting the GOOD Life, a Way to a Better Way.*
Author's Website: www.TheGoodFactor.com

Charity Awareness: *www.PhoenixRescueMission.org*

BRIAN SWANSON

THE MOMENT OF FORGIVENESS

We all know the quote, "...to forgive but not to forget." I believe this statement holds true in its general sense; however, it leaves us with much more to evaluate. There are different levels of mistakes. Some are easy to forgive and forget. Some emotionally tied mistakes can be much harder to forget.

Burrowing down into the many questions and theories of this quote would be difficult to cover here. I want to raise only one question for contemplation. "When do we forgive?"

However, before I dig into this question, I must qualify a couple of principles. Every mistake comes with a repercussion. An individual's feelings toward a mistake can have a significant impact. Mistakes can range from being sorry for accidentally stepping on someone's toe to trying to apologize for breaking someone's heart. Emotions can have an impact on all mistakes, hence the reason to owe someone a sincere apology.

I have pondered the question many times. But one time was set around the death of my adoptive mom. I was adopted at the age of three days old. I lived a good life and give credit to my mom and dad for the man I am today. I was always taught to be kind and respectful to people. It was drilled into me to follow positive morals and standards. That is an outstanding way to be raised. However, a parental adage comes to mind: "Do as I say, not as I do."

My mom was a violent and emotionally abusive disciplinarian. I remember one incident when I was young. I was school age, and my mom always got out of bed in the morning to take care of my breakfast before I jumped on the school bus. It was a typical morning with one exception. I had gotten out of bed, gotten dressed, and gone to the kitchen before she had an opportunity to get there and make my cereal.

Being the independent child that I was, I made my cereal and had my breakfast. Mom then came to the kitchen. She got very angry because I had trounced on her motherly duties. Rather than exclaiming that I was good and was growing up to become my own person, she picked up the cereal bowl and threw it. This is where things become debatable. I always believed that she threw the bowl at my forehead as her target, because that is where the melamine-style cereal bowl made contact. However, in the short time I had with her before her death, we discussed the incident. Her side of the story was that she meant to throw the bowl to the floor for effect, and it slipped out of her wet hands. Either way, I ended up with a nice dent in the middle of my forehead for a few days.

Mom was always getting angry at me for something. There was a time when I had left albums on the turntable. I had been told, probably numerous times, not to leave them at the top of the spindle because that would cause the albums, which happen to be Dad's, to warp under the weight. She came home and found I had left them there. At the drop of a hat, she got upset, took all the albums from the spindle, and broke them into pieces. Thinking back to that moment, I was upset because I lost my favorite music. Analyzing that memory today, it was my dad who paid the price for my mistake; they were his albums.

Before I move on to other examples that I feel are necessary to make my point to the question I asked, I will pause and ask you, should I have forgiven her for these angry outbursts at those moments? As is evident, I have not forgotten.

One time during the sixth grade, I remember a very serious situation. I was held up in my room waiting to leave the house for something. Dad was in the shower, and Mom was in the bathroom with him. I heard a loud crash of glass and a sudden, terrified, synchronous scream of mom and dad coming from the bathroom. I ran down the hall to find that the shower door had broken, and Dad was bleeding. Because everything is a matter of perspective, there were two stories of what had happened. One detail that was agreed upon is that Mom was in one of her angry moments again.

Mom's side of the story was that she moved the shower door, and it slipped out of her hand, crashing into the wall and breaking. There was the side comment of, "Those cheap-ass doors."

Dad's side was that it was simply an accident. No more, no less, no further explanation. My side was very different. Mom was mad and on one of her rants. She was upset at Dad and deliberately threw the door along its track into the wall. She hurt my dad! I will finalize this story with the fact that Dad had a few glass cuts from the shards and recovered quite quickly.

Do you remember having your or a sibling's mouth washed out with soap because of the escape of some bad language? Well, my experience was not just soap, but very hot Mexican peppers. Of course, the level of punishment rose because of my tolerance for the soap. I still chuckle at this. I had gotten one over on mom.

I knew my mother disciplined me more often and sometimes more violently than other kids. I always knew that family members witnessed some situations, but it never occurred to me that they would have witnessed stories that I do not remember. I was given one of those stories while I was taking care of her in her last days. They said Mom had dressed me in my Sunday-best clothes and brand-new shoes. We went to the country where my cousins lived.

As was typical, I went outside to play with the other kids. The shoes got dirty. Mom yelled and screamed at me for wrecking them. She probably used the word destroyed. She proceeded to take the shoes and throw them in the trash. Immediately after disposing of the shoes, we loaded up in the car and left very abruptly. A believable story from my perspective.

As we all know, life goes on, and so do the memories. There are many incidents within my life that revolve around my mother's angry and violent way of dealing with situations.

Returning to the initial question. When do we forgive? Do we forgive at the moment of the mistake or incident, or does it take months or years to forgive? I believe this answer is based on the individual. My experiences taught me to forgive in the moment. I rationalized that my mistakes were some sort of learning lesson. They were something I needed to evaluate and use for the rest of my life to become a patient, forgiving, and compassionate individual.

As mentioned, I was with my mom in her last four months of life. I made the trip out of state, leaving my understanding family behind to take care of her in her final moments. Dad had passed away years before. My cousins were overwhelmed with her demands, and I felt that it was my sonly duty to be there.

Since her death, I have evaluated and rationalized that I have not forgiven her after each moment. I had set the memories aside and moved on. To this day, I do not think that I have forgiven. Maybe I do not know what it means to forgive. I have simply justified her actions with the idea that she raised me in the manner that she thought was best. She was raised by discipline, and so was I.

After writing this, I think I have concluded that the statement, to forgive but not forget, can be rewritten. Forgive the best you can, but don't forget that love is shown in many ways.

BRIAN SWANSON

Brian Swanson is a dedicated entrepreneur, podcaster, bestselling author, and business owner. His specialty is within the world of learning, teaching, and business building. His experiences include working in restaurants, bars, finance, construction, as a comic bookstore owner, disc jockey, website creator, marketer, graphic editor, and owner of GalaxyFest (a popular local Pop Culture Convention). Brian has a passion for sharing his skills and experiences through writing, speaking, and co-hosting a long-running podcast, *Denim and Pearls.*

One topic he loves to share is his experience of searching for his biological parents. Finding them was a positive experience, and his willingness to share has helped many adoptees conquer their fears and begin their quest to find their parents. If he is not behind the computer or orchestrating an event, you can find Brian hosting or performing karaoke at numerous venues around the state any day of the week—that is, assuming he is not traveling around the world. Learn more about Brian here: *www.Facebook.com/DJWildLife* and *www.DenimAndPearlsLive.com.*

Author's Website: *www.GalaxyFest.com*

Charity Awareness: *www.SurvivalToThrivalSeries.com*

CHRISTOPHER MUSIC

THE HARDEST & MOST LIBERATING LIFE LESSON

As a fifty-seven-year-old man, I've had the incredible privilege of living a multi-varied life. I've walked many paths—multiple careers, complex relationships, unpredictable highs, and some brutal lows. I've traveled to over sixty countries to experience the gift of other cultures. I've made millions when I was thinking straight, and I've lost millions when common sense left the building. I've known the joy of real friendship and the sting of betrayal from false "friends" that cuts deeper than a knife.

When I turned fifty, life presented me with a cruel fork in the road. I had built a successful financial planning company from the ground up over the span of a decade. From the outside, everything looked fine as I was generally light-hearted with my staff and clients. But on the inside, I was unraveling. I wasn't happy as measured by *any* metric. My twenty-six-year marriage—something I poured my soul into—had run its course. And despite doing everything in my power to salvage it, I had to finally choose my own health—mentally, emotionally, spiritually, and physically—and that meant walking away.

Now, here's where it got even more complicated. My wife was also my business partner and CEO of the firm. When I made the decision to divorce, she didn't agree with it, nor did she agree with the idea that I could continue in the company that I had founded. There was no middle ground, no negotiated handshake solution. Just a clean break. So, I made the gut-wrenching decision to sell my interest in the companies, which were my creation, and with it, all my intellectual property, which included 24 trademarks and over 100 copyrights of original material. That decision felt like losing a child. And I don't say that lightly, as I've never known a loss that painful.

I had lost everything, which included my marriage, my home, my company, and my entire support system, including my community. I was zeroed out as a man, which is when all means of emotional support have been eliminated from access. So, I did what many men do when they don't know what else to do. I got into a thirty-five-foot motorcoach with my Jeep on the back and drove west. I needed to get away from everything and to disappear for a while. I ended up in Las Vegas when the COVID pandemic hit the Strip, and I was there when it looked like the zombie apocalypse finally happened!

What followed were years of anger, self-pity, and escape. I drank too much and produced too little. I let the pain consume me, and I justified it all. I told myself I had been treated unfairly. And of course I was, factually and demonstrably. But here's the part that took years to face—I had allowed it to happen. I made errors in who I allowed to gain access to my energy, guidance, and opportunities. I deferred power to those who misused it. I stayed way too long and compromised way too much. I had chosen to trust when I should've held my ground. But in my mind, it was easier, and infinitely more satisfying, to blame others rather than face my own altruism and weakness.

Then, one day, a friend looked me in the eye and said something I'll never forget: "You need to forgive them and move on."

Of course, I resisted. "Forgive? Are you kidding? What they did wasn't okay! That betrayal wasn't right by *any* standard!" But here's what I didn't understand at the time, and really what most people don't understand. Forgiveness isn't saying what they did was okay. It's not about giving them a pass. It's about giving up the anger. That's the Oxford English Dictionary definition: to "stop feeling angry or resentful towards (someone) for an offence or mistake."

And that changed everything for me.

I couldn't control what they did. I couldn't change the past. But I could take responsibility for my viewpoint, my attitude, my contribution to the situation, and how I chose to process it. It took years—too many years—but eventually, I let go. And in that release, I found something far more important than justification. I found a new mission.

The moral of the story is simple: I wasted too much time holding on to resentment when I should've been building the next version of me. I am at least two years late for my own rebirth and transformation, but I made it to this moment, full of hope and excitement for what is to come. And in hindsight, I wouldn't trade a single experience. Not one. Even the ones that ripped me to pieces (and there were a few), because every one of them contained a lesson I needed to learn—no matter how painful the delivery.

At the end of the day, life's too short not to forgive. But here's the real twist: the only person you ever truly need to forgive is yourself. Forgive yourself for not knowing better. Forgive yourself for trying too hard or not hard enough. Forgive yourself for staying too long or for giving too much. And a BIG one for me: Forgive yourself for betraying your own standards. It is in that forgiveness, that release of anger and pain, where real healing happens. But we must be ready for it, and that will take as long as it takes.

That's what I've learned.

And now, at this stage in life, I feel like I've finally stepped onto the path I was always meant to walk. It's a path of self-discovery for sure, but more than that, it's about contribution to my sphere of influence. It's about creating value for my friends and family, for the groups of which I'm a part, and for society at large.

If you're reading this and you're harboring any resentment—toward an ex, a friend, a business partner, a family member, or anyone with whom you have been associated—I ask you to do what I eventually had to do. Look in the mirror. Not with judgment, but with radical ownership, and ask yourself: What role did I play in the making of this situation? What did I ignore? Where did I tolerate too much? Where did I fail to act? And most importantly, "What can I do now to be the point of CAUSE, and not EFFECT, in creating better conditions for myself and those around me?"

Believe me, I know it's not easy. Nothing about this process is. But I also know this: it's the only path to true growth and the only way to become who you were meant to be.

Once you cross that line of ownership, once you forgive and let go, you will see what I see now: that forgiveness isn't weakness. It's power. It's the fuel of reinvention, and it opens the door to a life that isn't defined by what you've lost—but by what you're here to build next.

Learn the power of forgiveness and liberate yourself into your highest potential! You will be a better person for it.

CHRISTOPHER MUSIC

Christopher Music, MBA, RFC, CBEC, is a thirty-three-year veteran of the personal financial planning profession. He has owned, built, and sold two firms since 1992, resulting in the improvement of the financial destinies of thousands of families in the US. He is a Wall Street Journal/USA Today bestselling author and an award-winning international speaker on financial topics. A Certified Business Consultant, Registered Financial Consultant®, and Certified Business Exit Consultant®, he is committed to expanding his knowledge and expertise in the fields of personal finance and economics for the ultimate benefit of small business owners.

He has shared the stage and/or collaborated on projects with Grant Cardone, Forbes Riley, Steve Forbes, Brian Tracy, Erik Swanson, Robert Allen, Rudy Giuliani, Mel Robbins, and other leading coaches and consultants. Christopher currently lives his life virtually as a digital nomad, traveling the world full-time and working with healthcare practice owners as The Professional's Prosperity Mentor. He can be reached at CM@ChristopherMusic.com.

Author's Website: *www.ChristopherMusic.com*

Charity Awareness: *www.TheWayToHappiness.org*

CLEVELAND AUZENNE

FORGIVENESS: THE FREEDOM I DIDN'T KNOW I NEEDED

I didn't grow up knowing what forgiveness really meant. I heard people talk about it in church. I heard the phrase, "Just let it go." But nobody told me what to do when the pain was still fresh, when the damage was done, and when it kept showing up in my daily life—especially when it involved my son.

As a man, I was raised to be strong. That strength was often defined by silence. So, when I was hurt, when I was betrayed, when I was denied time with my son, I just tried to move on. That's what I thought forgiveness was—just pushing through. But I was wrong.

Forgiveness isn't pushing through. Forgiveness is sitting in the pain long enough to feel it, name it, and then release it—so it no longer controls your life. Forgiveness is freedom.

I remember breaking down on June 28 around 9 PM. My wife was right there with me. I cried out, "Why did they do this to me?" I wasn't just talking about one situation—I was releasing years of buried anger, confusion, and grief. That night marked the beginning of something I didn't know I needed: true forgiveness.

I had to forgive the mother of my child. I had to forgive the family members who stood by and watched. I had to forgive the system. I even had to forgive myself. One of the hardest moments was when my son was on the phone, and I heard his mother say in the background, "You won't have nothing to do with your daddy when you turn eighteen." That shattered me. But I had to forgive it. Not for her, but for me.

Napoleon Hill said, "Every adversity, every failure, every heartache carries with it the seed of an equal or greater benefit." That lesson became my lifeline. The heartbreak taught me to search deeper. The rejection taught me to stand taller. The betrayal taught me to anchor my peace within, not from others.

Forgiveness didn't come easy. There were moments I thought I had moved on, only to be triggered by a song, a smell, or a memory. That's how I learned the myth of forgiveness: it's not a one-time event. It's a practice. A choice. A process.

And sometimes, forgiveness happens without reconciliation. I've had to forgive people who will never say, "I'm sorry." People who still believe they were right. People who may never acknowledge the pain they caused. But I forgave them anyway. That's real strength.

I also realized the cost of unforgiveness. It sneaks into your life like a silent thief. You become guarded, skeptical, untrusting—even when you think you're fine. It changes how you see the world, how you treat others, and how you love. I didn't want that for myself. I didn't want to carry that heaviness any longer.

Therapy helped. Meditation helped. Talking to God helped. But most of all, I had to be honest with myself. I had to face the truth that forgiveness isn't for the weak. It's for the warrior who wants to be free.

There were times I never saw my son get on the school bus. Times I sat in courtrooms just to prove I was worthy of being a father. Times I paid child support without even getting a thank-you. And still, I showed up. Still, I forgave.

Because I knew this: If I didn't heal, I would bleed on people who didn't cut me. And I wanted to be a better man—for my wife, for my children, and for myself.

Forgiveness gave me that chance.

To the fathers out there who feel like giving up—don't. Keep showing up. Keep doing the inner work. Your story isn't just about pain—it's about power. Your child needs you to be the light, even when others try to keep you in the dark.

You are not alone. You are not broken. And you are not without options. Forgiveness is one of them.

Forgiveness doesn't mean forgetting. It means you no longer carry the weight. It means you learn to see the lesson without reliving the pain.

And for anyone reading this, ask yourself:

* What are you still carrying that's keeping you from peace?
* Who do you need to forgive, even if they'll never say sorry?
* What would your life look like if you finally let it go?

Forgiveness isn't weakness. It's wisdom. And it's the doorway to a life that isn't just surviving—but thriving.

This chapter isn't just for the ones who hurt me.

It's for me.

It's for every father, mother, son, or daughter who's ever held onto pain longer than they should have.

It's time to let it go.

Forgiveness is the freedom I didn't know I needed—but I'm so glad I found it.

CLEVELAND AUZENNE

Cleveland Auzenne is the proud owner of IRIDE Transportation, a company dedicated to providing safe and reliable non-emergency medical transportation services. As a Certified Instructor with the Napoleon Hill Foundation, he empowers others through the timeless principles of success, mindset, and purpose. Serving as Vice President of the Southwest Louisiana Black Chamber of Commerce, Cleveland is a passionate advocate for economic growth, small business support, and community advancement.

A devoted husband to his incredible wife and a loving father, Cleveland leads with integrity, faith, and a deep love for people. He is committed to uplifting those around him and helping individuals align with their highest potential—both personally and professionally. Whether mentoring entrepreneurs, volunteering locally, or speaking on the power of mindset and perseverance, Cleveland believes that service, gratitude, and love are the true currency of success. His mission is clear: to build, serve, and inspire from the inside out.

Author's Website: *www.IRidesTransportation.com*

Charity Awareness: *www.SurvivalToThrivalSeries.com*

DR. CURT COLLINS

FORGIVENESS IS THE THRESHOLD—CROSS IT & THE LIFE YOU DESIRE BEGINS

Life doesn't ask our permission before it delivers the moments that shape us. Joy arrives unexpectedly, but so does heartbreak. Connection lifts us, but betrayal can break us open. Loss, fear, and uncertainty; none of them wait for a convenient time. If anything, life seems to deliver its greatest challenges right when things finally feel stable.

But while we cannot control what happens, we can always choose how we respond. And that choice—quiet, internal, invisible to the world—is everything. It determines our emotional frequency. It determines whether we live life in effect or at cause. It determines whether we stay trapped in the past or step into the future we're meant to create.

For me, learning to raise my emotional frequency, moving from guilt, fear, and anger into courage, love, and gratitude, has been the foundation of success. It is the skill that allowed me to stop reacting to life and start creating it; to stop being pulled into the chaos of lower vibrations and instead live from a place of strength, clarity, and spiritual alignment.

Forgiveness is at the center of that shift.

Most people think forgiveness is about letting someone "off the hook," or pretending that what happened didn't hurt, but forgiveness has nothing to do with condoning the behavior. Forgiveness is about reclaiming yourself. It's about freeing your nervous system from the weight of the past so you can finally breathe again. It's about choosing the frequency you want to carry into your future, instead of dragging yesterday's wounds into tomorrow's possibilities.

As a chiropractor for over twenty years, I've seen the cost of unforgiveness every single day. People walk into my clinic carrying emotional burdens they've been holding for decades. From resentment toward parents, betrayal from partners, to shame from childhood moments they never processed; those emotional frequencies are not abstract. They show up in the body as chronic tension, headaches, digestive disorders, immune dysregulation, and fatigue that no amount of rest or adjustments can truly fix. The body always tells the truth about what the mind refuses to release.

We are, at our core, energetic beings expressing ourselves through physical form. What we hold within, we multiply, and what we multiply, we broadcast. When we vibrate at states like fear, anger, guilt, or resentment, our entire life reorganizes around that frequency. But when we choose love, compassion, and forgiveness, we consciously tune ourselves into gratitude. Then life responds in kind, and healing becomes possible, clarity returns, synchronicity reappears, and doors open that were previously invisible.

What many people don't understand is that emotions are not just feelings; they're frequencies. They're stored energetic imprints, especially the ones created in childhood before we had any ability to filter or defend ourselves. A child doesn't know how to evaluate whether something is true or fair; they just absorb it. Trauma becomes programming. Programming becomes identity. Identity becomes destiny, unless we intervene.

Forgiveness is the bridge that moves us upward and breaks the bonds that have quietly restricted our ascent. It releases the emotional gravity that keeps us tied to what hurt us, restoring our capacity to rise, expand, and live from the fullness of our purpose. Without forgiveness, we remain anchored to the past; with it, we reclaim the freedom to create our future.

But forgiveness is rarely a one-time moment. It's a practice, a return, a willingness to release the story again and again until its emotional charge dissolves. Some wounds peel away like a thin layer of dust, while others must be released in fragments—slowly, patiently, sometimes painfully. But each release brings more light. Each act of forgiveness clears another layer of the lens through which we see the world. Eventually, we begin to see not through the eyes of our wounds, but through the eyes of our wisdom. We begin to experience life without bracing for the next blow. We breathe deeper. We love more freely. We trust ourselves again.

Life has handed me more than a few experiences that required forgiveness. Life has challenged me in ways that tried to break me repeatedly. From watching my mother die of cancer when I was barely stepping into adulthood to walking through a divorce and losing all contact with my twelve-year-old daughter for over a decade, or from business partners who betrayed my trust, to insurance companies refusing hundreds of thousands in payments, catapulting me into bankruptcy in my forties, I have endured.

And just when I thought I was rebuilding after years of struggling, the chiropractic board attempted to take my license because I recommended a regenerative medicine procedure to a patient over dangerous surgery or addictive opioids.

I'll never forget the day they served me the accusation. I was in my office, celebrating a few recent wins, feeling like I'd regained momentum. When I opened the envelope and read what they wanted to do, strip me of the profession I loved, something unexpected happened.

Instead of feeling fear, a strange sense of joy and excitement bubbled up. I knew instantly:

- This will not break me.

- This will make me.

- This will take me higher.

- This will become the fire that purifies, not destroys.

And it all did. But only because I refused to hold resentment. I refused to carry hatred. I refused to let lower frequencies dictate my path. I chose forgiveness not to excuse what was done, but to free myself from the emotional gravity of the situation. I chose gratitude. Thankful even for the challenge, because I knew God was using it to sharpen me. To strengthen me. To elevate me.

Not everyone makes that choice. I've watched many people stay stuck for decades, repeating the same stories of what someone did to them twenty years ago, unaware that the real prison is inside, not outside. When you refuse to forgive, you chain yourself to the moment that wounded you. You carry it into every new relationship, every new opportunity, every new version of yourself you're trying to become.

Forgiveness is not for the other person. Forgiveness is for your freedom. Try this: silently forgive everyone you meet, even if you don't think they need forgiveness. It is a form of energetic hygiene, clearing your field so nothing heavy sticks to you. It's like an adjustment for the soul.

Forgiveness doesn't mean you forget. It doesn't mean you trust the person again. It doesn't mean you pretend it didn't hurt. It means you refuse to keep drinking the poison. You stop rehearsing the story. You stop feeding the frequency that destroys your clarity and blocks God's guidance.

When you fully forgive from the heart, not the mind, you step into a higher field of consciousness where healing flows naturally, love expands, gratitude amplifies, synchronicity increases, peace becomes normal, and the past loses its power over the present. Forgiveness is not a small decision. It is a spiritual act with generational consequences.

And in my own life, choosing forgiveness opened the door not just to survival, but to a life better than anything I had before. It led me to rebuild stronger. It attracted the love of my life. A woman whose support, devotion, and heart have been one of God's greatest gifts to me. Together, we've created a life rooted in joy, anchored in gratitude, and lifted by the belief that everything we've faced was preparing us for what we're now stepping into.

- Forgiveness is how you rise.
- It's how you regain your power.
- It's how you align with God's frequency and let His guidance lead the way.
- It's how you transform pain into purpose and setbacks into spiritual momentum.

The greatest freedom you will ever know is this. You cannot always choose what life gives you, but you can always choose the frequency at which you meet it. Forgiveness is that choice.

And it is the foundation of every miracle that follows. Go ahead and try to see for yourself. Release the anger, the guilt, the disappointment, and the stories you've carried for far too long. Lay it all down. Give God the space to move in the places where bitterness once lived. And then just watch. Watch what He puts in its place. Watch how He restores what you thought was lost. Watch how He fills the empty spaces with strength, clarity, love, and blessings you never saw coming.

Let forgiveness clear the soil of your heart, because what God grows there next will astonish you. It will amaze you in ways you couldn't have imagined.

DR. CURT COLLINS

Dr. Curt Collins is a visionary chiropractor, regenerative medicine expert, and founder of Tomorrow Doctor. Since 2001, he has specialized in upper cervical chiropractic care and integrative wellness, blending time-tested principles with new innovative therapies. As Clinic Director at Envista Medical Neck & Back Center in Bakersfield, CA, he leads a multidisciplinary team dedicated to restoring health and relieving pain through advanced treatments, including stem cell and regenerative medicine.

Dr. Collins also co-founded Level 3 Consulting, where he mentors doctors nationwide to scale practices, automate operations, and create lasting impact without burnout. Grounded in faith and driven by purpose, he believes health is our greatest wealth, our networks determine our net worth, and service is life's highest calling. Whether in practice, on stage, or guiding groups, his mission is to awaken human potential, elevate frequency, and inspire others to live a higher quality of life filled with health, happiness, and success.

Author's Website: *www.TomorrowDoctor.com*

Charity Awareness: *www.AmericanDreamU.org*

CYNTHIA DEL ROSARIO

HEALING BEYOND THE HURT: MY JOURNEY TO FORGIVENESS

There are moments when we carry so much pain that forgiveness feels like a foreign language—a dialect spoken by others, not meant for us. I know this because I've lived it. I know what it's like to live behind the walls of unresolved grief, rage, and betrayal. I know what it's like to feel your body stiffen every time someone tells you to "just forgive and move on."

But healing doesn't come from the outside in. Healing starts when we choose—moment by moment—to shift our energy from survival to release. And forgiveness... forgiveness is the bridge.

THE SCARS WE DON'T TALK ABOUT

I remember the first time I learned what it felt like to be judged, categorized, and dismissed for simply existing. A brown girl in a white world, a body in a system that told me I was too loud, too much, too complicated. I internalized those messages. I thought I had to be less of myself to be loved. That self-rejection was the first betrayal.

And later, life gave me real reasons to feel betrayed. Hurt by the ones who were supposed to protect me. Let down by systems that were supposed to support me. Betrayal after betrayal stacked itself like bricks around my heart. I told myself I was surviving, but I was also hardening. And I carried those walls with me—into motherhood, into leadership, into love.

Forgiveness, at that point, wasn't a possibility. It was a threat. Because to forgive meant I had to feel. And I wasn't ready to go there.

ENERGY SPEAKS WHEN WORDS CAN'T

In my work with communities, with survivors, with families fractured by harm, I've learned that energy always tells the truth. Even when our mouths lie, our energy exposes us. We carry the wounds of unforgiveness like a vibration that hums in our chest. We react, we defend, we numb, we lash out, we retreat.

And we attract more of the same.

I began to notice how unforgiveness shaped the environments I lived in. I started witnessing how tightly wound we all were— how rage, grief, and disappointment showed up in our posture, our parenting, our partnerships. I saw it in myself.

I was raising a daughter while still carrying my mother's pain, and her mother's pain. I was building community while still learning how to trust. I was preaching about liberation while still enslaved by my own resentment.

Something had to change.

THE MOMENT I CHOSE AGAIN

It wasn't a thunderclap or a big ceremony. It was quiet. I was folding laundry and crying into my hands. I was exhausted from being strong. Tired of holding it all together. And in that moment, something whispered in me:

"You don't have to carry this anymore."

I felt it. Deep. Like a vibration rearranging the molecules of my spirit.

I whispered back: "Then help me put it down."

That was the first real prayer I ever prayed for forgiveness. Not asking for anyone else to change. Just asking for me to be free.

Asking for a way to unhook my heart from the bitterness. And that's when I understood:

Forgiveness isn't something I do for them. It's the sacred act of reclaiming my own peace.

FORGIVENESS AS AN ENERGETIC RESET

In the same way we shift our frequency from fear to love, we can change from resentment to grace. Not because what they did was okay. Not because we forget. But because we are no longer available for that vibration.

Forgiveness doesn't erase accountability—it elevates the conversation. It moves us from the vibration of retribution to the frequency of release.

I started practicing forgiveness like an energetic hygiene. Like brushing my soul's teeth. Each day, I asked:

- What am I still holding?
- Who do I need to release?
- What parts of me still believe I deserved that pain?

And I got honest. Brutally honest.

FAMILY, BOUNDARIES, & THE SACRED NO

One of the most arduous forgiveness journeys I've ever had to walk was with my own family. The people who loved the ones who hurt me and me. The people I needed the most and sometimes couldn't count on. I had to forgive them—not to stay close, but to let go.

Forgiveness doesn't always mean reconciliation. Sometimes it means blessing someone from afar.
I learned how to set boundaries with love.

I learned how to say no without guilt.

I learned how to say yes to my peace, my healing, my voice.

And in doing that, I modeled forgiveness for my daughter—not as a weak surrender, but as a powerful reclamation of energy.

THE BODY REMEMBERS—SO WE MUST TEACH IT SAFETY

Unforgiveness doesn't just live in the mind. It lives in the body. It shows up in tight shoulders, flared tempers, gut issues, and insomnia. Our nervous systems carry the memory of harm.

That's why forgiveness must include the body.

I started dancing, singing, and crying when I needed to. Taking deep, uncluttered breaths. I told my body, "You are safe now." And slowly, she began to believe me.

Somatic forgiveness. That's what I call it—a full-body permission to heal.

FORGIVENESS IN COMMUNITY

When I work with women in community healing circles, I watch them carry ancestral grief, institutional betrayal, and personal heartbreak—all at once. I honor their stories, their rage, their survival. And then I remind them:

"We don't heal alone."

Forgiveness becomes possible when we're witnessed in our pain. When someone says, "Me too." When someone cries with us and doesn't rush us to be okay.

Community is the medicine. We bring our wounds to the circle, and the circle helps us transmute them.

I've forgiven pieces of my past by watching other women forgive theirs. That's the beauty of energetic healing—it ripples.

WHAT FORGIVENESS IS NOT

Let me be clear. Forgiveness is not:

- Approval of harm
- Forgetting what happened
- Forcing yourself to be okay
- Letting people re-injure you

Forgiveness is:

- Choosing peace over punishment
- Releasing yourself from the weight of bitterness
- Rewiring your nervous system for joy
- Reclaiming your energy, your power, your freedom

MY INVITATION TO YOU

If you're reading this, and you're still holding on to something heavy—I see you. If you've been told to "just get over it," but your spirit still aches—I honor you.

Forgiveness is not a one-time event. It's a daily practice—a radical act of self-love.

So today, I invite you to ask yourself:

What would it feel like to be free?

Not for them. Not for the ones who hurt you. But for YOU.

You deserve that freedom. You deserve that lightness. You deserve to thrive beyond survival.

Let forgiveness be your bridge.

Let healing be your home.

And may your energy rise to meet the version of you who no longer has to carry the pain.

With love,
Cynthia

CYNTHIA DEL ROSARIO

Cynthia Del Rosario is a visionary leader whose steadfast integrity and inspiring spirit fuel her dedication to serving communities and developing innovative solutions with lasting impact. With over forty years of industry experience, Cynthia's career spans a broad spectrum of content creation, marketing, production, distribution, talent and rights management, and business affairs. She has collaborated with some of the world's leading brands, including Verizon, GE Capital, Procter & Gamble, Pfizer, IBM, Pepsi, and American Express.

As founder of 7 Mile Global Ad Solutions, LLC, she leads efforts to transform how branded intellectual property is managed, creating platforms such as IP360 and the 7MG Academy. Alongside her husband, Patrick Neville—an Iraq War veteran and 9/11 First Responder—she owns a popular bar and restaurant, Whiskey River NY, that fosters connection, community, and memorable conversation.

Her proudest achievements are her two children, Kayla and Aidan.

Author's Website: *www.7MilesGlobal.com*

Charity Awareness: *www.T2T.org*

DANIEL KILBURN

WHEN THE SIRENS FADE

FORGIVING MYSELF FOR WHAT I COULDN'T PREVENT

A FOREIGN CONCEPT: MY JOURNEY BEGINS

Forgiveness. Some say it's the most powerful act a human can commit. But if I'm honest with you—it's a power I didn't grow up knowing. It wasn't taught to me in childhood, nor reinforced by the rigor of military life. For decades, forgiveness wasn't a concept I actively rejected; I just never thought it applied to me.

As I sat down to write this chapter, I searched the archives of my life for moments where forgiveness showed up. And surprisingly, there weren't many. Or rather, I hadn't recognized them. Because forgiveness, like an emergency evacuation plan, only proves its value when the sirens start screaming.

THE DUAL NATURE OF FORGIVENESS: OTHERS VS. SELF

Over the years, I've found it relatively easy to forgive others for small transgressions. A snarky text. A rude comment. An unfounded criticism. Those kinds of things are easy to brush off—probably because I've lived long enough to know everyone has bad days, demons, and disappointments.

But there's a threshold I struggle with: intentional harm. When someone deliberately causes damage—physical, emotional, or economic—it triggers something deeper. Especially when it's clear that their behavior isn't an exception, but a pattern. Forgiveness doesn't come easy then. I see it as surrendering to someone's toxicity. But maybe that's not what forgiveness is at all.

Because where I've truly struggled isn't in forgiving them—it's in forgiving myself.

THE UNEXPECTED MIRROR: WHAT THE SILENCE TAUGHT ME

Every day, I create content. I give free, life-saving information about emergency preparedness and financial resilience. I speak from my heart. And yet, most days? Silence.

The feedback is rare. Sometimes there's appreciation. Other times, bizarrely, hostility. People dismiss or even mock the information I offer. And that used to hurt more than I cared to admit.

Until one day, I asked a hard question: What if it's not about them? What if I need to forgive myself?

I needed to forgive myself for feeling unheard. For taking it personally. For believing that my worth was tied to likes, shares, and algorithmic approval.

I needed to forgive myself for all the times I thought, "Maybe I'm not doing enough," when in reality, I was doing more than most.

And I needed to forgive myself for the lives I couldn't save. That's the hardest one. When you live a life of service, especially in emergency planning, you witness loss. Sometimes, people don't act until it's too late. And I've blamed myself for that. But I'm learning… not everything is mine to carry.

REBUILDING WITH GRACE:
LEADERSHIP, LEGACY, & LETTING GO

We are all products of our culture, upbringing, careers, and relationships. But at some point, we must decide if those past blueprints serve our future. Forgiveness is part of that process. Not just letting go of grudges—but letting go of guilt, regret, and false responsibility.

Forgiveness has taught me this: it is not weakness. It's strategic surrender. Like clearing debris after a storm, it makes way for rebuilding.

When I began to forgive myself—for the silence, the backlash, the misunderstandings—I found renewed energy. I realized that I didn't need to change my message. I just needed to deliver it with more grace and less attachment.

Now, when I teach disaster planning or financial literacy, I understand that some won't listen until it's too late. And that's not on me. I show up anyway. I serve anyway. That's leadership.

FORGIVENESS IS FUEL

Forgiveness is not about forgetting. It's about remembering—without the poison. It's choosing to hold the lesson, not the pain. It's knowing that healing is a journey, not a destination.

If you're reading this and you've carried blame—whether for what someone else did, or what you didn't do—I invite you to set it down. The pack is lighter without it.

Ask for help when you need it. Many of us are waiting, arms open, ready to walk with you through the wreckage. Not because we've figured it all out, but because we, too, have chosen to forgive.

FAQ: FORGIVENESS FROM THE FRONTLINES

1. How do I begin forgiving myself when I feel responsible for others' pain?

Start by acknowledging the difference between responsibility and response. You can respond with compassion, but you are not responsible for every outcome. Write down what you can control—and what you can't.

2. What if the person who hurt me hasn't apologized?

Forgiveness doesn't require their permission. It's for you, not them. Waiting for their apology only prolongs your pain.

3. How can I forgive people who repeatedly harm others?

Forgiveness doesn't mean allowing ongoing harm. Set boundaries. Forgiveness is release, not reconciliation. You can let go without letting them back in.

4. Why does forgiving myself feel harder than forgiving others?

We're often our harshest critics. Self-forgiveness threatens our belief that pain equals penance. But you don't need to keep punishing yourself to prove you care.

5. Can forgiveness really lead to healing?

Yes. Forgiveness is the key that unlocks the cage of resentment. Healing begins when you stop feeding your pain and start nurturing your peace.

DANIEL KILBURN

Kilburn is a retired U.S. Army Senior Infantry Drill Sergeant, a seasoned speaker, and the founder of Emergency Action Planning LLC. With a heart for service and a mission to safeguard families and communities, Daniel dedicates his life to teaching the principles of resilience, preparedness, and financial literacy. His powerful voice and grounded wisdom stem not just from years of military discipline but from real-life experiences navigating natural disasters, personal challenges, and transformational growth. Daniel's work centers on helping people rediscover their sense of purpose and security, especially during life's most uncertain moments.

An award-winning Toastmaster and bestselling co-author, Daniel brings authenticity, clarity, and compassion to every page he writes. Through his words, he challenges readers to reflect, rise, and resonate on higher frequencies—starting with love and gratitude. For additional information, Daniel's contact information can be found here: www.linkedin.com/in/DanielKilburn

Author's Website: *www.EmergencyActionPlanning.com*

Charity Awareness: *www.WoundedWarriorProject.org*

DANIELE G. LATTANZI

WHEN FORGIVENESS STARTS WITH YOU

"You can't drive a car looking in the rearview mirror."
~ Daniele G. Lattanzi
(A reminder I've returned to many times in my own life.)

A DIFFERENT WAY TO THINK ABOUT FORGIVENESS

Most of the time, when people hear the word *forgiveness*, they instantly think of forgiving others: someone who said something hurtful, someone who disappointed them, betrayed their trust, or didn't show up when it mattered. And yes—those situations matter. Forgiving others is essential.

But in the context of **survival to thrival**, I've learned something that many people overlook:

If you want to thrive, the first person you need to forgive is yourself.

That's not a motivational poster. That's a practical reality. Many of us are generally good people—we try hard, want to do the right thing, and often give others the benefit of the doubt, especially people we love, work with, or believe in. But when it comes to ourselves, we are ruthless. We replay our mistakes, criticize our decisions, and punish ourselves mentally. We tell ourselves stories like, "I'm not good enough," "I should've known better," "I always mess it up," or "I don't deserve to win." If we keep repeating those beliefs, we create a dangerous pattern: we **build our future on top of self-judgment.** That's not thriving. That's surviving with a heavy backpack full of regret.

THE PROBLEM IS NOT WHAT HAPPENED—IT'S WHAT YOU KEEP HOLDING

Here's the part that's difficult to accept:

Sometimes, what happened in your past was real. You made a mistake, failed, or life didn't go as planned. People left. You lost money. You trusted someone you shouldn't have. Those things can be painful. But the real trap is this: **holding on to the past becomes a habit.** And once it becomes a habit, it starts operating like a quiet poison, affecting your confidence, your decisions, your health, your relationships, your performance, and your ability to lead. In other words, it becomes a lifestyle. That's why my motto on forgiveness is simple: **let it go.** Not because it didn't matter or was "fine," but because holding onto it is destroying your ability to move forward.

WHY SELF-FORGIVENESS IS THE FOUNDATION OF THRIVING

This is where many people get confused.

They think forgiving yourself means you're making excuses. No.

Forgiving yourself means you're acknowledging something happened—and choosing not to let that event define your identity. Own the mistake. Take responsibility for what you did wrong, learn from them—but most importantly, move forward. If you keep putting yourself down, you will bring that energy into every area of life. You won't be good in a relationship if you think you're a failure, or lead your family well if you're constantly insulting yourself internally. You won't show up powerfully at work or build health if your mindset is stuck in shame. You can forgive other people, but if you don't forgive yourself, you still show up as broken. And broken energy creates broken results. So yes—self-forgiveness is not selfish, soft, or optional. **It's the starting point of becoming operational again.**

THE BODY CAN HEAL—& SO CAN YOUR MINDSET

I've said it before, and I'll repeat it:

The human body has an incredible ability to heal itself—if you give it what it needs. The same is true of your mindset. You have an innate ability to thrive. You are not defined by one mistake, one season, or one bad chapter. You can rebuild, adjust, and grow—but only if you stop holding onto the version of yourself that you're punishing. Letting go is not denial; letting go is a strategy.THE LOSER-TO-WINNER SHIFT

I want to be very clear here.

When you hold onto self-judgment, guilt, and shame, you take on what I call **a loser mindset**. Not because you *are* a loser, but because your thinking becomes trapped in the psychology of losing. A loser mindset repeats, "It's over," "I can't," "I always fail," "I'm not that type of person," or "I don't deserve better." In contrast, a winner mindset asks, "Okay, that happened… now what? What can I learn? What's my next step? How do I rebuild? How do I improve?" Forgiveness is what helps you shift from loser thinking to winner thinking—because it removes the identity poison. Once you remove that poison, you start making better decisions.

A PRACTICAL TOOL:
WRITE DOWN FIVE "KICK-ASS" MOMENTS

Let me give you a simple exercise—because mindset is not magic. Mindset is training.

Here's the exercise:

Write down five moments in your life when you were a "kick-ass" person.

It can be anything:

- A time you overcame fear.

- A time you handled a crisis.

- A time you showed discipline.

- A time you achieved a goal.

- A time you did something hard.

- A time you stepped up for someone

• A time you built something meaningful.

And if you can't find five, write down one. Because even one is enough to prove something: **If you've done it once, you can do it again.**

That's the whole point.

Self-forgiveness becomes easier when you stop staring at your failures and start remembering your capabilities.

Because confidence is not arrogance.

Confidence is memory.

MY "AHA" MOMENT: MY BACK INJURY & THE CHOICE TO BECOME OPERATIONAL

I want to tie this into a real moment of my life—because forgiveness is not a theory. Years ago, I had a severe back injury that lasted months and disrupted everything. At a certain point, I was told, "You may not be able to walk again." At first, it was devastating. I went through the emotional spiral: anger, fear, frustration, and worst-case scenarios. What I realized was that if I stayed in that negativity, nothing would improve. Negativity affects actions, discipline, effort, and belief. The "aha" moment happened when I let go of the idea that "this can't be fixed" and replaced it with, **"I can do something about it."** Maybe not perfection, perhaps not a complete reset, but something. That mindset shift changed my behavior—I stopped collapsing mentally, started focusing on micro-steps, building a plan, and asking better questions. Slowly, I improved. Strangely, that was forgiveness too. Because in those moments, it's easy to blame yourself: "I should've been stronger," "I should've trained more," "I should've prevented this." But the truth is, life throws curveballs. Thriving requires you to stop attacking yourself and start rebuilding yourself.

THE THRIVING QUESTION

So here's the question I want you to reflect on: What are you still holding onto that is preventing you from moving forward? Is it guilt, shame, regret, a past failure, a relationship mistake, a business decision, or a moment you wish you could redo? You don't have to pretend it didn't happen. But you do have to decide: are you going to carry it forever? Because you cannot thrive while holding on.

If there's anything I want you to remember, it's this: forgiveness isn't only about other people. Self-forgiveness is the foundation of thriving. Letting go is not weakness—it's a strategy. Your past can inform you, but it should not imprison you. Write down proof that you're capable and use it to rebuild your confidence. Becoming operational again starts with a mindset. Thriving isn't a destination; it's a decision you make daily. And forgiveness—especially forgiving yourself—is one of the strongest decisions you will ever make. So let it go. Not because it didn't matter, but because your future matters more.

DANIELE G. LATTANZI

Daniele G. Lattanzi is your Practice Growth Partner with over twenty-five years of experience helping small businesses and healthcare practitioners transform their activity into thriving, scalable companies. His entrepreneurial journey builds on extensive management, finance, marketing, e-commerce, and business development expertise. Fluent in four languages—English, Italian, Portuguese, and Spanish—Daniele's linguistic skills have been instrumental in his international coaching and business operations across Italy, Europe, and North and South America.

As the Co-Founder and CEO of Effective Practice Management and Holistic Health Solutions since 2016, Daniele has dedicated himself to empowering private practice owners and their teams to unlock their full potential by providing proven practice management training and coaching. Follow him at: *www.Instagram.com/DG_Lattanzi*

Author's Website: *www.EffectivePracticeManagement.com*

Charity Awareness: *www.SurvivalToThrivalSeries.com*

DAWNESE OPENSHAW

FORGIVENESS: THE KEY TO FREEDOM

"Without forgiveness, there's no future."
~ Desmond Tutu

We all carry scars. Some are visible, most are invisible. They live in the folds of memory, in the tightness of the chest when a certain name is mentioned, in the tears we refuse to let fall. Pain has a way of attaching itself to our hearts like heavy chains.

And if courage was the first step in moving from survival to thrival, forgiveness is the master key that unlocks the prison door.

THE POISON & THE CURE

In survival, forgiveness feels impossible. We replay betrayals on a loop: the parent who abandoned us, the friend who lied, the partner who broke trust, the boss who humiliated us, or even our own choices that turned sideways. Survival clings to pain because it feels like protection—*If I never forget, I can never be hurt like that again.*

But here's the truth I've learned: holding on doesn't protect us, it poisons us. Survival uses resentment like a shield, but thrival invites us to set it down. Thrival asks us to breathe again, to reclaim our power, to choose peace over punishment.

Forgiveness is not weakness—it is strength dressed in softness. It's not condoning what happened—it's choosing not to let what happened control the rest of your life.

Or as I often remind myself: *Stop rehearsing your pain and start practicing your possibility.*

MY STORY OF FORGIVENESS

I remember a season of my life where anger became my closest companion. A deep wound—one I didn't ask for, one I didn't deserve—shaped how I saw myself and how I trusted others. For years, I told myself that holding on to the anger kept me strong. I thought if I let it go, it meant what they did was "okay."

But the truth? I wasn't strong. I was stuck. My light dimmed. My joy dulled. And no matter how much I achieved on the outside, inside, I was chained to that pain.

Forgiveness came slowly. It came in pieces: through counseling, through journaling, through messy tears, through the quiet whisper of Spirit reminding me, *"You were made for more than this pain, and you are being refined by it—like the refiner's fire."*

The day I chose to forgive, not because they deserved it but because I deserved the freedom I longed for, I felt my soul exhale. Forgiveness didn't change the past, but it changed something inside me—and that changed everything.

One of the most radical experiences of forgiveness in my life came from childhood sexual abuse. Beginning at the age of seven, I carried a wound that shaped how I saw myself and how safe I felt in the world. For years, I believed I could never forgive the one who hurt me.

And yet, through years of inner work, the Spirit's whisperings, and the slow practice of release, I reached a place where I could look them in the eyes, be in their presence, and even give them a hug.

That doesn't mean what happened was ever okay. It means I chose freedom over chains. Forgiveness made the impossible possible.

What feels impossible today may be the very place where your freedom is waiting.

THE MYTHS OF FORGIVENESS

We often resist forgiveness because we've been taught the wrong things about it. Let's clear the air:

- **Myth: Forgiveness means forgetting.**
  Forgiveness doesn't erase memory; it releases the charge. You may remember what happened, but the memory no longer rules you.

- **Myth: Forgiveness means reconciliation.**

  Sometimes it does. But often it doesn't. Forgiveness can be one-sided. You can forgive and still choose distance.

- **Myth: Forgiveness makes me weak.**

  Forgiveness takes more courage than revenge. Weakness is letting bitterness control your story.

- **Myth: Forgiveness is for them.**

  Forgiveness is for *you*. It's your gift to your nervous system, your peace, your future.

As I like to say: *Forgiveness is choosing your freedom over their offense.*

THE LAYERS OF FORGIVENESS

Forgiveness is not a one-time event. It's a process, like peeling an onion. Sometimes, you peel one layer, only to find another wound beneath it. That doesn't mean you failed; it means you are human.

Here are the layers I've seen in myself and others:

- **Forgiving Others:** The obvious one—letting go of what someone else did.

- **Forgiving Circumstances:** Life doesn't always go the way we dreamed. Sometimes we must forgive the loss, the diagnosis, the detour.

- **Forgiving Ourselves:** The hardest one. We hold ourselves to impossible standards. Thrival demands self-compassion.

- **Forgiving God (or Life Itself):** Though it may sound radical, many of us quietly carry resentment against the Divine for "allowing" pain. Releasing this restores connection to Source.

Each layer invites us deeper into freedom.

THE TURNING POINT

Forgiveness is both a decision and a practice. For me, it wasn't a lightning bolt—it was a slow dawning. The day I could look back at my pain and whisper, *"I am stronger because of you,"* was the day I knew I was free.

"True forgiveness is when you can say, 'Thank you for that experience.'"
~ Oprah Winfrey

This doesn't mean I celebrated the hurt. It means I claimed the wisdom it gave me without letting the wound define me. That moment of gratitude became my doorway from surviving to thriving.

THE PRACTICE OF FORGIVENESS

So, how do we forgive when it feels impossible? Forgiveness is both an inner posture and an outer practice.

- **Name the Wound:** You cannot heal what you won't acknowledge. Write it, say it, cry it. Let it be seen.

- **Choose Release:** Say out loud: "I choose to forgive." Even if your heart isn't there yet, the choice begins the process.

- **Feel the Emotions:** Anger, grief, sadness—let them move through your body. Forgiveness is not bypassing. It's metabolizing.

- **Shift the Story:** Instead of "they ruined me," try "I am stronger because I learned." Reframing doesn't excuse—it empowers.

- **Create Ritual:** Write a letter and burn it. Place a rock in water as a symbol of release. Rituals give the subconscious closure.

- **Practice Daily:** Forgiveness is like exercise. One workout doesn't make you fit. One act of forgiveness doesn't free you forever. Keep choosing.

As I remind my clients: *Every time the old wound resurfaces, you get to choose again. That's not failure. That's freedom in progress.*

REFLECTIVE QUESTIONS

- What part of my story is still holding energy that no longer serves me?
- What freedom might open if I chose to forgive today?
- Who do I become when I live unchained from resentment?
- How can forgiveness be an act of love for myself first?
- What is one small step I can take toward release right now?

A MANTRA FOR FORGIVENESS

"I release what was. I reclaim who I am. I rise free."

THE RIPPLE EFFECT

Here's the beautiful paradox: when you forgive, the ripple goes beyond you. Your children feel it. Your community feels it. Even the person you forgave may feel it, though they never hear the words. Energy shifts.

Unforgiveness keeps us stuck in survival. Forgiveness tunes us to freedom, possibility, and love.

Forgiveness doesn't rewrite the past. It rewrites you. And in that rewriting, you discover the freedom, the power, and the love that is the very heart of thrival.

DAWNESE OPENSHAW

Dawnese Openshaw is a visionary leader, master transformational and relationship coach, and passionate advocate for conscious living and loving. As Founder of Lead the Change, she empowers individuals, families, and organizations to lead with emotional, social, and relationship intelligence. Dawnese is the co-creator of the Global Leadership Experience, a life-changing training for those ready to align with their purpose and live a vision-led life.

A lifelong student of leadership since reading Dale Carnegie's *How to Win Friends and Influence People* at fourteen, Dawnese shares her experience and wisdom gained from daily living and supporting individual and organizational growth for over thirty years.

She and her husband, Scott, are celebrating thirty years of marriage, are proud parents of three amazing adult children, and are brand-new grandparents. Dawnese believes that when people live in alignment with their values, relationships thrive —and when relationships thrive, *magic happens.*

Author's Website: *www.LeadTheChange.org*

Charity Awareness: *www.SurvivalToThrivalSeries.com*

DHARMI SHAH

SORRY FOR THE THING I SAID IN 2004

THE GRACE OF LETTING GO

Let's be real—"forgiveness" is one of those words that feels like it should come with a warning label. It's heavy. Like, sit-in-your-feelings-and-eat-a-pint-of-ice-cream heavy. For most of my life, forgiving others came easier than forgiving myself. And honestly, even that had its limits.

Do I believe in kindness? Absolutely. Do I believe every person deserves my forgiveness? Not so sure. I'm not one of those people who think you have to forgive someone to be free. I feel pretty free, thanks very much—and I didn't send everyone who hurt me a get-out-of-jail-free card. Some people? I simply love from a distance... a very safe distance. And maybe that's a form of forgiveness, too.

But the toughest part of all of this? Forgiving myself. That's where the real work began.

WHY IS SELF-FORGIVENESS SO HARD?

Now here's where it gets tricky—self-forgiveness.

Why is it so much easier to forgive other people but torture ourselves with the replay button in our heads? I could be minding my business, sipping coffee, and suddenly I'm remembering something awkward I said five years ago, like it just happened.

It's wild how quickly we offer grace to others, but withhold it from ourselves. I've had entire inner monologues about how someone didn't say hi the "right" way—and suddenly I'm convinced I did something wrong. Spoiler: I didn't. That's just the overthinker's brain doing what it does best.

These days, I'm practicing self-forgiveness in real time. I remind myself that I'm human, still learning, still growing. Sometimes, we say or do things that don't land quite right. That doesn't make us bad—it makes us human. I remember, years ago, apologizing for something that still makes me cringe. It wasn't life-altering—it was a moment, a sentence I wish I could unsay. But that moment taught me that sometimes, the hardest person to face... is you.

WHEN LIFE THROWS A CURVEBALL

There were seasons where I blamed myself for everything. When life took a hard turn, I didn't just feel disappointment—I felt shame. Deep down, I thought maybe I brought it on myself.

"Is this karma?" I'd ask. "Did I miss a sign? Did I say the wrong thing to the universe?"

But what I've come to believe is this: some chapters have to end for new ones to begin. Sometimes things fall apart not because we failed, but because we were meant for something different. Something better. And when that realization sinks in, we start to make peace with the past.

We begin to say, "Whatever the lesson was, I forgive myself for how I handled it."

GRACE OVER GUILT

Forgiveness doesn't always look like a huge emotional breakthrough. Sometimes, it's the simple decision to stop beating yourself up.

It's choosing rest over spiraling. Silence over self-criticism. Saying to yourself, "You did the best you could."

That's what grace feels like. It's not flashy. It's not loud. But it's powerful. It gives us room to breathe again. It softens the way we show up for ourselves.

And grace reminds us that we don't need to keep punishing ourselves to prove we care. We're allowed to let it go.

WHEN THE UNIVERSE HAS OTHER PLANS

Let's have a moment of honesty—the universe doesn't always play nice. I've tried all the things. Vision boards. Meditation. Gratitude lists. Still, life shows up with plot twists and no warning.

And in those moments? I've definitely yelled into a pillow or dramatically questioned my choices.

But eventually, I realized that part of forgiveness is also forgiving life for not going the way I planned. It's forgiving timing for being off. It's forgiving myself for not having it all together when I thought I should.

And if you can laugh through it—even just a little—consider that progress. As someone once told me, "If you don't laugh, you'll cry." So, now I do both. And then I order takeout.

WE'RE ALL STILL LEARNING

Forgiveness isn't a one-time thing. It's a practice. Sometimes, we get it right. Sometimes, we trip and fall face-first into a pile of old guilt. But we get back up.

Because we're still learning. Still growing. Still figuring it out.

We are all doing our best with what we have—and that's enough. If we can give love and compassion to others for their missteps, then we can certainly give it to ourselves.

So, if you're holding on to something that keeps whispering you should've done better—here's your permission to let it go.

LET IT BE

Forgiveness isn't about pretending something didn't happen. It's about deciding not to carry it forever.

So, breathe deep. Offer yourself some grace. And remember—you're doing better than you think.

Forgiveness isn't a destination. It's more like a series of green lights after a long stretch of red ones. Sometimes, you don't even realize how much you've been holding onto until you start to release it—bit by bit, layer by layer. And even then, it's not about suddenly feeling healed. It's about feeling lighter.

There are still days when old thoughts sneak back in, when overthinking tries to take the wheel. And that's okay. That doesn't mean we've failed at healing. It means we're human, still navigating the road. The trick is learning to hear those thoughts and gently letting them pass, like clouds in the sky.

Sometimes, forgiveness is just deciding not to drag yesterday's emotional baggage into today's peace. It's choosing to stay soft when the world asks you to be hard. It's waking up, making your coffee, and saying, "Today, I'm giving myself grace—even if I have to keep reminding myself every hour."

And if all else fails? Breathe. Stretch. Laugh. Call that one friend who always gets it. Healing is never one-size-fits-all—but it's always possible.

The truth is, overthinking can feel like a full-time job. You find yourself replaying conversations, obsessing over the tone of a text, and wondering if you said too much—or not enough. I may never get the chance to apologize for everything I've said or done wrong, including whatever I blurted out in 2004—but I can forgive the version of me who didn't know better. Forgiveness is what pulls you out of that cycle. It's the gentle reminder that you're allowed to move on, even if your brain wants to stay stuck on repeat.

We're not meant to carry every interaction like it's a suitcase we can never unpack. At some point, we get to set it down. We get to say, "That moment has passed. I'm choosing peace now."

Some days, forgiveness looks like writing it all out. Other days, it looks like not explaining yourself to anyone. And sometimes, it just looks like staying in bed a little longer and deciding not to feel bad about it.

No one tells you that forgiving yourself might be the most radical act of self-love you ever commit to. But once you do, life opens up in new ways. You find space to laugh louder, breathe deeper, and live freer.

So, give yourself that permission. Every single day, if needed.

Forgiveness is one of those things that doesn't always announce itself. It doesn't come with a grand reveal or some dramatic soundtrack. Sometimes, it arrives quietly—through a sigh of relief, a better night's sleep, or the way your body finally relaxes when you stop clinging to the past.

There's something beautifully unspoken about the peace that comes with finally letting go. It's not about pretending it didn't happen. It's not about rewriting history. It's about choosing to remember it differently—without carrying the weight.

And yes, some days you'll still think about it. Some days it might still sting. But that doesn't mean you're not healing. That doesn't mean you haven't grown.

It just means you're human. A beautiful, evolving, emotional human who is learning to move forward without dragging every piece of the past along.

And honestly, that's worth celebrating.

MY RECIPE FOR FORGIVENESS

If forgiveness came in a to-go box, it'd probably have a label like this:

- An abundance of grace.

- Friends who gently pull you back from overthinking spirals—even if snacks are required.

- A heaping spoonful of "I messed up, and that's okay."

- A full cup of self-love, stirred often.

- And a generous sprinkle of humor—because sometimes, you just have to laugh at the mess.

DHARMI SHAH

Dharmi Shah is a globally recognized award-winning entrepreneur, celebrated for her transformative leadership and exceptional impact across industries. As the visionary founder of The Corporate Experience, a cutting-edge marketing firm, Dharmi curates unparalleled experiences that help businesses grow and thrive, all while forging lasting bonds that drive sustained success.

She is also the mastermind behind Refresh and Revitalize, an award-winning coaching brand dedicated to empowering women, cultivating a powerful community where they uplift, inspire, and support one another to reach their fullest potential.

Dharmi founded Evenings of Elegance, an elite event production company that spent over two decades creating extraordinary, high-profile events, leaving a lasting impression on every client. A culinary connoisseur, Dharmi finds pure joy in the kitchen, believing that the dinner table is where cherished memories, laughter, and joy come together, building profound connections with every shared meal.

Author's Website: *www.DharmiShah.com*

Charity Awareness: *www.TinyHeartsRememberedInc.org*

DIANNE SUSI

BEING THE PEACEKEEPER DOESN'T MEAN BEING A PUSHOVER

People often ask me how I stay so calm, how I don't hold grudges, and how I don't seem to let anything stick. The truth is simple: I live in forgiveness—always have. Maybe not in the dramatic, fall-to-your-knees kind of way some people talk about, but in a quieter, everyday kind of way. I learned a long time ago that if you want to be at peace in this life, you can't carry around the weight of everyone else's wrongdoings. You can't make their shame or their mistakes yours. And you sure can't wait around for an apology that may never come.

Forgiveness, for me, isn't a single moment. It's a lifetime posture. It's the way I walk through the world. I don't wait to be hurt and then decide to let it go. I start with forgiveness, before the wound can take root. Not because I'm a doormat, not because I'm naïve, but because I've learned that holding onto resentment doesn't just harden your heart; it slows your healing.

As a middle child, I took on the role of peacekeeper. My job in the family dynamic was to keep things smooth at all costs. I can remember being a child, and if my sister did something wrong and was punished for it, I would often get looped into that punishment, not because I had done anything wrong, but because my father didn't want her to go through it alone. He would ask me to do the extra chores with her, and I did. Not out of obligation, but because I wanted to be a good kid. I wanted to make things easier on everyone. That's where my peacekeeping instincts were born.

I wouldn't call anyone in my life a bully, even if I was treated unfairly at times. What I've come to understand is that some people lead with dominance or defensiveness. But I've always chosen to lead with peace. And that has made all the difference.

For me, the relationship has always been more important than being right. It's not that anyone "got over" on me; I just believed that if there was love or friendship between us, that mattered more than winning an argument. I've never needed to be right. I've needed to stay in alignment with what feels true and kind. That's why I've often softened first, apologized first, or let things go when others wouldn't. Not because I was weak, but because the connection meant more to me than control or ego.

I've carried that energy through my entire life. Into friendships. Into motherhood. Into marriage.

And then, of course, into divorce.

My ex-husband betrayed me in every way a person could be betrayed. Lies, cheating, manipulation; it was all there. I lived through the unraveling of a marriage, the destruction of a home, and the crumbling of trust. But in the wake of it all, I did not let bitterness define me. I raised my daughter with love, built a new life with grace, and forgave him long before he ever said a word.

And yet, decades later, I finally received the thing most people wait years for: an apology. A real one; acknowledgment. He admitted to the ways he had mistreated both me and our daughter. And while it didn't undo the past, it offered a kind of closure that made forgiveness feel even more worthwhile. But the truth is, I didn't need it. I had already let it go.

Forgiveness, to me, is not weakness, nor is it avoidance. It's the opposite; It's a strength, it's clarity, it's choosing peace when pain is easier.

People often confuse my calm with being a pushover. They see my kindness, my softness, my easygoing way, and they assume I'm someone who can be walked on. But I'm not a rug. I don't let people use me. I simply don't take on other people's projections. And when people show me who they are, especially if who they are is angry, unkind, or unwilling to evolve, I let them go with love, and without resentment.

That's what happened with a dear friend of mine, someone I had known for fifty years. I would've never imagined that our friendship would come to an end. I had been the peacekeeper in that relationship, too. The one who softened first. The one who apologized when things felt off, even if I hadn't done anything wrong. But in the end, when I finally spoke my truth, instead of meeting me with care and reflection, she pushed back hard.

She held onto stories that weren't true. She tried to create drama in a space where I had worked hard to keep peace. And I realized: I was done. I had done everything I could. And so, I cut the cord with confidence, with clarity, and with peace.

Because sometimes, forgiveness looks like walking away.

Sometimes, it looks like knowing when a relationship has run its course.

Sometimes, it means acknowledging that the loss is not yours. It's theirs.

My daughter has often told me that she wishes she could speak the way I do about people who have hurt her, that she admires how I never spiral into self-blame, or let other people's actions make me question my own worth. And I think that comes from something deeper.

I learned forgiveness from my mother.

My mom went through a lot in her life. Family members stole money from her. She had every reason to hold a grudge, to stay angry, to replay old wounds. But she didn't. She would say, "If you just keep talking about the past, you'll never be happy." And she meant it. She lived it. She forgave and forgot. She let go, and I watched her do it again and again.

She taught me to do the same.

I don't stay angry. I don't stew. I don't beat myself up.

I forgive.

Because staying angry is like taking poison and expecting it to hurt the other person.

That doesn't mean I don't take responsibility when I'm wrong. I do. I apologize. I own my part. But if something goes sideways in a relationship, I don't assume it's my fault. I don't carry what isn't mine.

Forgiveness, at its core, is about freedom.

It's how I stay connected to myself. It's how I protect my peace. It's how I continue to live with grace, no matter what other people choose to do.

If you're reading this and carrying a heavy wound—from someone who never apologized, someone who disappointed you, or from someone who hurt you—I want to tell you something I've lived:

You don't have to carry it. You don't have to wait for the apology. You don't have to keep going over the story to understand it.

You can forgive them. You can release it. You can set yourself free.

Forgiveness doesn't mean they were right. It means *you're ready to move on.*

Let it go. Let it soften. And let yourself feel what it's like to finally be light again.

You deserve that.

We all do.

DIANNE SUSI

Dianne Susi is a service-driven advocate with a passion for helping others live with dignity, stability, and compassion. She began her career as a claims examiner at an insurance company and later spent thirty-three years in the financial department of a major hospital. Her job was to ensure that every patient left with their claim paid, so they could focus on healing without financial stress. She took great pride in making sure every file that crossed her desk was handled with care, accuracy, and humanity. Alongside her professional work, Dianne also built a housecleaning and home organizing path that allowed her to raise her daughter, Natalie—and simply have fun. Later in life, after her husband Claudio started a pet-sitting business, Dianne became a devoted animal lover, helping walk dogs and welcome them into their home. Their first dog, Primo—a fiery little Maltese all of seven pounds—ruled over every animal who entered their house, but grew to love the familiar ones. Since retiring from the hospital, Dianne now spends her days gardening, caring for backyard birds, and keeping their dog Richie happy and healthy. She often says that if she ever came into great wealth, she'd devote it entirely to rescuing and supporting animals in need. Follow Dianne on social media: *@diannesusi*

Charity Awareness: *www.BVSPCA.org*

EILEEN E. GALBRAITH

FROM BETRAYAL TO SELF-FORGIVENESS

Why do we allow others to treat us poorly? Why do we accept what is clearly unacceptable? These are the questions that haunted me in 1998, the year my life cracked open.

After fifteen years of marriage, I found out my husband was cheating on me. There was no warning sign, no subtle unraveling. The truth didn't trickle in gently. It hit like a freight train.

One moment, I was living what I thought was a stable life. The next, I was staring at the wreckage of everything I believed in. My world imploded. My identity as a wife, partner, and companion dissolved overnight. I hadn't just lost a marriage—I had lost *myself* in the process.

I couldn't eat. I couldn't sleep. I couldn't focus. I lost thirty pounds in thirty days and nearly lost my job. But more than anything, I lost my will to go on. I married to *be married.*

Divorce was never part of my plan. The heartbreak was so severe, I spiraled into a darkness I never thought I'd face. I even attempted to take my own life—believing there was no light left for me on the other side of this pain.

I felt rejected, abandoned, and utterly worthless. My inner voice was brutal. *You weren't enough. You should have seen it coming. You're not lovable.* The betrayal pierced me deeply, but it was the shame and self-blame that truly destroyed me.

Looking back now, with all the perspective I've gained, I realize how much of my suffering came not just from what happened, but from how I internalized it. I made *his decision* about *my worth.* And that nearly broke me.

For a long time, I believed forgiveness was about absolving the other person—letting them off the hook for their wrongdoings. But that belief kept me stuck. Because how could I possibly forgive someone who blew up my life and walked away without remorse?

It wasn't until I began to awaken from the fog, until I started to understand that *what happened was happening for me, not to me*, that I saw forgiveness differently. Not as a gift for him, but as liberation for *me.*

Forgiveness was never about excusing his choices. It was about reclaiming my power.

It started with forgiving him—not because he deserved it, but because I deserved peace. I was tired of carrying around the poison of anger and resentment. Every time I replayed the betrayal in my mind, I relived it. I was keeping myself chained to a moment that no longer existed.

But even more transformative than forgiving him was the moment I chose to forgive *myself.*

Forgiving myself was the hardest part. I had to face all the ways I had abandoned myself long before he did. I had to confront the places where I gave too much, spoke too little, and stayed too long. I had to let go of the idea that being "the weaker one" made me less valuable. I had to embrace that vulnerability does not equal weakness—it means I loved deeply, and that in itself is strength.

For so long, I beat myself up for not seeing the signs, for being "naïve," for staying, for crumbling. I judged myself more harshly than anyone else ever could. But here's the truth: I was doing the best I could with what I knew at the time. And when we know better, we do better.

That's what forgiveness offered me, a new lens through which to view my past. Not with blame or bitterness, but with compassion.

The day I forgave myself was the day I began to heal.

I looked in the mirror and saw someone who had been through the fire and survived. Someone who had been broken but was now rising. I began to speak more kindly to myself. To rewrite the story that I had been telling in my mind. No longer was I "the woman he left"—I was the woman who found her own way back.

I stopped beating myself up over his decision and started focusing on *my own.* I chose to live. I chose to grow. I chose to rebuild.

And in that choice, I found something even deeper than forgiveness—I found freedom.

Forgiveness is not a one-time event. It's a daily decision to release the grip of the past. Some days, I still felt the sting. But each time I chose to extend grace instead of shame, love instead of blame, I reclaimed another piece of myself.

And slowly, my life began to change.

I began to understand that we don't forgive others because they ask for it or deserve it because our hearts can't carry that much pain forever. Forgiveness is an energetic cleanse. It's the moment we decide to stop bleeding for a wound someone else caused.

But what about self-forgiveness? That's where real magic lives.

Because when we hold on to guilt or shame, we are punishing ourselves for someone else's betrayal. We are keeping ourselves in a self-imposed prison. And we deserve to be free.

Forgiving myself allowed me to soften. It allowed me to be human. To say: *I didn't know then what I know now—and that's okay.* It helped me see that my compassion for others had to begin with compassion for myself.

And it taught me something else: boundaries *are born from forgiveness.* Once I forgave myself, I started setting healthier limits. I stopped allowing others to treat me poorly. I learned to recognize what was unacceptable and walk away from anything that didn't align with my worth.

I also stopped being ashamed of my story.

Because my story, though painful, is powerful. It's shaped who I've become. It's deepened my empathy. It's given me tools to help others navigate their darkest moments. And it's made me fiercely committed to honoring the woman I am today.

Forgiveness was never about pretending it didn't happen. It's about remembering it differently—without the pain taking center stage. It's choosing to focus on the growth, not the wound.

So, to anyone who feels like they're stuck in their own heartbreak, wondering how they'll ever breathe again, I see you. And I want you to know healing is possible. Forgiveness is not weakness—it's a radical act of strength. And self-forgiveness? That's your soul calling you back home.

You don't have to carry the weight of someone else's decision forever. You can set it down. You can honor the love you gave and still walk away. You can cry and still be strong. You can forgive and still protect your peace.

And above all else—you can forgive *yourself.*

You deserve to be free.

FORGIVENESS REFLECTION EXERCISE: RELEASING THE WEIGHT

Find a quiet space where you won't be disturbed. Take a few deep breaths, placing your hand gently over your heart. Close your eyes and tune in to the emotion you've been holding—anger, shame, guilt, sadness. Now, bring to mind the person or situation that hurt you. This may be someone else, or it may be *you.*

Ask yourself: *What have I been carrying that no longer serves me?*

Then, write a letter—not to send, but to release. Say everything you need to say. Let the truth pour out, uncensored.

Next, read your words out loud or in your mind. Afterward, speak these affirmations:

- "I forgive you for not being who I needed you to be."
- "I forgive myself for abandoning my needs."
- "I choose peace over punishment."
- "I release the past and reclaim my power."

Tear up or burn the letter (safely), symbolizing your release.

Finally, breathe deeply. Feel the weight begin to lift. Forgiveness doesn't mean forgetting—it means freeing your heart to heal.

Repeat this as often as needed. Healing is not a single act; it's a practice. And today, you took one bold step toward freedom.

EILEEN E. GALBRAITH

With an innate talent for connecting with others, Eileen champions a philosophy rooted in dialogue, believing fervently that communication is the linchpin of a better world. Throughout her journey, mentors consistently hailed Eileen's joy in service, her intuitive grasp of people's desires, and her aversion to conventional sales tactics. For Eileen, sales were never about coercion; they were about understanding needs and offering solutions with sincerity and empathy.

However, it was adversity that propelled Eileen into the realm of entrepreneurship. Confronting personal crises, she discovered a reservoir of resilience and empathy within herself, prompting her to extend counsel to other women facing similar challenges. Thus, her accidental foray into entrepreneurship birthed two ventures in the early 2000s, now united under a single banner. Today, Eileen is not just a sought-after speaker and multi-time Amazon Bestselling Author; she is the visionary behind "Implement to Impact," a coaching enterprise dedicated to empowering women entrepreneurs with a focus on fostering time freedom, wealth creation, and a supportive community.

Author's Website: *www.ImplementToImpact.com*

Charity Awareness: *www.SurvivalToThrivalSeries.com*

ERIC D. JACKSON
CHOOSE FORGIVENESS

. . . .

"Forgiveness frees us from surviving the past;
It unburdens our present experiences,
So we can greet the future and others with kindness,
With a confident, peaceful spirit of thrival."
~ Eric D. Jackson

We all need reminders, maybe even help, to be **forgiving**. We all *desire* to **thrive** and to flourish.

The etymology of "forgive/ness":

To "give, grant, allow; remit (a debt), pardon (an offense); completely, fully - given; to give or receive; the sense of "to give up desire or power to punish."

In order to step into our future *'courageously'* (like in the first book of the *Survival to Thrival* series), *out of our comfort and survival zones*, we need to first let go of the past (not hold onto) if we are to really flourish... now *and* into the future.

We need to deal with whatever is anchoring us to the past (either in comfort or in conflict) before we can truly be free to greet a better future—the future we envision for ourselves.

I like that the origins of the word "forgiveness" include both to give and to receive. Forgiveness is the gift we not only give to others, but also receive from ourselves. We cannot control how others process their past experiences, but when we forgive, we demonstrate humility. We don't only "give up the desire or power to punish" others, but we also stop punishing ourselves. We pardon the debt and the offense that would also weigh us down.

Perhaps we can even become *"UN-Offend-Able"* as author, Brant Hansen writes,

"God has a way for us to live, a humility that He has called us to, and it's the way that we humans happen to really flourish. It's <u>how</u> you will flourish."

In the first book of this series, I wrote, "Courage is 'to seize—to grasp to oneself:

In order to prosper, flourish, grow, increase, and mature—to grasp (to) oneself, and to seize the life you want to live will require the courage, the inner strength, and a brave heart—your free will—to meet the dangers and troubles outside of your comfort zone."

In this book, we are considering another side of the coin of thrival and *flourishing*, which is to release, *rather than* to cling to; to "give up" or "to give in," to become "forgiving," fully and completely.

That frees up our energy from wasted and negative, releasing any drama, so that we can move forward, *and maybe even upward... not just for ourselves but together*. Perhaps coming to a place of forgiveness allows for a new and improved reality, even with those we have forgiven?

Offense and anger are not ours to cling to or to possess. God (if you choose to believe) says that He will take care of these things, and that we already have an offer of forgiveness for ourselves, so we should do the same for others. We do not want to take ownership of offenses and anger, but rather release them, release others, and release ourselves.

I also wrote last that, "We cannot be victims if we are to be victorious!"

Both in courage and in forgiveness, we cannot be victims, especially of our own making.

"When we cannot come to a place of forgiveness, we become victims, even to ourselves."
~ Eric D. Jackson

We could say that it takes courage to be forgiving, to be kind, to be tenderhearted, to even have the most open perspective of family, all freely and completely.

To thrive and live victoriously, we must be able to freely express the best version of ourselves, and that means the freest, unburdened, and "unoffendable" version.

How can we truly experience kindness, as well as become a kind person ourselves, if we are not forgiving first?

It is one thing to have done the hard work from within to become a better version of ourselves, but if we are still guarded, perhaps untrusting, and even jaded about the world around us, how can we truly be kind to others?

Emotions do get the best of everyone at some point—literally everyone.

I have personally struggled with this. I have done a lot of the deep work on myself, and I cherish the drama-free, love-filled core, immediate home I get to share with my wife and son.

But I will admit that it can be extremely difficult to make that kind of peace with the complicated world and people outside of that innermost sanctuary. And what I have found most recently is that I was still anchored in the past to some remaining negative experiences that prevented me from living and giving freely and completely. How are you doing personally with all of this?

Me? I was guarded most of my life based on my own experiences and observations, and that clouded or tainted my perspectives... my abilities to see clearly, think clearly, and act better.

No matter how positive, caring, or supportive I actually was... No matter how loving, building up others, and ready to serve, as I did show up to give... There was still something missing. It limited my ability to be truly kind. It limited my experiences and my ability to truly thrive, not just for myself and with my core household, but everywhere and with everyone.

Lacking forgiveness impairs our ability to move from *Survival to Thrival*.

We might gather from Travis Bradberry, author of "Emotional Intelligence 2.0, that EQ is the most critical gift that parents can give their children, which most determines their future successes. Having a high EQ accounts for 90% of top performers. Having "Self-Awareness" and "Self-Management," along with "Social Awareness" and "Relationship Management skills," equips people to navigate a complicated world more successfully, filled with complicated people.

Generally speaking, people want to do business and life with people they like. Specifically, you've probably heard it phrased as "know, like, and trust." I've even heard it said this way, "know, LOVE, and trust." People will go all the extra miles for (and with) someone they love, and that sounds like thriving to me!

We have to develop the skills that allow us to love others better, and to be loved, if we are to move beyond survival and into a life of Thrival.

As I have been growing and maturing, I have chosen to take this to heart and really inquire within myself what it means to be likable—to be kind. I have been improving my own practices of kindness. It's not just some random act because you felt like it, and maybe because it was convenient or you felt good about doing it.

I am starting to cherish more and more the sweet gentleness of being kind to a person, no matter what is spinning in my world or theirs. What I've been practicing at home for over twenty years I am now getting better at practicing in the world around me, and that is to create a space that protects tenderness and unity, and honors other people around me (maybe even admires or finds their individual value and worth).

Depending on the person and situation, that may be very challenging, and definitely easier said than done sometimes (many times).

As it relates to forgiveness, kindness as a gift and a sacrifice (fully and completely), is likely going to be needed when we least feel like it, and it probably isn't going to feel good or convenient - at least not at first. And it never means that the other party/ies are going to join you in choosing forgiveness.

But we can invite people to move forward and upward with us, to take the high road, and not to otherwise move backward and downward in our relationship, and that's not productive at all for anyone.

"We cannot control others, but at least we can still create an open space and invitation to protect the unity we do share in a way that honors everyone."
~ Eric D. Jackson

We will never solve all the problems or have all the answers. We may not be able to heal all of the old wounds and ties. And I know from personal experience, we may never see the relationships we always hoped would be there, and be there in healthier ways, ever come back again. That's really hard to process, to reconcile, to deal with, or even find balance and peace with. It's all very imperfect, like I wrote in the last book on Courage:

"We are living in an imperfect world, with imperfect people, making imperfect choices, getting imperfect results."
~ Eric D. Jackson

Courage helps us to create more good than should be possible based on this math.

Forgiveness also helps us to allow for good to come out of imperfection in each other.

In the next book in this series, Survival to Thrival, perhaps we will find that Perseverance helps us to hold on long enough, while still doing good, to truly experience a life of Thrival.

Say that for *yourself,*

"There is an old truth that used to be me,
And the present truth is I am who I am today, Choosing
Forgiveness, taking agency of me and my role in healing
imperfections as best I can all around me—
Because I am becoming the future version of me that THRIVES
in ALL that I am."

Forgiveness allows us to look into the mirror and see ourselves clearly where we are at right now, to accept ourselves up to this moment in all the good, bad, and the ugly… and to choose what steps we need to take next to move us forward and upward into the life we want to thrive in.

That same Forgiveness allows us to see others as they are… *and more importantly, it allows us to accept others…* extend grace to others… to show others dignity, respect, and even honor… to give them space to be who they are, and *encourage them in their journey of forgiveness—From Survival to Thrival.*

Cheers! To your journey forward and upward, thriving in Forgiveness!

ERIC D. JACKSON

Eric D. Jackson is dedicated to aiding business leaders in achieving the transformations they desire in life, work, and finances. As a speaker, coach, and trainer affiliated with the Maxwell Leadership Team and SCALE Architects of Predictable Success, Jackson showcases his expertise in leadership and finance. Additionally, he manages his own insurance and financial services practice and is eagerly anticipating the release of three book projects. In his role as a Financial and Leadership Coach, Jackson assists leaders in expanding their influence, strengthening their teams, and amplifying their impact. He is a certified Coach, Trainer, and Speaker with Maxwell Leadership, a licensed SCALE Architect by Predictable Success, and a Licensed Financial Services Partner with certifications as CLU and MLO. Jackson is the principal and recruiter for Leadership Life Finances LLC, offering commercial benefit solutions for business leaders through "It's Your LIFE," catering to their insurance, financial, and training needs. He also serves as the Principal at Transformational Leadership & Culture Intn't LLC. Jackson is also an established publisher, known for his journal/planner and success series, *Forward & Upward*.

Author's Website: *www.ItsYourLife.com/links*

Charity Awareness: *www.KidInTheCorner.org*

GENESIS GOMEZ

THE APOLOGY I NEVER GOT & THE PEACE I CHOSE ANYWAY

Forgiveness has never been black and white for me, because sometimes I offer it freely and quickly. Other times, it takes time, distance, and silence, especially when there's no apology at all.

My abuelita used to tell me it was a trait I shared with my abuelito: that soft heart, that clean-slate instinct. She said he would forgive and forget just as fast as someone could say, "I'm sorry," and in her eyes, I carried that same spirit. That always stuck with me. Especially because, out of all the adults on my mom's side of the family, she was the only one who loved me for me—no conditions, no strings, just love.

I miss her often. And I think part of me still forgives the way I do because she saw that as something beautiful. I wanted to live up to that.

But as I've grown, and especially as I've healed, I've come to understand that forgiveness is not always clean. It's not always soft. And when there's no apology, no ownership, no acknowledgement of harm… It's not fast. It's:

- Slow

- Messy

- Layered

- Exhausting

Forgiveness without an apology is something you do for yourself, not to excuse someone, not to reunite, not to forget. But because you deserve your own peace. That's the kind I've had to practice the most.

People have hurt me more than once. Sometimes the same people, in the same ways, because they knew I would forgive them. Sometimes I think they confuse my silence for softness. My grace with naivety.

And when I did finally speak up, when the pain built up and I reacted emotionally, those moments were often used against me. I wasn't seen as someone hurt. I was suddenly the problem. My reaction became the excuse they needed to avoid accountability. They never asked why I broke down. They only pointed out how I broke. And that left me not only wounded, but ashamed. Embarrassed. Like I had to ask for forgiveness for finally expressing what I had tried so hard to hold in.

Someone close to me once told me they wished I wouldn't forgive so easily. That I should keep a tally. They're not wrong in feeling that way. I've been burned more than once because I gave people more chances than they earned. But still, I find it hard to hold on to anger if someone truly admits their wrongdoing. If they say, "I'm sorry," and mean it, I let go. I move forward. I don't bring it back up. I don't need to.

That is, unless the behavior keeps happening.

Because an apology without changed behavior isn't really an apology, it's damage control. And if someone continues to hurt me in the same way after claiming to be sorry, I will bring it back up. Not out of spite, but out of truth. Because if you're choosing to repeat the harm, then I have to choose to protect myself.

Eventually, if nothing changes, I have to do what they won't, draw the line. That doesn't mean I didn't forgive you. It means I no longer allow you access to keep hurting me under the guise of "moving on." I've learned that forgiveness and boundaries are not opposites; they're partners. And peace doesn't just come from letting go, it also comes from knowing when to walk away.

But when there's no apology at all? When they act as if nothing happened? When they gaslight you into thinking you imagined the pain? That kind of forgiveness takes even longer. Even when I do get there, I don't forget the way I do when someone takes responsibility. Something about that kind of wound leaves a scar, not because I didn't heal, but because I had to do it *alone.*

I've spent a lot of time trying to figure out what forgiveness means when it's one-sided. When they never owned it. When they got to move on, while I stayed behind, picking up the emotional debris.

For a while, I thought not forgiving meant I was bitter. That I was holding on too long. But I've realized… the longer it takes to forgive, the deeper the hurt must have gone. That's not weakness, that's evidence that your heart is fully alive, even if it's been bruised.

I've also come to see that forgiving others doesn't mean I owe them closeness. I can forgive you and never let you close again. I can forgive you and block your number. I can forgive you and still say, "You no longer have access to me."

Forgiveness, for me, has become less about reconciliation and more about liberation. I'm not trying to go back to how it was. I'm trying to set myself free from the weight of needing it to ever be different.

I think a lot of us grow up believing forgiveness is about restoring the relationship. But that's not true. Sometimes, the most loving thing I can do for both of us is release it without ever expecting a redo.

There's also the kind of forgiveness I don't talk about enough, the kind I've had to give myself.

Forgiving myself for what I tolerated. For how long I stayed. For the ways I tried to be perfect so they would treat me better. For the times I lashed out because I didn't yet know how to sit with my pain. For the way I gave everyone else grace, but starved myself of it.

That kind of forgiveness took even longer. Because when you're in survival mode, you make decisions you later question in your healing. And if you're not careful, you start resenting yourself more than you ever resented them.

But I'm learning. I'm learning that I did the best I could with what I knew then. And now that I know better, I don't have to hate the version of me that didn't.

I can look back and see her, scared, tired, over-functioning, longing to be loved, and say, "You didn't deserve what happened to you." And I forgive you for not knowing how to stop it sooner.

Forgiveness is not a feeling. It's a decision. And sometimes, it's a decision I have to make over and over again, even about the same person.

Because healing isn't linear. Triggers come back. Memories resurface. New layers reveal themselves as I grow.

But every time I choose forgiveness, even if it takes me a while, I'm choosing peace. It's not perfection, nor is it approval —just peace!

So no, I don't always forget. Especially when someone never made it right. But I no longer need an apology to heal.

Because the truth is... I've stopped waiting for people to make it right when I've already made it right within me.

That's forgiveness. That's survival turning into thrival. That's the peace I chose, even when the apology never came.

GENESIS GOMEZ

Genesis Gomez is a speaker, author, entrepreneur, and the founder of Reigning Resilient Queens, a movement committed to helping women rise through life's hardest chapters with strength, self-worth, and vision.

With a career spanning the worlds of modeling, public speaking, financial services, and end-of-life planning, Genesis brings compassion and clarity to every space she enters. Her journey reflects what it means to rebuild, to lead with heart, and to use every experience—personal and professional—as fuel for a deeper purpose.

Featured in national media and recognized for her authentic voice, Genesis continues to empower others to grow forward with grace and grit.

Author's Website: *www.GenesisGomez.com*

Charity Awareness: *www.ElevatingConnections.org*

JAMI LAH

THE GIFT OF LETTING GO: FINDING FREEDOM

There's something almost mystical about forgiveness that I've come to understand over the years; it operates on a level that most of us struggle to access. Sometimes, we catch glimpses of that clear signal of grace, but more often than not, we're stuck in the static of hurt, anger, and confusion.

Before I go further, I want to acknowledge something important. I feel extremely blessed and have had a really good life, a loving family, supportive parents, and more gifts than I could have ever asked for. I understand that my perspective on forgiveness might feel difficult for some who have faced deeper wounds or more challenging circumstances. This is simply my experience, and I'm deeply grateful that even though life hasn't always been perfect, it has been good to me, and that shapes how I see the world.

I've come to believe deeply that we're all walking our own paths, each of us navigating through experiences that are beyond our complete understanding. There's a grand design at work, call it the universe, God, divine timing, or simply the mysterious unfolding of life, that places people and situations in our lives for reasons we may never fully understand. When someone says something hurtful or when actions leave me questioning, I try to remember that they, too, are on their journey. They're operating from their own understanding, shaped by their experiences, their wounds, their fears, and their view of the world. This doesn't excuse harmful behavior, but it helps me see beyond the immediate pain to something larger.

Years ago, I read Colin Tipping's "Radical Forgiveness," and it fundamentally shifted how I understood this whole concept. Tipping suggests that perhaps, and I know this might sound crazy, the people who hurt us are actually playing a role in our spiritual evolution. Maybe they're here to teach us something we couldn't learn any other way. I'm not saying we should be grateful for abuse or that we should stay in harmful situations. What I'm suggesting is that there might be a higher perspective available to us, one that can transform our pain into growth.

This perspective becomes especially important when it comes to family, where I've established clear priorities. Mine has always been family first. When someone in my family says something that stings or acts in ways that don't make sense to me, I return to this foundation: they are my family, and the love for my family comes first. This doesn't mean I don't stand up for myself—boundaries are still essential. But it means I'm willing to dig deeper, to extend grace more readily. When extended family dynamics get complicated, or when misunderstandings arise, I remind myself that we're all figuring out this thing called "life."

I've learned to ask myself powerful questions that have transformed how I respond to difficult moments: "What if I don't understand the full picture? What if there's pain I can't see? What if they're struggling with something they can't articulate?" But perhaps the most transformative question I've discovered is this: "Are they doing or saying this out of love or fear?" When I can see that someone's hurtful behavior might be coming from their own fear, insecurity, or pain rather than bad intentions, it becomes so much easier to extend compassion instead of defensiveness.

Growing up with loving parents taught me that forgiveness within families may look different than forgiveness with strangers. There's a deeper commitment, a willingness to work through things because the relationship matters more than being right. This foundation of love has made forgiveness feel more natural to me, though I recognize not everyone has had this same gift.

Looking back at the challenges that have required forgiveness, I can see how they changed me, often for the better. The disappointment that redirected me toward something better. The misunderstanding that taught me to communicate more clearly. The conflict that helped me find my voice. Some situations forced me to become very resourceful, finding solutions and strengths I didn't know I had.

I'm not suggesting that pain is good or that we should seek it out, but when we're in the midst of difficult experiences, there's often growth happening that we can't see at the moment. Sometimes, the very people who challenge us become our greatest teachers, not because of their intention, but because of how we choose to respond.

This perspective has helped me release resentment. When I can see that my challenges have contributed to who I've become—stronger, wiser, more compassionate—it becomes easier to let go of the anger toward those who played a role in that growth. Because ultimately, forgiveness is less about the other person and more about the peace I choose to live in. Holding onto anger, resentment, and hurt keeps me trapped, and I like to live in joy. When I forgive, I'm not condoning wrong behavior or pretending everything is fine. I'm choosing to free myself.

What I've found is that forgiveness helps me more than holding on ever could. When I carry resentment, I'm the one who suffers. The person who hurt me often has no idea I'm still carrying that weight. Forgiveness is the gift I give myself, the permission to be free.

Forgiveness isn't just a grand gesture reserved for major betrayals. It's a daily practice woven into small moments, forgiving the driver who cuts me off, recognizing they might be rushing to the hospital, or forgiving myself for harsh words spoken in anger, knowing I'm still learning too. When I feel hurt or angry, I try to pause and breathe before reacting, applying those same questions: "What if there's more to this story? Are they acting out of love or fear?" This approach has saved countless relationships and prevented unnecessary pain.

What amazes me about this process is its ripple effect. When I choose to forgive, it doesn't just free me, it often transforms the relationship itself, creating space for healing, understanding, and deeper connection. I've watched forgiveness heal family wounds that seemed permanent and restore friendships that appeared beyond repair. When we operate from this place of grace, we give others permission to do the same.

This doesn't mean everyone will meet us there. Some people aren't ready or willing to make that shift. But that's not our responsibility. Our job is to choose the path that serves our highest good and trust that love will find its way.

As I continue on this journey from survival to thriving, forgiveness remains one of my most essential practices. It's not a destination I arrive at but a choice I make, again and again. Some days I'm crystal clear, receiving that pure signal of grace. Other days, I'm fumbling with my emotions, catching only fragments of peace. But here's what I know for certain: every time I choose forgiveness over resentment, understanding over judgment, love over fear, I'm not just healing myself, I'm contributing to the healing of the world and adding more love.

The path we're all walking is mysterious, filled with lessons we may never fully understand. But when we can trust that there's purpose in our pain, wisdom in our wounds, and growth in our challenges, forgiveness becomes not just possible, but natural.

It becomes the response of a heart that has learned to see with eyes of love. And in that seeing, in that choosing, in that daily practice of grace, we discover something beautiful: forgiveness isn't just about letting others off the hook. It's about setting ourselves free to thrive.

JAMI LAH

For more than twenty years, Jami Lah has built international strategic partnerships that create exponential impact and brand awareness in the United States and abroad. As an innovator and connector, she leverages her vast network of CEOs, investors, and thought leaders in commercial real estate, technology, and start-up sectors to facilitate global change. She is currently the Founder and Executive Director of TEDxStGeorge and Producer for TEDxSanDiego. She has also produced TEDxOnBoard, TEDxCincinnati, and TEDxSemesterAtSea. Through these platforms, Jami has created numerous immersive events whose talks have garnered millions of views, advancing ideas on sustainability, health, wellbeing, AI, and emerging technologies.

Through her Lifelong Learning Worldwide initiatives, she creates transformative experiences, curates educational travel opportunities, champions powerful storytelling, and explores AI applications that empower individuals globally. Jami's exceptional ability to identify synergies between stakeholders establishes her as a trusted innovation catalyst, while her strategic vision transforms possibilities into tangible outcomes, benefiting organizations and communities alike.

Author's Website: *www.Jami-Lah.com*
Charity Awareness: *www.SurvivalToThrivalSeries.com*

LADY JEN DU PLESSIS, DC

FORGIVENESS IS THE DOOR I CHOOSE

For years, my default was to power through—matter-of-fact, strong, pleasant, on point. That strength served me well in a male-dominated industry. I learned to lead with facts, with reports, with results. I knew how to do the job, and I did it with excellence. But there's a subtle danger in excellence when it turns into a shield. "Don't say that. Don't say it that way." Perform. Perfect. Prove.

And then there's the other way—the one I keep choosing now: live. That choice has a frequency to it. Presence. Accountability. Love. Gratitude. And in this volume, one more frequency gets the spotlight: forgiveness.

I used to think forgiveness was a single act—something I could check off a list. It isn't. For me, forgiveness is an ongoing practice of setting down weights I was never meant to carry, and releasing the silent armor that made me feel safe when I was a little girl trying to manage chaos I didn't create. It's not loud; sometimes it's barely a whisper.

THE BURDEN YOU DON'T HAVE TO CARRY

I grew up learning to anticipate danger. I learned to read rooms. I learned to gauge a person's tone in one or two words. That's what happens when your home feels more like a battleground than a sanctuary. In that environment, you collect burdens without even realizing it. You pick up other people's moods, expectations, disappointments—and you start believing that if you can be good enough, they will change.

That's the first lie forgiveness exposes: "It wasn't my job to carry this in the first place."

I can love my family and still put down what isn't mine. I can be strong and still be soft. I can be matter-of-fact and still keep my hands open. Survival taught me to clench. Thrival asks me to release.

Forgiveness isn't pretending it didn't happen. It isn't excusing or erasing. It's not even reconciliation with another person— sometimes that isn't possible or wise. Forgiveness is me saying, "I won't drink this poison anymore and call it protection." I won't keep rehearsing pain and calling it preparation. I won't keep holding my breath in rooms where I've already outgrown the air. By refusing these habits, I affirm the principle of truly honoring my boundaries—choosing peace over the false comfort of familiar pain. This commitment shifts my focus from past injuries to present possibilities, embracing a life where freedom flourishes.

A FRESH, TENDER DOOR

Recently, I received news that pulled me backward into an old hallway of questions—so fresh I'm not ready to hold a microphone and speak it aloud. I will say this: it touched my family story in a way that made me do the math, rewind timelines, and wonder what was true and who knew what, and when. That's the kind of news that tries to wake up the little girl in you—the one who thinks she needs to fix everything quickly and quietly so no one gets hurt.

I cried. I remembered how easily resentment masquerades as armor—how quickly we reach for it when something feels unfair, and there are more questions than answers. And then I chose the simplest step I could take: I picked a meaningful day as an anchor to start a gentle conversation. Some clarity came. Some relief. Some threads are still loose. The tenderness is still here.

I'm not ready to *speak* that story on a stage or write it. But expression carries a boundary for me: forgiveness is not a gossip column. It is not another trial. It's a door I walk through for my own freedom. I can forgive from afar. I can release the burden without creating a new one.

That's the second lie forgiveness exposes: closure is not a prerequisite for freedom. I don't need anyone to know, agree, or apologize to reclaim my energy. Forgiveness is an inside job.

WHERE RESENTMENT TRIES TO LIVE

Resentment is sneaky. It tells you that holding a grudge will finally even the score; that if you carry this long enough, they will somehow feel what you felt. But you know the truth: resentment is a kind of poison you swallow while hoping it harms someone else. It doesn't. It corrodes your peace. It eats at your joy. It keeps you rehearsing conversations in the shower with people who aren't even there. Beneath this sneakiness often lies fear—fear of being vulnerable again, fear of acknowledging the hurt we carry. Recognizing this can be the first step towards healing.

When I notice resentment trying to pull a chair up to my table, I ask: "What, exactly, am I drinking right now? What story am I repeating that keeps me small, angry, tight? And then I choose a different story: I can forgive without forgetting. I can remember without reliving. I can honor my experience without hauling it into every room I enter."

That's how I protect my energy and my heart.

THE ARMOR & THE LIGHT

In an earlier chapter of my life, I wrote about armor, the silence, the perfectionism, the isolation, and how poking even one small hole in that armor lets the light through. That visual stays with me because it is precisely how forgiveness feels. I do not have to rip everything off at once; I can soften one place in me that has been hard for a long time. I can tell one true sentence to someone I trust. I can set down one brick. That's enough for today. Tomorrow I can set down another.

Before moving on, I ask myself gently, 'What needs kindness now?' and allow my body to answer. This self-compassion pause reinforces my step-by-step release and models the practice for others.

Forgiveness is not me telling the world that what happened was "fine." Forgiveness is me telling my body, my nervous system, my future, "We are not staying in this scene."

CONFESSION, RELEASE, RELIEF

I'm Catholic. Confession is part of our rhythm. People sometimes misunderstand it as punishment or performance. To me, it's release. When a whole congregation is willing to lay down burdens, the entire church breathes easier. Forgiveness works the same way in a family, a company, a community, or a circle of friends. When we lay it down, we stop making everyone else carry our unspoken stories—the energy in the room changes. Imagine, at the end of a long day, when everyone in the household gathers to share their day's worries, then sets them aside, collectively choosing peace. Or when a work team acknowledges past miscommunications during a meeting and, together, agrees to move forward positively. Let yourself visualize the relief that fills the room when honesty is shared and burdens are lifted.

No, I don't need to track people down on the street and say, "Do you know what you did to me?" The point isn't to shift my pain into their hands and watch what they do with it. The fact is to place it somewhere safe and let it go—so I can walk out lighter and love more honestly.

THE PRACTICE THAT KEEPS ME FREE

I'm a pragmatic person. I like to think of forgiveness practices not simply as theoretical concepts, but as tangible actions I can incorporate into a typical Tuesday afternoon. Picture a day when things feel chaotic yet charged with opportunity: There I am, using simple practices to navigate a series of challenges. Here's what forgiveness looks like in my daily life—a set of practical steps that guide me back to freedom:

1. Name the hook.

I ask, "What's hooking me right now?" A comment? A memory? A tone? Naming it shrinks it from a storm to a sentence. When it has a name, it has a boundary.

2. Choose a phrase that returns me to myself.

I keep a steady anchor: Stop proving, start living. When resentment tempts me to rehearse the past, that phrase brings me back to the life I'm actually living.

3. Make room in the body first.

If my shoulders are up by my ears, forgiveness won't land. I soften my jaw, drop my shoulders, and open my hands. I let my body vote for freedom before my mind does. Pause and breathe here, allowing the body to fully embrace this release before moving forward.

4. Forgive from a distance when needed.

Forgiveness does not require proximity. Sometimes the kindest, cleanest release is the quiet one. A prayer. A journal line. A deep breath with a simple, "I'm done carrying this."

5. Root-dig, don't weed-whack.

If something keeps popping up in a relationship, we address the root—not just the symptom. We can disagree, cry, resolve, and then have dinner. Resolution resets the room.

6. Build small rituals that remind me who I am.

I have a few—like what I wear on stage or the bracelet I put on (or take off) to signal authenticity rather than performance. They're not about fashion. They're about integrity.

7. Respect the boundary of tender stories.

Some stories are still raw. They may not be for microphones yet. I honor that. Forgiveness doesn't force me to bleed publicly. It lets me heal privately.

When proving tries to sneak back in, forgiveness has a way of exposing hidden proving patterns. Proving says, 'Do more, and they'll see you.' Forgiveness says, 'Do less and set yourself free.' Proving tries to use anger as fuel. Forgiveness recognizes anger as a flare—beneficial for attention, harmful as a lifestyle.

In my work, I have often been the token woman in the room. I know how easy it is to turn that into a proving contest—facts versus facts, reports versus reports, results versus results. There's nothing wrong with facts; I still use them. But facts are not a shield, and results are not a personality. When I choose forgiveness, I prefer to let go of the fight over who's right and return to what's true. What's true is that I can do the job.

Forgiveness separates my value from the scoreboard. It lets me lead with grace without abandoning clarity. It keeps me from dragging old arguments into new rooms.

FROM SURVIVAL TO THRIVAL
(ONE DOOR AT A TIME)

Survival training taught me to scan for danger. Thrival trains me to look for light. Survival taught me to clench. Thrival teaches me to release. Forgiveness is the door between those two rooms, and every time I walk through it, I prove to myself that freedom is not an accident—it's a practice.

I will continue to honor what is tender and private. I will continue to share what serves others. I will continue to forgive from afar when that's what wisdom requires. I will continue to set down what isn't mine and carry what is—love, gratitude, presence, accountability.

If any of this resonates, please hear me: you don't have to rip the armor off. Just poke one hole. Let one beam of light in. Say one true sentence to one safe person. Forgive one small thing today. And then do the next small thing tomorrow.

LADY JEN DU PLESSIS

A dynamic leader renowned for transforming powerhouse businesses into companies that run smoothly without the need for daily intervention by its leader, Lady Jen Du Plessis is known as The Team Building & Scaling Architect who boasts over forty years in finance and over $400 million in revenue generated. She knows exactly how to build wealth through strategic team scaling, sustainable systems, and high-impact leadership, and has helped over 8,000 entrepreneurs leap from practitioners to thriving enterprises to achieve the pinnacle in their business.

She is a celebrated 22X Amazon #1 Bestselling Author, podcaster, and TV host who delivers real transformation, not just fast profits, so her clients achieve both business success and personal fulfillment. She cherishes her life in the countryside, enjoying local wineries, ballroom dancing, humanitarian efforts, boating, and quality time with family.

Author's Website: *www.JenDuPlessis.com*

Charity Awareness: *www.SurvivalToThrivalSeries.com*

JOANNA RUSSELL

THE POWER OF FORGIVENESS: HEALING BEYOND SURVIVAL

Courage gets us through the storms, but forgiveness—deep, genuine forgiveness—sets us free to truly thrive. Over the last few years, my own healing journey has been about more than just surviving; it's been about investing in myself and doing profound transformational work that has opened my heart and mind in ways I never imagined. One of the most powerful tools I've used is the Hawaiian process of *ho'oponopono*—a beautiful visualization technique that helps clear the mind and heal the heart. It's a practice rooted in love, responsibility, and forgiveness, and it has helped me release long-held pain and embrace peace.

Throughout my journey from survival to thriving, I've come to realize that forgiveness isn't just about absolving others; it's about freeing ourselves from resentment, regret, and pain that keep us stuck in the past. I've learned that forgiveness begins with acknowledgment—recognizing the wounds and giving ourselves permission to feel the pain without judgment.

I carry a deep compassion for my mum, who was fighting her own battles—struggling with depression, trauma, and the limitations of her circumstances. Despite her emotional absence at times, I know she tried her very best. She loved in her own way, and her efforts, even if imperfect, came from a place of love and survival. Understanding her struggles has softened my heart, allowing me to see her as human—imperfect, resilient, and doing her best with what she knew.

The inner journey—learning to forgive others—was one of the most challenging, yet most freeing parts of my life. I remember holding onto resentment, believing that anger protected me. But I also realized that carrying that pain was like lugging around a heavy weight everywhere I went. Forgiveness didn't happen overnight; it was a process of peeling back layers of pain, understanding that everyone acts from their own wounds. When I finally made the decision to forgive my mum—many years earlier—I carried that forgiveness deep within me, but I hadn't yet found the right words to express it fully.

When she became unwell, I was overwhelmed by a profound sense of regret and pain—regret that I hadn't been able to articulate my forgiveness openly and in real time, so we could have talked it through and perhaps found some closure together. It was in that moment, lying beside her in the hospital in the middle of the night as I watched her slip away, that I truly understood how much healing still awaited me. I realized how important it was to finally release that last lingering regret, so I could truly begin to find peace within myself.

For those reading this, I ask you to reflect: What are you holding onto that no longer serves you? What wounds are you carrying that might be waiting for your forgiveness? Healing is a process, and it begins with the courage to face our pain, to feel it fully, and to choose compassion and understanding. Remember, forgiveness isn't about forgetting or excusing—it's about freeing yourself from the chains of the past and stepping into the light of your own resilience and hope. Your journey is uniquely yours, but you are never alone. The power to heal lies within you—are you ready to embrace it?

Forgiveness doesn't mean forgetting or pretending the hurt didn't happen. It's about releasing the hold that pain has over our present and future. It's a gift we give ourselves—the freedom from carrying the weight of past hurts. And I can tell you, that peace is worth every effort.

But forgiveness isn't only about others. It's equally about ourselves. I've learned that the hardest person to forgive is often the one in the mirror. For so long, I carried guilt and shame for the choices I made, for the roads I took, for the mistakes I thought defined me. Self-forgiveness was an act of radical kindness—learning to accept that I am human, that I am enough, and that my past does not determine my worth or my future.

That process of forgiving myself was the most powerful lesson I ever learned. It's what allowed me to shed shame and step into my own truth. I began treating myself with compassion, nurturing the parts of me that felt broken or unworthy. And in doing so, I unlocked a new level of resilience—one rooted in love, not shame.

In recent years, I've dedicated myself to deepening my inner work—pursuing transformational healing that goes beyond surface-level change. Incorporating the Hawaiian practice of *ho'oponopono* into my self-care routine has been a vital part of my healing journey. It serves as a beautiful and powerful reminder that we are all deeply interconnected, and that by healing our hearts and minds, we create ripples of positive change that extend far beyond ourselves—touching every aspect of our lives and the lives of those around us. Through this process, I've learned to forgive not only others but also myself—for the times I felt I failed, the regrets I carried, and the pain I held onto.

This practice has helped me release old wounds and make space for love, compassion, and growth. It has shown me that even when life has been difficult, love and forgiveness are always within us—waiting to be embraced. This journey of forgiveness has been essential to my evolution, enabling me to live more authentically and courageously.

In my coaching practice, I see how forgiveness can transform lives. Clients who have carried decades of pain, regret, or bitterness find liberation when they decide to let go. They realize that forgiveness isn't a one-time act but a continual choice—an ongoing process of choosing love over resentment, understanding over judgment, peace over pain.

So, how do we cultivate forgiveness?

PRACTICAL STEPS TO EMBRACE FORGIVENESS

1. **Reflect & Acknowledge:** Take time to write about your feelings. Name your pain, your anger, your disappointment. Recognize what's holding you back.

2. **See the Other Person's Humanity:** Try to view the situation from their perspective. Remember, everyone acts from their own wounds, their own struggles. They do their best with what they knew at the time.

3. **Let Go:** Decide to release the pain—this is a gift to yourself. It doesn't mean you forget or condone what happened; it means you choose peace.

4. **Use Visualization:** I've found that visualization techniques like *ho'oponopono* help clear the mind and heart. Visualize yourself releasing the pain, forgiving yourself and others, and filling that space with love and light.

5. **Be Gentle with Yourself:** Forgiveness is a process. Celebrate every small step forward, even if it's just a tiny shift in your mindset.

THE FREEDOM OF FORGIVENESS

Forgiveness is a gift—a liberation from the past that frees us to live fully in the present. It's not always easy. Sometimes, it feels like releasing a piece of ourselves. But I promise you, once you begin, the weight begins to lift. And with that freedom, we find the courage to live more authentically, more fully.

Reflecting on my own story, I see that forgiveness was the bridge that took me from merely surviving my wounds to truly thriving in my life's purpose. It's a courageous act—one that requires vulnerability, patience, and love. But the rewards are profound: peace, clarity, and a renewed sense of possibility.

YOUR TURN: EMBRACE FORGIVENESS

Today, I invite you to consider where forgiveness might be waiting in your life. Is there someone you need to forgive? Or perhaps, yourself? Remember, forgiveness isn't a destination; it's a continuous journey—one that shapes who we are and who we become.

Because when we forgive, we don't just heal the past—we free ourselves to live fully in the present. And that, my friend, is the essence of true thriving.

JOANNA RUSSELL

Joanna Russell is a Senior Executive Coach and founder of Ajile LLC, recognized for expertly blending traditional leadership development with holistic coaching to drive organizational transformation and strategic growth. With nearly two decades of high-level experience in the UK healthcare sector as a Specialist Senior Social Worker, Joanna distinguished herself by managing complex cases, navigating intricate legal frameworks, and overseeing significant budgets—demonstrating advanced business acumen and operational leadership. Her transition from senior case management to executive coaching marks a natural evolution in her commitment to developing leaders and fostering organizational excellence.

Now based in the U.S., Joanna partners with high-achieving professionals to restore motivation, elevate performance, and enhance leadership effectiveness. She also leads peer advisory groups and has served as Director of Coaching for a personal development company, designing impactful coaching frameworks. Joanna's warm, relatable, and deeply empathetic approach guides clients through sustainable transformation, helping them reconnect with purpose, set healthy boundaries, and thrive at the highest levels of leadership.

Author's Website: *www.AjileLLC.com*

Charity Awareness: *www.ThistleFarms.org*

DR. JOEL PARKER

THE JOURNEY TO FORGIVENESS

FORGIVENESS

Forgiveness is the intentional process of letting go of resentment and negative feelings toward someone who has wronged you—freeing yourself from anger, bitterness, and the desire for vengeance—without necessarily excusing the behavior, forgetting the hurt, or reconciling. It brings profound mental, emotional, and physical benefits: reduced stress, anxiety, and depression, and a greater capacity for peace and compassion.

When the "someone" we need to forgive is ourselves, the process becomes even more transformative—and often harder. Self-forgiveness is not about denying responsibility; it is about releasing the chains of guilt and regret so we can move forward, embrace life fully, and rediscover the joyful, adventurous spirit we knew in youth.

It is life-changing, and, yes, easier said than done.

THE WEIGHT OF UNFORGIVEN SCARS

Life rarely unfolds as a series of perfectly planned events. It has sharp edges; it leaves scars. The mistakes we make—real or perceived—can become emotional traps, invisible chains of guilt that tether us to the past and dim our engagement with the present.

I remember my childhood pet chipmunk, who lived in the back section of the family piano. Every day I'd take him out to play; he'd stuff almonds in my ears for safekeeping. One morning, while I was at school and my mother was cleaning, he fell into the toilet and drowned. My mother tried desperately to revive him, but he was gone. The devastation and regret stayed with me for years. Even now, decades later, I feel a flicker of unease when I see a toilet seat left up—a small, lingering scar chaining me to that long-ago loss.

Reflection: Think of a mistake that still haunts you. How has it shaped your choices today?

ACKNOWLEDGING HUMAN IMPERFECTION

We are all flawed. As we pursue our goals and dreams, interacting with the world and those around us, we make imperfect decisions—sometimes because we lack information, sometimes because we're blindsided by circumstances beyond our control. A mistake-free life is an illusion. Denying our fallibility only prolongs suffering and can close us off from new experiences. Paradoxically, the pursuit of "perfection" can become its own cage.

Reflection: Recall a time you judged yourself harshly for being "only human." What would you say to a friend in the same situation?

TAKING FULL RESPONSIBILITY

True self-forgiveness begins with responsibility: recognizing your own role in events without excuses or blame-shifting. This shift—from shame and regret to self-respect—is the foundation of healing.

Responsibility is not always simple. A child in an abusive home has limited choices; survival itself becomes the priority. Yet even in the harshest circumstances, reclaiming some point of causation can open a path forward.

I once counseled a colleague who through some mistakes had ended up living on the streets in one of the city's most desperate areas. Through small acts of responsibility— accepting a childcare job that provided food, shelter, and a shower—she began to rebuild. She resisted the pull of the environment around her and eventually pursued education, becoming a veterinarian. Owning what she could control changed everything.

Reflection: What past action do you avoid admitting? How might accepting it free you?

FEELING THE REMORSE WITHOUT DROWNING IN IT

Remorse has its place—it can keep destructive impulses in check—but there is a line where it becomes more harmful than helpful. On one extreme lies the sociopath with no remorse; on the other, the person paralyzed by the slightest perceived mistake.

My grandfather died shortly after routine prostate surgery. The surgeon undoubtedly felt deep remorse, yet hopefully not enough to abandon his calling and deny future patients his skill. My grandmother, early in life, struck a pedestrian while driving. No one died, but the guilt was so overwhelming she never drove again—an understandable but ultimately limiting response.

The key is balance: feel the remorse, reflect on what you might have done differently, then set a boundary on rumination. This is closure.

Reflection: Where in your life does guilt feel overwhelming? What small step could limit its hold?

MAKING AMENDS WHERE POSSIBLE

Actions speak louder than words. Amends are tangible steps that restore a sense of causation and integrity.

Imagine scraping another car's door while backing out of a tight spot. The amends might include repairing the damage, adopting new habits to prevent recurrence, and setting a time limit on self-reproach (perhaps 48 hours). Small, concrete actions create closure.

Reflection: Are there any amends you've delayed? Imagine the relief of acting on it.

CULTIVATING SELF-COMPASSION

Self-compassion is treating yourself with the same kindness you would offer a loved one. Most people are fundamentally good, yet capable of harmful actions. The very capacity to feel regret springs from that inherent goodness. Recognizing this separates the action (which may have been wrong) from the self (which remains worthy).

I once counselled a newly graduated veterinarian who, in her first year of practice, made some mistakes that ended up on a public Facebook site. She was gutted, devastated, and on the brink of tears as we spoke. I took the time to show her the necessity of cultivating self-compassion.

When we fail, we can either extend compassion and rewrite the narrative toward responsibility and growth, or we can spiral into self-loathing. Shared human goodness lights the path out of endless regret.

Reflection: How do you speak to yourself in failure? Try rewriting one harsh thought with compassion.

LETTING GO OF THE PAST'S GRIP

Without releasing the past, there is no space for new creation. That scar, that failed exam, that ended relationship—recognize it as a momentary event on your timeline. Journaling can help: define the experience, acknowledge the regret, and write a new personal policy that grants closure.

Visualize life without that weight. The future becomes an open landscape for new dreams.

Reflection: What "scar" do you cling to? Visualize releasing it —what opens up in its place?

LEARNING & GROWING FROM THE MISTAKE

Mistakes are teachers, not life sentences. The old "school of hard knocks" rarely built resilient people; more often, it left them hobbled.

Years ago, I founded a dog-gear company, "Canine Equipment–Gear fer Dogs™." It was exhilarating, but it drained cash from my profitable veterinary practice. I sold it at a small financial loss and with some pride. Yet the lessons—how to bring an idea to market, manage cash flow, negotiate with buyers—were priceless. Those insights fueled later, more successful ventures.

Lick your wounds, yes—but extract the wisdom and carry it forward.

Reflection: From your biggest regret, what wisdom have you gained? How has it made you stronger? What can you use for your next venture?

REDISCOVERING THE JOY OF YOUTH

Self-forgiveness returns us to the unfiltered curiosity and lust for adventure we knew as children. Growing up on Vancouver Island, I inherited a small boat with a 3-horsepower motor that frustrated me endlessly. One sunny afternoon, in a burst of creativity, I moved the gas tank to the front. The boat leapt onto a plane, skimming the water like water-skis—pure, exhilarating joy.

That's the modern equivalent: cut the ties to past failures and rediscover playfulness, wonder, and the willingness to dream and risk delight.

Reflection: What childhood activity brought pure joy? How could you revive a version of it now?

EMBRACING LIFE'S ADVENTURE ANEW

Imagine a life shaped not by the fear of mistakes, but by responsibility, self-forgiveness, and boundless possibility. A life where you leap out of bed eager for the day, regardless of age. It won't always win universal approval—you may outgrow old relationships and find new ones—but the adventure is yours to claim.

Reflection: Imagine your life without self-imposed limits. What adventure calls to you today?

ACTIONABLE STEPS TO SELF-FORGIVENESS & RENEWED JOY

Here are the practical take-home steps distilled from the journey:

1. Acknowledge the mistake fully and take undivided responsibility—no excuses, no blame-shifting.

2. Feel genuine remorse, reflect on what you could have done differently, then set a clear boundary on rumination to avoid drowning in guilt.

3. Make amends where possible—through direct action, behavioral change, or internal restitution.

4. Cultivate daily self-compassion: speak to yourself as you would to a dear friend; recognize your inherent goodness, separate from past actions.

5. Release the past through journaling, visualization, or ritual—create closure and free mental space for new dreams.

6. Extract the lesson: identify the wisdom gained and consciously apply it to future choices.

7. Reclaim youthful joy: schedule play, curiosity, and small adventures; revive a childhood pleasure in some form.

8. Commit to the practice: self-forgiveness is ongoing— repeat as needed, and choose adventure over safety every time it matters.

Empowering Final Note: True self-forgiveness returns you to the adventurous spirit of youth—curious, resilient, and ready to live fully. The decision begins today, with you.

DR. JOEL PARKER

Dr. Joel Parker, a veterinarian since 1984, became a private practice owner in 1986. He grew his practice, guided by solid management principles, into a Standing Ovation Practice™—a practice that delivered an above-and-beyond expected experience. He later founded Veterinary Endoscopy Solutions and Canine Equipment™. After fifteen years, he sold the businesses and started Veterinary Practice Solutions in 2004, a veterinary management consulting firm, innovated with "Whiteboard Wednesdays" on YouTube, and early online webinars. In 2024, he launched Parker Business Systems (PBS), a boutique-style consulting firm specializing in transforming privately owned veterinary practices into Standing Ovations Practices™.

He, above all, leads a purposeful life, helping others achieve time and financial freedom.

He lives with his family between Clearwater, FL, and Vancouver, BC. He enjoys sports cars, great coffee, strumming a ukulele, and playing with his unique, small, weird dogs.

Author's Website: *www.TheStandingOvationPractice.com*

Charity Awareness: *www.TheWayToHappiness.org*

J.S. KOVACH

FORGIVENESS & FAMILY

"Nobody loves me!"

The sun had gone down hours ago, and it was pitch black in our cabin. My family was camping in Yellowstone National Park for a family reunion, and my immediate family of nine was crammed into one of the individual cabins that Grandpa had rented for each family. While camping was nothing new to us, staying in a cabin felt like "glamping," since we usually camped in old Coleman tents.

"That's not true," my mother said from somewhere in the dark. The cabin could have been cozy, but to me, it only felt suffocating. My siblings and I shared bunks—seven kids ruined any "cozy" feeling—I was cramped, my sister's breath was hot on my face, and my brothers had been picking on five-year-old me, knowing I was an easy target.

My mother had what she must have considered a good idea at the time: "Everyone who loves Jillian, raise your hand!"

There was silence in the darkness. It was so dark that you couldn't see your hand in front of your face—and, of course, no one could see whether anyone in the cabin raised their hand to prove their love for their little whiny sister.

My brother, nine years older than me, laughed and shouted, "Mom made a funny!" My other brothers laughed. Mom told them to hush up. I cried myself to sleep.

To this day, my family will not let me live this story down. It's been brought up at family gatherings for years—decades. For years, I've laughed beside them and pretended that it didn't bother me. I pretended to agree that I had been dramatic—an overreactive, attention-seeking little turd.

However, throughout the years, deep down, I've believed that statement to be true: Nobody loves me.

I am the fifth of seven children—when I was born, I had three older brothers and an older sister. We were all separated by three years. My brothers were thick as thieves, and my sister, having been raised by those three hellions, was "one of the boys." I came along, and I was the princess. I was the baby sister, doted on hand and foot by my parents and adoring older siblings.

Then, three years later, my mom decided to have not only one, but two more sisters—at the same time! "The twins" were a surprise—my mom, a Colorado mountain hippie, didn't believe ultrasounds were safe for babies, so she'd never had one. It was around seven months into her pregnancy that the midwife was palpating her extra-large stomach and exclaimed that she swore she felt two heads.

Of course, we didn't know they'd be girls (remember, no ultrasounds), and nothing could have been worse (in my opinion) than another sister to replace me—except for two more sisters to replace me! Suddenly, I was no longer the princess, the baby, or the focus. (To add insult to injury, I grew up with brothers who reminded me that I wasn't the actual middle child of seven—I was the "butt-end" of the middle.)

Two years later, in that cabin, in the darkness where I couldn't see if my siblings loved me, it all came to a head. I'd had enough. I was certain nobody loved me.

To be fair, my childhood was actually pretty idyllic. My best friend lived down the street—her sisters were the same age as my sisters —and we all spent the summers pretending we were "lost girls" in my large, wooded backyard, "surviving" on wild berries and mud pies. We built lean-tos and decorated them with rusty cans and other trash we found in the woods. One man's trash was a lost girl's vase for wildflowers.

My family loved movie night, and from an early age, I wanted to be a famous actress. I wanted the glitz and glam and for everyone to know my name. When I finally recognized that I was terrified of the spotlight and shyer than an opossum caught off guard, I abandoned that dream. On the big screen, I watched others live my dream, knowing that could never be me.

My next dream was to become a famous author. If I wasn't playing outdoors and getting my knees dirty, my nose was in a book. Eventually, the stories and characters in my imagination demanded to be written into reality, and I wrote my first 80,000-word novel at the age of twelve. I followed that with three more novels, the longest of which was around 120,000 words. My father, a professional copyeditor and published author himself, would read and edit my manuscripts. He wasn't gentle on me—the first several drafts were so redlined you could hardly read the actual manuscript.

He was also encouraging and supportive. I learned so much from him. He helped me craft pitches to literary agents, fanning my hopes for publication. I wanted to be like Christopher Paolini—a homeschooled kid who wrote *Eragon* at the age of fifteen. While I received only rejections, many agents were impressed by the skill with which I wrote for a twelve-year-old.

At first, these rejections didn't deter my dreams; I just knew I needed to write more and pitch more. However, my pre-teen insecurities and those demons in my head from that night in Yellowstone crept in… and I eventually stopped writing regularly. In novels, I read about others living their dreams. I shelved my dreams and put other people's dreams onto my shelves—literally.

While I felt supported in some ways by my parents, I was still the fifth of seven kids—a lot of mouths to feed for a single-income family barely making it. My mother homeschooled all seven of us. This meant she never had a moment for herself and barely a moment for each of us. She was keeping us fed, keeping us from killing each other, and keeping us educated to the best of her ability. There wasn't any time, energy, or money for much more.

My mom homeschooled all of her children until they went to college. Both she and my father were educated and encouraged all of their children to prepare for and attend college. While my mother encouraged her daughters to become educated just like her sons, our deeply religious background instilled in us even more deeply that we daughters should prepare to become mothers. Education was for "just in case." Just in case our husbands lost their jobs. Just in case our husbands died tragically.

By the time I graduated high school (unofficially officially), I didn't know what I wanted to be when I grew up. I knew I needed to take either the ACT or the SAT to get into a university, but I'd never taken a standardized test, and my math skills were weak. I wasn't as smart as my siblings (I told myself). My older sister earned her associate's degree in high school and was accepted to a prestigious university, while my only familiarity with algebra was how to spell it. I didn't want to put myself through a personal hell for a random degree that would get me some random job I would never enjoy.

So, I put off college until the pressure from my family grew too great. All of my siblings had college degrees, and I couldn't be the only one without. Two of my brothers are lawyers. My older sister had her master's by the same age I was when I started college. Another sister is a nationally recognized interior designer.

I graduated in April of 2020 and had been accepted into a master's program for that autumn, but COVID-19 shut the university down and gave me enough pause to drop out, even when the program went fully online.

Those childhood demons never left me. I'd graduated from college, but it took everything out of me. I'd graduated with what I considered an easier but actually interesting degree, but it wasn't a degree that gave me any job security. It wasn't a law degree, as two of my brothers had.

For years, I've drifted between jobs. I worked beside wonderful people, many of whom barely graduated from high school. Formal education doesn't define the virtues of anyone —this just made me wonder why I busted my ass for that degree if it wasn't necessary.

My husband and I recently moved to a new city in a new state —thousands of miles from any family or friends. I was starting a new job—again. I was starting over—again.

My most recent employment, however, has presented me with an opportunity and a pathway to the next step up. Every job before this had been a lateral move—this new pathway could set me up for something in my field with a significant pay raise and elevated status. I didn't know an opportunity like this existed.

I've come to the realization that my demons are what have been holding me back. I haven't fully believed in myself for a very long time. I've let preconceived notions about my place as "the butt end of the middle" child determine how far I pushed myself—how big I let myself dream.

I could be angry that I'm nowhere near where twelve-year-old me thought I would be in my thirties. I have been angry. I still am—but I'm realizing that I can be angry and do nothing new, or change my habits and take myself seriously for once.

I can be angry at how I felt my family unfairly treated me, but now I know that they were doing the best they could with what we had. I've learned to forgive them for perceived slights. We've discovered ways to connect and move on from differences. I have a healthy relationship with my siblings and parents these days.

As much as I need to forgive my family, I need to forgive myself for not believing in my dreams enough. I need to forgive myself for letting myself down. I need to forgive myself for not believing I could do and be more.

Forgiveness allows me to step into a career that gives me purpose. By forgiving myself, I can believe in and actualize a future where I am thriving.

J.S. KOVACH

J.S. Kovach is an award-winning author and in-demand copyeditor of over two dozen bestselling books, including collaborative works with celebrities such as Erik Swanson, Sharon Lecter, and Brian Tracy.

She wrote her first 80,000-word novel at the age of twelve, which garnered critical acclaim from top YA literary agents. She has since written four YA novels and multiple short stories, and her research essay, "Outdoor Recreation Increases Self-Confidence in Women," was selected for publication in her university's Student Leadership Journal.

Her passion for writing, reading, and editing blossomed into a thrilling career in the editorial and publishing field, where she serves as Editorial Manager at Integrity Publishing International.

When her nose isn't in a book, she is usually found outdoors hiking, kayaking, or camping with her husband and three dogs: a Newfoundland mix, a Borderspaniel, and their rescue "foster fail" mini longhaired dachshund. If you're looking for a copyeditor, please contact her at *Kovach.Edits@gmail.com*.

Author's Website: *www.JSKovach.com*
Charity Awareness: *www.ACLU.org*

JULIE DELGADILLO

FORGIVENESS IS THE BRIDGE

I remember standing by the window one quiet evening, the warm glow of the fading sun casting long shadows in the room. The murmurs of the bustling city below drifted up to where I stood, lost in my thoughts. As I watched the world outside continue its dance, it suddenly struck me that I had always viewed forgiveness as something you offered after the pain was gone.

I believed forgiveness was the final chapter, something you earned once the hurt faded, once the apology came, once the story wrapped itself up neatly. But then came a day at work that changed everything. During a particularly challenging project, I encountered a team member who consistently refused to meet deadlines. Frustrated, I found myself holding onto every missed commitment, expecting an apology that never arrived.

As the project dragged on, tension mounted, and I realized I was not only hurting our team dynamic but also my own peace of mind. It was in a moment of quiet reflection, staring out at the bustling city from my office window, that it struck me:

forgiveness doesn't come at the end of healing. I let go of waiting for that apology and chose to address the issue constructively. Forgiveness became the turning point that freed me from the weight of resentment, allowing me to lead with a fresh perspective.

When you work in service-based leadership—especially with underserved communities—you don't just witness hardship. You carry it. You hold it. You absorb disappointment, broken systems, missed promises, and moments when people let you down, even when they meant well.

If you don't learn how to forgive, you don't just stay hurt—you stay stuck. And stuck is where survival lives.

WHEN SURVIVAL TEACHES YOU TO ARMOR UP

In survival mode, forgiveness feels dangerous.

Survival teaches you to protect yourself, to remember every misstep, to stay guarded so you're not hurt again. It teaches you to keep score of effort, of sacrifice, of who showed up and who didn't. I often found myself thinking, "I can't let that happen again." This internal dialogue, like a mantra, reinforced my armor and made survival feel like the only safe path. I lived there longer than I care to admit.

There were seasons in my career when I felt like I was carrying more than my share. I showed up early. I stayed late. I followed through. And when things fell apart—when a system failed, when expectations weren't met, when trust was broken—I felt the weight deeply.

One missed meal. One broken promise. One moment where someone depended on us and we didn't deliver. Those moments don't just hurt professionally. They hurt personally.

I remember sitting alone after a long day, replaying everything in my head—not to blame others, but to understand how it happened. And what I realized was this: if I held onto that pain without forgiveness, it would turn my compassion into calcified caution. Leaders burdened by such cautious defensiveness don't heal communities.

FORGIVENESS IS NOT APPROVAL

One of the biggest misconceptions about forgiveness is that it excuses behavior. It doesn't.

Forgiveness does not mean what happened was okay. It does not mean there aren't consequences. It does not mean you forget the lesson.

Forgiveness means you refuse to let the pain define you. To put this into practice, try a simple two-minute exercise each day. Sit quietly and take a few deep breaths, letting go of the hurt. Visualize handing over the pain to a higher purpose, releasing the emotional weight with each exhale. As you do, silently affirm to yourself: 'I choose to be defined by growth, not pain.'

This small daily ritual can help reinforce the decision to choose forgiveness as an ongoing, active choice.

In leadership, I've had to forgive people who never apologized. I've had to forgive systems that moved more slowly than the needs they served. I've had to forgive myself for decisions I made with the best information I had at the time.

That last one was the hardest. Self-forgiveness is where most of us get stuck.

THE QUIET WEIGHT OF SELF-BLAME

When you care deeply, you replay everything.

"What if I had caught it sooner?"

"What if I had said no instead of yes?"

"What if I had trusted my gut?"

I've asked myself all of those questions.

In the nonprofit world, when something goes wrong, the stakes are high because people are depending on you. Seniors waiting for meals. Families waiting for shelter. Volunteers giving their time. Donors trusting your word.

When something fails, it's easy to internalize it as personal failure. But forgiveness taught me something powerful: responsibility and self-punishment are not the same thing.

You can own your part, correct the process, and still choose compassion for yourself. That choice is what moves you out of survival.

FORGIVENESS AS LEADERSHIP DISCIPLINE

Leadership is not just about vision and execution. It's emotional stewardship (tending to team morale daily). You set the tone—not just for what gets done, but for how people feel while doing it.

I've learned that unforgiveness shows up whether you name it or not. It manifests in tension, guarded conversations, the lack of trust, and exhaustion that no amount of rest seems to fix. Forgiveness clears energy.

It creates space again—for creativity, connection, and courage.

I remember a season when my team was stretched thin. Morale was low. Everyone was doing their best, but frustration lived just under the surface. Instead of pushing harder, I chose a different approach.

We paused. We talked honestly—not about metrics or logistics, but about how things felt. One team member voiced what many of us felt, saying, "I'm tired of feeling like a cog." We acknowledged disappointment. We named fatigue. And we chose forgiveness—for each other and ourselves.

That moment shifted everything—not because the workload disappeared, but because the weight lifted.

FORGIVENESS IS A BOUNDARY, NOT A WEAKNESS

Here's something forgiveness taught me that changed how I lead:

> *"Forgiveness does not mean unlimited access."*
> ~ Unkown

You can forgive someone and still change how you engage with them. You can release resentment and still set boundaries. You can move forward without reopening the same wound. Consider the formula: forgiveness plus boundary equals sustainable trust. This simple equation can serve as a reminder for leaders to embed the practice of maintaining trust while setting healthy boundaries.

There were times I had to forgive while also choosing a new direction and changing roles. Shifting responsibilities. Stepping into alignment instead of obligation.

One of the most healing decisions I ever made was choosing a position that brought me closer to home, closer to family, closer to peace. It wasn't a retreat—it was a recalibration.

Forgiveness permitted me to choose alignment over approval.

FORGIVING THE TIMELINE

Another form of forgiveness we don't talk about enough is forgiving where we are.
The timeline we thought we'd be on.

The version of ourselves we thought we'd be by now.

I've met so many incredible women who feel behind—behind in career, behind in life, behind in confidence. And I always tell them the same thing:

"You're not late. You're right on time."

Forgiveness releases comparison. It releases shame. It releases the pressure to perform healing instead of living it. When you forgive yourself for not being "there yet," you open the door to thrival.

FORGIVENESS IN SERVICE

When you serve people long enough, you learn that everyone is carrying something.

- The senior who seems short with you.
- The volunteer who cancels at the last minute.
- The donor who changes direction.

Forgiveness allows you to see people beyond the moment.

One of the most excellent gifts service has given me is perspective. When you sit across from someone whose life has been shaped by hardship, you realize quickly that grace is not optional—it's essential.

Forgiveness keeps your heart open enough to continue serving without becoming cynical.

And cynicism is where purpose goes to die.

FROM SURVIVAL TO THRIVAL

Survival asks, "How do I protect myself?"

Thrival asks, "How do I stay open?"

Forgiveness is the bridge between the two. It doesn't erase what happened, but it transforms what happens next. Forgiveness is choosing not to carry yesterday into today. It's choosing alignment over resentment. It's choosing to lead with integrity rather than inflict injury. Forgive, align, and lead light every day.

I've learned that the most empowered leaders are not the ones who never get hurt. They're the ones who heal well.

A PRACTICE, NOT A MOMENT

Forgiveness is not a one-time decision. It's a daily practice. Some days, it's easy. Some days, it's a choice you make over and over again. But every time you forgive yourself, someone else, the process, you reclaim energy. You reclaim clarity. You reclaim your future. That's what thrival looks like. To make forgiveness a habit, end your day with a simple 30-second check-in. Close your eyes, take a deep breath, and identify any lingering weight from the day. Name it, acknowledge it, and then, as you exhale, consciously let it go. This micro-ritual helps reinforce your forgiveness practice, transforming it from an idea into a tangible, daily habit.

If you're reading this and carrying something heavy, I want you to hear this:

You don't have to minimize the pain to release it.

You don't have to forget to forgive. You don't have to wait for an apology to move forward. Forgiveness is not for the other person. It's for you.

It's how you loosen survival's grip and step fully into the life you're meant to live.

Ask yourself:

- What am I still carrying that no longer serves me?
- Who do I need to forgive—including myself?
- What would open up if I released this weight?

Write this down and return to it often:

"I choose forgiveness.
I choose alignment.
I choose to move from survival to thrival."

Forgiveness isn't weakness. It's leadership. It's healing. It's freedom. And it's how we rise.

JULIE DELGADILLO

Julie Delgadillo is a confident, enthusiastic, witty, and sought-after passionate servant leader and mentor with over twenty years of experience in non-profit management, leadership development, and confidence coaching. Julie is the Director of Meals on Wheels and the previous Executive Director of Corazón U.S. & Mexico. Julie is a firm believer in leading by example and actively engages in developing community leaders. It's not uncommon to catch her rolling up her sleeves and wearing a tool belt to personally contribute to building homes in Mexico for deserving low-income families. Julie's strengths and passions are rooted in empowering women to be confident in every area of their lives. Julie has personally coached and developed teens and women from around the globe, serving as an International Ambassador for the economic development of women. Julie is also a former International Beauty Queen and a long-time Hunger Relief Advocate. When she is not out conquering the world, you can find her discovering new brunch spots, listening to audiobooks, or in the aisles of TJ Maxx, Marshall's, or HomeGoods. Let's Connect: *www.Linkedin.com/in/JulieDelgadillo*

Author's Website: *www.linktr.ee/SheConquersTheWorld*

Charity Awareness: *www.SurvivalToThrivalSeries.com*

JULIE JONES

FORGIVENESS BEGINS IN THE MIRROR

Forgiveness is often misunderstood. We are taught to forgive others, to let go of resentment, to offer grace, and to take the high road. But the deepest and most transformative forgiveness is not outward. It is inward. Forgiveness is not for anyone else. It is for you.

When we don't forgive, we get stuck. We replay the past. We carry guilt like a weight we were never meant to bear. And while we are standing still, life continues to move forward. Doors remain closed, not because God is withholding blessings, but because our hands are full.

I know this because I lived it.

For years, I carried the guilt of divorce. Not just one divorce, but two divorces. Fundamentally, I don't believe in divorce. I was raised to believe that commitment meant endurance, sacrifice, and perseverance through hardship. I watched my parents model this beautifully. Their fifty-seven-year marriage weathered storms, disagreements, and difficult seasons, yet their commitment never wavered. I wanted that kind of marriage. I prayed for it. I believed in it with my whole heart.

When my marriages ended, the guilt was overwhelming. I found myself saying, "If only I had prayed harder." "If only I had tried longer." "If only I had been more patient, more understanding, more forgiving."

I took responsibility for everything that went wrong. I carried shame that was never meant to be mine alone. I ignored the truth that marriage requires two willing participants, not just to create it, but to repair it.

That guilt kept me trapped.

It kept me in relationships longer than I should have stayed. It closed doors to new opportunities, professionally and personally, because deep down, I believed I didn't deserve better. I told myself that leaving was failure, even when staying was costing me my emotional and mental health.

The cost of staying was far greater than the cost of leaving.

Communication had broken down. Connection had faded. We found ways to coexist without truly being together. I convinced myself that enduring a toxic situation was more honorable than facing the reality of divorce. It wasn't. It was avoidance disguised as virtue.

And I paid for it—with my peace.

Guilt has a way of distorting reality. It clouds judgment. It erodes confidence. It silences intuition. Over time, I became disconnected from myself. I lost clarity. I lost trust in my own discernment. I stopped believing I could hear God's guidance, not because He wasn't speaking, but because guilt had turned down the volume.

Eventually, I hit a brick wall.

I was emotionally exhausted, spiritually depleted, and stuck in the past. Life felt heavy. Opportunities passed by because I wasn't open to receiving them. I was surviving, not thriving.

That's when I turned inward. I stopped trying to justify the past and started seeking healing from it. I prayed not for answers, but for forgiveness. Not just forgiveness from God, but forgiveness for myself.

And then something shifted. Learning to forgive myself didn't mean rewriting history or pretending the pain didn't exist. It meant releasing the belief that I was permanently broken or unworthy because of it. It meant acknowledging that every chapter of my life, even the painful ones, had shaped the woman I was becoming.

I began to understand that forgiveness is not denial. It is clarity. It is not weakness. It is strength.

It is not forgetting. It is freedom.

As I released guilt, space opened up.

I could think clearly again. I could feel again. I could trust my instincts, the quiet, steady knowing that comes when you are aligned. I didn't hear an audible voice, but I felt guidance. A calm certainty. A deep sense of peace that told me I was exactly where I needed to be.

With that clarity, new doors began to open.

Opportunities I never could have forced appeared naturally. Relationships rooted in mutual respect and emotional health found their way into my life. My confidence returned. I found myself by finding alignment within my core. Most importantly, I found purpose in my pain.

Today, I work with women who are carrying the same burdens I once carried: guilt, shame, regret, and self-blame. Women who feel stuck because they believe their past disqualifies them from a better future seek guidance from my experience. Together, we find that forgiveness isn't about feeling guilty about what happened. It's about what happens next.

We were never meant to carry guilt alone. God does not ask us to punish ourselves for our humanity. He offers forgiveness freely when we seek Him. Healing begins when we accept that gift and extend it inward.

Forgiveness clears the clutter. It opens doors and makes room for something new.

So, I'll ask you the same question I had to ask myself:

What burden are you carrying?

What part of your life is on hold because guilt is standing in the way?

What blessing might be waiting on the other side of forgiveness?

You don't have to carry it alone, and you don't have to stay stuck.

Life is too short to live in unforgiveness, especially toward yourself.

JULIE JONES

Julie Jones is a Dallas-based business protocol and etiquette expert, corporate trainer, and sought-after public speaker. A certified graduate of the renowned Protocol School of Washington®, Julie brings a unique blend of experience as both an educator and entrepreneur. She spent fifteen years in education before building and successfully selling a plumbing company—proving her ability to lead, teach, and build from the ground up. Her passion lies in addressing a critical gap in today's professional world: the development of soft skills. Julie believes that success requires more than degrees or determination—it's about building trust, communicating with confidence, and forming lasting relationships. Julie now works with professionals of all ages to refine their business image and interpersonal skills. Her client roster includes major corporations such as American Airlines, JW Marriott, and Grant Thornton, as well as prestigious universities like SMU, Texas Tech, and Tulane. She also coaches student-athletes, emerging professionals, and high school leaders, preparing them to thrive in the modern workplace.

Author's Website: *www.TodaysProfessionals.com*

Charity Awareness: *www.SurvivalToThrivalSeries.com*

KIMBERLY STEVENS

THE KIND OF FORGIVENESS THAT SAVES YOUR LIFE

FORGIVENESS & THE GIRL WHO LEARNED TO SURVIVE

Forgiveness has never come easily to me. I am not one of those people who can shrug off a harsh word or a broken promise and walk away feeling light again. I carry things. I absorb things. I grew up learning to read the emotional weather in every room I entered, and I learned early how to contort myself into whatever shape would keep the peace. That kind of childhood didn't teach me forgiveness. It taught me survival.

For a long time, I believed the two were the same. I believed that staying quiet, small, and agreeable was a form of forgiveness. It took most of my adult life to realize that it was something else entirely. It was self-abandonment. It was the little girl still inside me folding her feelings into a tight square and tucking them away so no one would be bothered. It was the ache of a little girl who wanted to be seen and heard but settled for staying under the radar so she wouldn't get in trouble.

Growing up that way taught me that forgiveness was tangled with fear. I learned to believe that if I spoke my truth, love might leave me. If I said, "You hurt me," I feared someone would call me oversensitive or dramatic. If I told the story the way it actually happened, I worried it would make someone else uncomfortable. So I stayed quiet, accepted their version of the truth, and silenced my own.

Over time, I began to believe their narratives more than my own memories. I learned to doubt my instincts and question my own perceptions. I learned to carry the shame other people placed on me. And beneath all of it was the oldest fear of all, the fear that maybe the wound really was my fault, that their interpretation was right, and my perspective did not matter.

This is how I lost myself and learned not to trust myself.

This is how I began to believe that my voice was too much, my feelings were inconvenient, and my truth was expendable.

Thankfully, somewhere in the middle of that fear, Christ whispered something I didn't understand: "You are forgiven." Not because I earned it or behaved well enough to deserve it. But because He loved me first. His forgiveness didn't just cover what I had done. It uncovered what I had lost: myself.

I didn't realize it then, but that whisper was the quiet catalyst that would one day lead me to forgive others and to forgive myself for the years I stopped trusting my own voice, accepted their story as the truth, and kept giving parts of myself away to keep the peace.

I needed forgiveness not just for my actions, but for the way I had stopped trusting who God made me to be.

I began forgiving because I had been forgiven. It didn't happen all at once. It grew slowly, long before I understood what it was becoming, a quiet restoration of the self I had buried under fear, silence, and shame.

My journey with forgiveness didn't begin with courage. It began with grace.

THE LONG WALK TOWARD LETTING GO

Forgiveness, for me, is not forgetting. I am not sure forgetting is even possible. Our bodies remember things long after our minds try to move on. I can still feel the sting of labels beaten into me that landed like stones in my heart. Irresponsible. Incapable. Bitch. I can still feel the ache of being misunderstood, dismissed, or told who I was before I ever had a chance to discover it myself. These memories have not disappeared simply because I decided to rise above them.

Forgiveness, for me, is looking at what wounded me and saying, "You don't get to name me anymore."

People often say forgiveness is a moment, but I have found it to be more like a long walk. Sometimes it is steady. Sometimes it limps. Sometimes it circles back to the same mile marker I thought I had already passed. But as long as I keep moving, I know I am on the right path.

Christ's forgiveness gave me the courage to take the first step. The long walk that followed was learning to forgive others first, and now I am learning to forgive myself.

THE DOORWAY OF SELF-FORGIVENESS

I think of the moment I stood in the pumping room after my daughter Torrey's diagnosis, reliving the worst chapter of my life, which was the diagnosis and death of her older brother, Braden Michael. Torrey was only a few days old when doctors told us she had the same rare metabolic disorder that stole Braden's life.

I went to the pumping room to pump while we waited for confirmation of her diagnosis. I saved the milk carefully, holding on to hope. But the moment the doctor confirmed she had Citrullinemia, I walked back into that room and dumped the milk down the drain, and with it, I poured out every hope I had allowed myself that she would have a life. I didn't think. I didn't pause. It was a reflex of pure self-protection as I relived the grief from a death I thought I would never have to face again.

I was convinced the story was repeating itself. I was sure God was preparing me for another funeral. Forgiveness was the last thing on my mind.

And then I walked out of the pumping room and met borrowed faith. Our pastor's wife Janie looked at me with a strength I didn't have and said words that steadied my shaking heart: "This is not Braden. This is Victoria Faith. You will fight for her." That moment didn't teach me how to forgive. It taught me why I needed to. I needed to forgive myself for collapsing under the weight of painful memories. I needed to forgive the terror that overtook me. I needed to forgive the part of me that believed God had abandoned me when, in truth, He had carried me.

Forgiveness, in that moment, was not an act. It was a release of past fear so I could go forward and fight for my daughter's life.

FORGIVING THE WOUNDS THAT SHAPED ME

There is another category of forgiveness that touches our childhoods, our mothers, our fathers, and our grandmothers, the kind that reaches back before we were old enough to understand what wounded us or why.

I had two grandmothers with two very different legacies. One lived with grace. The other lived with bitterness. One softened. One hardened. One believed in possibility. The other believed in pain. As a child, I didn't know I was watching two futures. As an adult, I realized I was choosing one.

Christ's forgiveness was the lens that helped me see what bitterness really does. Bitterness keeps us circling the same injury. Grace lets us walk out of the room.

I had to forgive people who never apologized. People who did their best and still caused deep pain. People who didn't know how to love gently because gentleness was never offered to them.

Christ didn't ask me to excuse them. He asked me to release the hold their wounds had on my identity.

Because I am forgiven, I forgive. Even when it is quiet. Even when it is private. Even when it changes nothing about the relationship, but everything about my heart.

MONEY, POWER, & THE SHAME THAT LOOPED FOR YEARS

There was another place I had to learn forgiveness, one I didn't understand for most of my life. Money. Not because I didn't have it, but because spending it made me feel powerful. Power was something I never had growing up. Every purchase felt like proof that I wasn't trapped anymore. It felt like I finally had a voice, a choice, and a sense of control.

But almost immediately, the guilt would slam into me. I would feel ashamed for feeling powerful at all. Then I would swing to the opposite extreme and try to fix it by overpaying the debt, draining the accounts, and punishing myself for wanting anything in the first place.

Underneath all of it lived a deeper terror, the fear of losing everything. Because I had. I lost my home to foreclosure. That foreclosure broke something in me, and part of the spending and guilt cycle was me trying to outrun the shame of that season.

So the cycle kept looping. Power. Guilt. Overcorrection. Depletion. Fear. I kept trying to pay off emotional debt with financial decisions. Forgiving myself became the only way to break the cycle. Christ's forgiveness steadied me so I could finally say, "I do not have to bankrupt myself to atone for the girl who grew up without power, or the woman who once lost everything."

THE FUTURE THAT FORGIVENESS OFFERS

Without forgiveness, I live in a state of blame, trapped in the shadows of what already happened. I stay tethered to the past, rehearsing the moments I wish I could rewrite and compounding their shame over me. Why did I do that? Why didn't I know better?

But I cannot change the past. Forgiveness is what releases me from trying. It is the only way to stop looking backward and start looking ahead. When I forgive myself, I reclaim my future and allow myself to receive the gifts today offers without the stain of yesterday's shame.

Forgiveness doesn't pretend the past was different. It simply refuses to let the past decide who I become tomorrow.

RESILIENCE HELPED ME SURVIVE; FORGIVENESS HELPS ME LIVE

For years, I prided myself on being resilient. I could swim through anything. Literal oceans. Emotional storms. Medical emergencies. Even grief that stretched to the highest heavenly places. I have proven I can endure.

But survival is not the same as living.

Resilience is grit. Forgiveness is grace.

Resilience says, "I will keep going."

Forgiveness says, "I will be restored."

Christ's forgiveness created space for restoration in me. It softened what was rigid. It quieted what was loud. It healed what was breaking. Resilience kept me from drowning. Forgiveness let me breathe again.

THE FINAL WORD

I don't forgive because people deserve it.

I forgive because Christ forgave me.

His forgiveness didn't erase my story. It redeemed it and gave me the courage to release what was too heavy to keep carrying. Forgiveness is not surrender. It is freedom.

Forgiveness is how I rise.

It is how I breathe.

It is how I honor the unconditional love of a Savior who met me long before I knew I needed Him.

Forgiveness is not simple.

It is sacred.

And it has saved my life more times than I can count.

KIMBERLY STEVENS

Kimberly is a results-driven keynote speaker who empowers teams to harness grit and gratitude to achieve their goals and exceed expectations. With a powerful personal story of resilience and a proven track record of success, she inspires organizations to take small, daily steps that create big, measurable outcomes—both professionally and personally. As a record-holding collegiate athlete and an award-winning insurance agency owner, Kimberly understands the power of determination, adaptability, and strategic action. Her career began with sixteen years in pharmaceutical sales, helping patients navigate insurance complexities.

Her passion for turning challenges into opportunities led her *to Extend the Wav*e, a movement bringing hope, encouragement, and connection to children and families in hospitals nationwide. Inspired by the Hawkeye Wave, Extend the Wave ensures that families facing difficult medical journeys feel seen, supported, and are never alone. Through this initiative, Kimberly is proving that a simple act of kindness can create a ripple effect of impact across the nation.

Author's Website: *www.ExtendTheWave.org*

Charity Awareness: *www.ExtendTheRose.org*

LATONYA AUZENNE

FORGIVE. REBUILD. RISE.

··

A LOVE STORY BUILT ON PRINCIPLES, TESTED BY PAIN, & TRANSFORMED THROUGH PURPOSE

We didn't fall in love by accident. We met on purpose. In purpose. For a purpose.

The setting was simple—a bookstore—but the energy was divine. Two souls searching for something more. Not just love, but *alignment*. Not just companionship, but *clarity*. We were both tired of surface. Both ready to evolve. We weren't drawn to each other's masks—we were pulled by each other's truth.

From the beginning, we had something different: a hunger to grow. A shared desire to *become* better versions of ourselves— not just for us, but for our children, our community, and the legacy we would one day leave behind.

It was the kind of love that requires courage. And commitment. And forgiveness.

Because love without healing eventually turns into war. And leadership without alignment becomes a burden.

BLENDING LOVE, LEGACY, & LOSS

We came together as a blended family—hopeful, united, and deeply committed. But blending doesn't mean seamless. It means *layered*. It means learning how to lead children who carry stories and wounds you didn't create. It means facing energy that was shaped before your love ever arrived.

What we didn't expect was the resistance—not just from the world, but from *within our home*. Some of our children, influenced by outside forces and old patterns, became mirrors of misunderstanding. They reflected the fear, judgment, and criticism we had spent years escaping.

And we were trying to build a business at the same time.

There were days it felt like we were battling on all sides— loving each other, raising children who didn't fully see us yet, and facing an industry that wasn't ready for the frequency we brought.

THE BUSINESS WE BUILT FROM BELIEF

We started our transportation company with nothing but a vision, a prayer, and a set of principles. We believed in serving with excellence, leading with integrity, and building a culture of respect and safety.

We applied the exact teachings of Napoleon Hill—even before we were officially certified:

- A Definite Major Purpose
- Faith and Autosuggestion
- Organized Planning
- Persistence

We weren't guessing our way through business. We were *building by design.* And it worked—fast.

Our company grew. Our reputation spread. Clients noticed our professionalism. Health plans respected our vision.

We invested back into the business. We hired a seasoned Safety Manager, Oscar Watson, a Greyhound legend with over twenty-seven years of experience. We brought in a Louisiana State Trooper to train our drivers and shift the safety culture in real time.

But success—especially fast, purpose-driven success—can become a trigger for those still in survival mode.

WHEN YOU LEAD WITH LIGHT, SHADOWS PUSH BACK

The NEMT industry wasn't ready.

We thought others would be inspired by our effort to raise the standard. Instead, many saw it as a threat.

Some providers had been operating for years without structure, training, or purpose. For them, it wasn't about transformation —it was about territory. They weren't thinking about service. They were surviving. And a survival mindset doesn't easily make room for elevation.

Still, we tried. We hosted calls. We encouraged collaboration. We spoke about mindset, leadership, and unity. I even scheduled an office meeting to lift the region's morale during a tough time in the market.

But days before the meeting, I received a cold, negative text from a provider I didn't even know. Another provider, with influence, scheduled a competing meeting for the *same day* and told others not to attend mine.

It hurt. Deeply.

I wasn't there to compete—I was there to uplift. My message was about mindset. About how we can choose peace, clarity, and structure, even under pressure. Yet somehow, I became the target.

That morning, I sat on the edge of my bed in tears, wondering:

Why am I doing this? Why do I keep trying to give when so few want to receive?

THE REAL LESSON:
FORGIVENESS IS FREQUENCY WORK

That moment taught me something powerful.

Forgiveness isn't emotional. It's energetic. It's not about who's right. It's about what's real. And what's real is this—you cannot lead and carry bitterness at the same time.

We had to forgive—not just the people, but the pain. We forgave our children for what they couldn't yet understand. We forgave our peers for the slander, the gossip, the false stories. We even forgave the industry—for its chaos, its culture, and its resistance.

Because the truth is, once your mind is defeated, nothing else works. No vehicle. No funding. No partnership. As Napoleon Hill said:

"A quitter never wins—and a winner never quits." "When defeat comes, accept it as a signal that your plans are not sound. Rebuild those plans, and set sail once more toward your coveted goal."

We didn't quit. We forgave.

We rebuilt. And we rose.

BECOMING CERTIFIED TO TEACH
WHAT WE LIVED

That pain led to a breakthrough. My husband and I both became **Certified Napoleon Hill Instructors**, side by side. We now teach the very principles that helped us build, heal, and thrive:

- Faith over fear
- Purpose over pressure
- Love over ego
- Planning over panic

We teach them in our business. We teach them to our family. We teach them to anyone who will listen.

Because success is not about status—it's about **alignment with divine law**.

It's about who you become while building.

FROM SURVIVAL TO THRIVAL

We are no longer surviving.

We are thriving.

But our thriving didn't come from comfort—it came through **forgiveness**.

We had to release everything that wasn't ours to carry:

- The lies

- The projections

- The envy

- The weight of being misunderstood

We chose love, not for applause, but for peace. We chose integrity, not for validation, but for legacy.

We chose to keep rising—together.

FINAL WORD

To the one reading this who has ever been **betrayed while trying to help**, who has felt alone while building, who has been doubted for thinking bigger, who has had to heal while leading—this chapter is for you.

You don't need everyone to understand your vision.

You just need to trust the **frequency of your calling**.

And when you forgive, when you rebuild, when you rise—you become unstoppable.

We did.

And now, we help others do the same.

LATONYA AUZENNE

Latonya Auzenne is a purpose-driven entrepreneur, certified Napoleon Hill instructor, and NeuroChange Practitioner dedicated to transforming lives through mindset mastery and business empowerment. As co-owner of IRIDE Transportation, she helps deliver safe and reliable non-emergency medical transportation across Louisiana. Latonya is also a passionate speaker, author, and direct sales leader, using her voice and personal story to inspire others to rise above adversity and reclaim their power.

Raised in Shreveport and now rooted in Lafayette, she brings a deep commitment to faith, integrity, and community impact. Latonya serves as Secretary of the Greater Southwest Louisiana Black Chamber of Commerce, where she champions minority-owned businesses and economic equity. Through workshops, coaching, and public service, she equips others with the tools to live their dreams and create lasting success. With a heart for healing and a bold vision for the future, Latonya is living proof that with belief and action, transformation is possible.

Author's Website: *www.CEOLatonya.com*

Charity Awareness: *www.CasaStLandry.org*

LAURIE K. SCHWARTZ

THE SAT'S: THE CONTINUATION OF OUR DAUGHTER'S SAGA

Our daughter completed the untimed SAT exam, and her tutor from the private school for children with learning disabilities mailed it to the SAT center in New Jersey. He had performed this process many times for many, many children. Back then, the SAT center had its own zip code. I attempted to research whether this was still true, but to no avail —things change over time.

Time passed, and many of our daughters' friends received their SAT scores and college admissions. We were still waiting. On a Saturday afternoon, while our daughter was away on a weekend school trip, I retrieved the mail. Among the usual envelopes was a package addressed to her from the New Jersey Environmental Agency. I assumed she had a project for school and contacted them for information. I opened the package and to my shock, out came her raw SAT exam.

I was stunned. I immediately called her tutor at the private school, and he advised me to bring it to him right away. He was flummoxed. Having administered and mailed countless SAT exams to their center, he had never encountered this before.

It appeared that the Post Office misdelivered the package because it had the correct address on it. What made no sense was that instead of forwarding the package onto the SAT center, whose address was on the front of the envelope or to the return address of the tutor at the private school, which was in the proper place on the envelope, The New Jersey Environmental Agency inexplicably opened it and returned it to our daughter's home address, which was inside the envelope and written on the test. We are now at the crosshairs of the United States Postal Office and the New Jersey Environmental Agency and both of their inefficiencies.

When I arrived at the tutor's school, he was so upset about this and promptly remailed the exam with a letter of explanation to the SAT center. And so, we waited again for her score. Weeks went by, and there was no response from them. I called the SAT center several times to inquire about the scores and was told they were still being processed.

By this time, all her friends had received their scores and had committed to their choice of college, some already getting dorm assignments. Frustrated, I continued calling the SAT center, determined to get an answer as to our daughter's score. Finally, I insisted on talking to a supervisor. My husband, an attorney, joined the call and firmly stated that we paid for the exam and have a right to know her score. If they refuse to provide it, he told them, we will take other actions.

They finally told us, after weeks of wasted time, that the test was contaminated and that they could not give us a score. They knew this for weeks and never told us sooner. We were dumbfounded. It was incredulous. I said, "Are you suggesting we cheated and changed answers on the test? Because nothing is further from the truth." They responded, "No, that is not what we are saying." I replied, "Then why are you withholding her scores if you're not concerned about us changing her answers? Of course, that is what you think."

They said they would verbally give us a range, but not in writing. It was a very good range. Obviously, they didn't want us to have anything concrete in our possession. They probably thought, how could a student who had done so poorly on her PSATs do so well on her SATs? It was a legitimate question; however, we knew what changed for her to be successful and they didn't, nor did they care to ask. That was extraordinary to me—they didn't care to ask how this happened. This was the SAT center that had so much power over our children's future.

After moving past this very unfortunate, unfair experience, which took a toll on our daughter and me, we have now reached the next step: Getting her into our state university, where her father and brother went, and where our taxes went. The university did not want to accept her without her written SAT scores. She was accepted by another good out-of-state university, even without her SAT score. They predicated their acceptance on her excellent school grades, her extracurricular activities, and recommendations. The problem was that it was an out-of-state university—an excellent school—but the cost far exceeded that of our own state university.

I had to take new actions and was fortunate to contact a dear friend who sat on the Board of Regents of the University. Thanks to his connections, we secured a meeting with the Head of Admissions. Despite our contact and our daughter's National Honor Society membership and strong grades, they accepted her only under a contingency agreement. She had to maintain a certain grade point average, or they would not allow her to stay. We accepted the terms.

It was so late in the admissions process that most of the dorms were already filled. She was placed in the athletic dorm. Within weeks, she was miserable—she did not fit in with the other students in the dorm because she was not athletic, and she was not near any friends, many of whom were at the university, but it was a huge campus. Being persistent and going through different channels we were able to make a move into a more appropriate dorm.

She was at the university for four years, excelled in her studies, and was a member of the College Honor Society. From the third grade, when she took the first California Achievement Test (CAT), the concept of forgiveness never entered our minds. We never could have imagined what was up ahead for her. It was a grueling fourteen-year-long journey. We felt very upset that some of these things occurred, and that we had little control over them, like the USPO mistakenly delivering her SATs and the New Jersey Environmental Agency not forwarding the packet onto the SAT center where it was correctly addressed.

In hindsight, we could see how some of the situations imposed upon us served us well in future situations. But we didn't know that at the time. If anything, it made my daughter and I stronger and more confident in our persistence and values. But I am getting ahead of myself, trust me, there is more. We can be forgiving of the school counselors who made what they thought was the best assessment of the situation with the limited information that we all had.

Hindsight being 20/20, we could see how these challenges ultimately shaped character. At the time, we had no idea how some of these struggles would prepare us for future battles. But we persevered and, in the end, my daughter succeeded—not because the system helped her, but in spite of it.

Dr. Viktor Frankl's book, *Man's Search for Meaning,* detailed how he created the theory of Logotherapy. Dr. Frankl was an Austrian Psychiatrist, Neurologist, and Concentration Camp survivor. Most of his family, including his parents and pregnant wife, were murdered during World War II and the Nazi atrocities. He was in four different Concentration Camps, including the Auschwitz death camp.

At the end of the war and after his liberation, Dr Frankl reflected on his own and others' experiences and felt that if a person can live through adversity and, in his case, ultimate adversity and still achieve meaning and growth from it, then the experience can have value.

In our case, it seemed that the totality of the experiences was invaluable. Obviously, there is no comparison to the two situations; however, the lessons gleaned from the experiences were elemental in future life lessons, which was the basis for Dr. Frankl's Logotherapy.

LAURIE K. SCHWARTZ

Laurie Koller Schwartz is a passionate advocate, devoted mother, and accomplished business leader. She is a graduate of the University of Baltimore in Maryland. She and her late husband, Michael, moved to Scottsdale, Arizona, where she rehabilitated and sold homes. Prior to that, she was a member of the Board of Directors of the International Association of Near-Death Studies (IANDS) and later the founder of NOVA—the Network Of eVolutionary Advancement. In both of those capacities, she coordinated national and international conferences on death, near-death studies, and reincarnation. Her professional strength is matched only by her fierce dedication to her family of three children, daughter-in-law, son-in-law, and five grandchildren.

Laurie strives to inspire readers with themes of resilience, courage, and the power of persistence. Her contributions to *The Book of Survival to Thrival* spotlight her belief in fighting for what's right—even when the system falls short—and her commitment to empowering others with compassion, strategy, and unwavering love. She lives by the principle that true success is measured by the lives we lift along the way.

Charity Awareness: *www.HOV.org*

DR. LÉ SANTHA NAIDOO

THE HEALING POWER OF FORGIVENESS: WHEN GRACE MEANS GROWTH

Forgiveness is not a destination—it's a journey that begins with the courage to look inward and the wisdom to understand that healing cannot happen while we're still carrying the weight of resentment. My path to understanding the transformative power of forgiveness began in the most unexpected place: in the mirror, facing the person I had been hardest on my entire life—myself.

For most of my existence, I had been my own harshest critic, my most relentless judge. Every perceived failure, every moment of imperfection, every time I fell short of impossible standards became another stone in the wall I built around my heart. I carried guilt that wasn't mine to bear and shame that had no business living in my soul. But it wasn't until I was forced to confront the deepest wounds of my past that I truly understood forgiveness wasn't just about letting others off the hook—it was about setting myself free.

The journey began with a four-year-old girl standing at her grandfather's funeral, watching flames consume the body of the man who had loved her unconditionally. My Thatha's suicide had planted seeds of guilt so deep they took root in my very identity. In my young mind, I somehow believed that if I had been better, more lovable, more worthy, he would have chosen to stay. The questions that haunted me were simple but devastating: "What could I have done to change his mind? What did I do that was so wrong?"

These thoughts didn't just visit me—they haunted me for decades, becoming an ever-present whisper that shaped how I saw myself, how I navigated relationships, and how I understood love. I carried the crushing belief that I had to earn love and approval, as if by being perfect enough, I could retroactively prove that I was worth staying alive for.

For years, I lived under this weight, trying to fix everyone around me, believing that if I could heal the world, maybe I could heal the wound in my own heart. I became the person who felt responsible for everyone else's happiness, carrying burdens that were never mine to carry, all while neglecting the most important relationship of all—the one with myself.

The breakthrough came during one of the darkest periods of my life, when my health was failing, my body was rebelling against years of neglect, and I found myself staring at a reflection I barely recognized. I was exhausted—not just physically, but spiritually. I had given everything to everyone else and had nothing left for myself. It was in that moment of complete depletion that I finally heard the voice I had been ignoring for so long: my own.

As I began learning more about my grandfather's life through family stories, a different picture emerged. I discovered the 1949 riots, where he and his cousin had hidden in mango trees, watching homes burn and fearing for their lives. I learned about the mental health challenges he faced, the immense responsibilities he carried, and the burdens that had nothing to do with a four-year-old's behavior. Slowly, painfully, beautifully, I began to understand that his decision wasn't a reflection of my worth—it was the result of pain so deep that he couldn't see any other way out.

This realization didn't come all at once. Forgiveness, I learned, is not a single moment of enlightenment but a series of choices, made over and over again, to release what no longer serves us. Some days, the forgiveness felt real and transformative. Other days, the old guilt would creep back in, and I would have to consciously choose compassion over condemnation, understanding over judgment.

The process of forgiving myself for carrying guilt that was never mine opened the door to forgiving others who had caused pain in my life. There was the friend who had betrayed my trust, leaving me feeling violated and confused. For years, I carried anger toward him, letting it poison my ability to trust others. But as I learned to forgive myself for the innocent mistakes of childhood, I found space to forgive him for his own brokenness, his own poor choices that had nothing to do with my worth.

There were the doctors who dismissed my concerns about my son's health, making me feel like an overprotective mother rather than a physician with valid medical concerns. The frustration and helplessness I felt during those months of fighting for proper care had left me bitter and distrustful of the medical system I had devoted my life to serving. But forgiveness allowed me to see that their dismissiveness came from their own limitations, their own fears, their own humanity. It didn't excuse their behavior, but it freed me from carrying the weight of their mistakes.

Perhaps the most challenging forgiveness came in learning to release resentment toward those closest to me who had cut me off when I began setting boundaries and living authentically. When I stopped being the person everyone expected me to be and started being who I truly was, some relationships couldn't survive the transformation. The pain of losing people I loved simply for being myself was excruciating. But forgiveness taught me that their rejection wasn't about my worth—it was about their own discomfort with change, their own fear of what my transformation meant for their lives.

The physical manifestation of this emotional and spiritual healing was profound. As I released years of stored resentment, guilt, and shame, my body responded in miraculous ways. The chronic pain that had plagued me for years began to subside. My energy returned with a vitality I hadn't felt in decades. My relationships deepened as I learned to show up authentically rather than performing roles I thought others wanted me to play.

Forgiveness also taught me the importance of boundaries—not as walls to keep people out, but as loving limits that protect my energy and allow me to show up fully for what truly matters. I learned that saying no to what doesn't align with my values isn't selfish; it's necessary for maintaining the peace I had worked so hard to achieve.

The ripple effects of this forgiveness work extended far beyond my personal healing. As I learned to be gentler with myself, I naturally became more compassionate with my patients, my family, and everyone I encountered. My son, watching me navigate this transformation, learned early that mistakes don't define us—how we respond to them does. My husband witnessed firsthand the power of a woman who had stopped apologizing for taking up space in the world.

Today, forgiveness remains a daily practice. When old patterns of self-criticism arise, I consciously choose self-compassion. When others disappoint or hurt me, I work to see their actions through the lens of their own pain rather than taking it personally. This doesn't mean I accept poor treatment or ignore red flags—it means I don't carry the weight of other people's choices as if they were my own.

FORGIVENESS

The most profound lesson forgiveness taught me is that we cannot heal what we refuse to feel. For years, I had buried my pain under layers of achievement, service, and perfectionism. But healing required me to sit with the discomfort, to feel the full weight of my grief and guilt, and then to consciously choose to release it with love.

If you're reading this and carrying your own burden of unforgiveness—whether toward yourself or others—I want you to know that liberation is possible. It doesn't happen overnight, and it's not always linear, but it is always worth it. Start small. Start with one moment, one choice, one breath at a time. Choose compassion over condemnation. Choose understanding over judgment. Choose freedom over the familiar weight of resentment.

Forgiveness isn't about forgetting or excusing harmful behavior. It's about refusing to let someone else's actions or your own past mistakes determine your future. It's about reclaiming your power and choosing peace over pain. The world needs your healed heart, your authentic voice, your unique gifts. But first, you must forgive yourself for being beautifully, imperfectly human.

The journey from survival to thrival begins with this sacred act of forgiveness.

LÉ SANTHA NAIDOO

A revolutionary force in medicine, Dr. Lé Santha Naidoo transcends traditional healthcare with her triple board certifications and visionary approach to wellness. As founder of Avyanna Wellness Institute and "The 100 Club," she delivers bespoke health optimization to an exclusive clientele, transforming lives through personalized and precision care. Rising from adversity to international acclaim, her journey to becoming a pioneering physician and her health advocacy captivate audiences worldwide on major television networks (*NBC*, *ABC*, *CBS*, *FOX*) and global stages. Her bestselling memoir, *Fat to Fabulous*, stands as a testament to her extraordinary resilience.

Receiving many honors for her community service, leadership, and ranking as America's Best Concierge Physician, Dr. Lé Santha's brilliance extends beyond medicine—she's a fierce mentor, philanthropist, and catalyst for human potential. Her unique blend of medical mastery and profound compassion creates not just physical healing, but profound life transformation.

Author's Website: *www.LeSantha.com*

Charity Awareness: *www.MercyChefs.com*

LISA CANNON

THE LONG ROAD TO FORGIVENESS

Who knew it would happen?

I come from a big family—seven siblings in total. When Mom was alive, we were the kind of family that showed up. Birthdays, holidays, even the in-between days—we gathered. We laughed, debated, shared meals, and, sure, disagreed. But the love was always there, woven into every occasion like a familiar thread.

My next-oldest sister and I were especially close. Fridays became our tradition—Mom's day. We'd take her to lunch, just the three of us. It wasn't fancy or grand, but it was sacred in its own way. A routine that whispered, *You are loved.*

As time went on, life changed in quiet but undeniable ways. Mom's bones, like so many in their nineties, began to betray her. First, a broken arm. Then a broken leg. Each injury pulled her a little further from her independence. Each rehab stay was a little more isolating.

Her last rehab stint came just as the world was exhaling from the long, held breath of COVID. The facility was considered "top-notch," but even the best weren't immune to the staffing shortages and frayed nerves of a pandemic aftermath. Nurses got sick. Care faltered. And my Mom—so used to hallway chats, friendly neighbors poking their heads in, her kids and grandkids stopping by—found herself alone in a quiet room for hours on end.

Meals were delivered to her bedside. No more chance meetings in dining halls. No small moments to break up the day. Visiting hours were limited to times when most of us were still working. I know she felt the silence like a weight.

Then came the moment I'd always known might arrive. My sister reminded me: *You and your ex said you'd take Mom if it ever came to this.*

But I wasn't that person anymore. I was divorced. In a new relationship. Caring for a partner's special needs son. Life had changed—but my love for my mother hadn't. We were best friends. And if she needed me, I would find a way.

So, I did.

I made plans. Moved my home office into my son's old room while he was away at college. Converted my office into a cozy bedroom, right next to the bathroom. We had a family conversation, and the decision was made: Mom would come home to live with my family and me.

What followed was an ordeal I couldn't have predicted.

The rehab facility was silent, unwilling to help. No discharge plan. No medication list. No support. I waited three weeks in limbo before I finally told the charge nurse, "In five days, at 10 AM, on Sunday, I will be here to take my mother home. Please have her ready."

No one called. No confirmation. No communication.

But when I arrived, there she was—dressed, packed, ready. She had told every aide, every nurse, every visitor: *My daughter is coming on Sunday. I'm going home.*

They didn't believe her. Thought she was confused, senile. But they were wrong.

She remembered. She *knew*.

Despite the facility's failure, one nurse showed me a quiet kindness. She handed me my mom's medications with clear instructions and even tucked in extra supplies—bandages, gauze, the little things that showed she cared. I will never forget her for that.

And just like that, we left.

That's when something strange happened—something more painful than I was prepared for.

The family disappeared.

No calls. No visits. Silence. Unless I reached out first, I heard nothing. It was as if, by bringing Mom into my home, I had made her invisible to them.

I reached out—again and again—telling them they were always welcome. No need to call ahead. The carer was there if they wanted to take her out, or I could arrange time for them alone with her. Nothing. Just silence. If I didn't plan a lunch or drive her to them, she didn't see them.

I took her to every doctor appointment. Managed the rotating cast of carers. When we were between helpers, I begged my sisters to stay with her. But caregiving, it seems, didn't fit into their schedules. My brother could only handle an hour at a time.

Sometimes, when one of my sisters would pick her up, I'd pretend to feel unwell. I'd let them go without me, hoping they'd feel freer, more at ease. I even sat at the far end of the table during lunches that I did attend, giving them space to be with her. But nothing changed.

And then she passed.

The grief, already immense, became complicated by the tension that followed. No one wanted to finalize her funeral plans, though Mom had laid everything out years ago. At the viewing, they stood in corners—apart, distant, awkward. It broke me.

I was angry. Angry that no one came. Angry that I had carried this burden alone. Angry that even now, two years later, no one called. I reached out once to each sibling after she passed, but the responses were clipped, cold, or silent altogether.

My sister—my closest ally once—refuses to speak to me. My brother, who lives nearby, talks occasionally. I think he's sad too, perhaps lost in his own grief. Maybe we all are.

Forgiveness is a big word.

It's a heavy word.

And it's not easy.

Some days, I want to call them. Other days, I want to shout. I think about knocking on their doors, but I don't. I'm afraid of what I'll find—anger, blame, more silence.

So, I hold my grief. I hold my memories. And I try to hold grace.

Forgiveness isn't about them—it's about me. It's about letting go so I don't drown in the weight of resentment. And though I haven't mastered it yet, I try. Every day, I try.

Some days, I cry thinking about it. Some days I miss them. Some days I feel free. But each month, each step forward, it gets a little easier.

Forgiveness is a journey. Mine is still unfolding. I hope that my story empowers you. Gives you the grace to know that, truly, forgiveness is a journey.

LISA CANNON

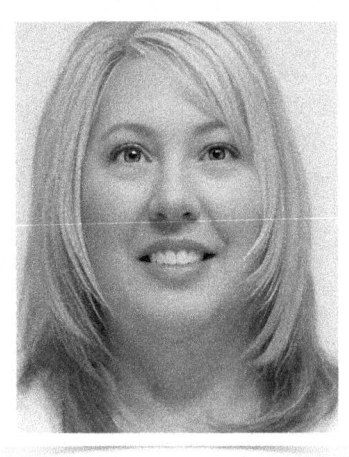

Lisa Cannon is the founder of 4SuccessU, a coaching and consulting company committed to helping women entrepreneurs build profitable, purpose-driven businesses. With over twenty years of experience in coaching, training, consulting, and public speaking, Lisa has empowered thousands of professionals to gain clarity, confidence, and direction through her signature blend of strategic systems, intuitive insight, and practical mindset tools. Having navigated her own share of personal and professional transitions, Lisa brings a deep, authentic passion for helping others step into their next level.

Her specialty lies in guiding clients through pivotal transitions —helping them shift from stuck to strategic, scattered to focused, and overwhelmed to thriving. Lisa's coaching style is straightforward and results-driven, yet always grounded in empathy. She's also a published author and widely respected for her no-fluff, heart-centered approach. Her motto? Life is short—show up boldly, lead with purpose, and become the greatest version of yourself.

Author's Website: *www.4SuccessU.com*

Charity Awareness: *www.SurvivalToThrivalSeries.com*

M.A. FULTS
FORGIVE TO LIVE

. . . .

FORGIVENESS

No discussion of forgiveness can be done without a discussion of mercy and grace. Sounds like religion, doesn't it? It is not religion or "religious," it is, in fact, truth. Why? Because without mercy and grace, forgiveness doesn't exist.

But then, what are mercy and grace? A few years ago, in reading Ron Carpenter's book, *The Necessity of an Enemy,* he provided a simple-to-understand and remember definition of both.

MERCY

Mercy is not receiving what we deserve. My reading in Romans chapter three this morning included verse twenty-eight, where Paul reminds us that we all have sinned, we've all hurt others, we've all done something for which we deserve punishment. Oops, that is from the Holy Bible, but it is also truth. Every one of us has erred, every one of us has caused damage, or hurt, to another person, through a lie, through cheating, or through stealing; possibly even through physical or mental abuse. When others extend mercy to us, it means the punishment we deserve for the hurt is not received by us. Does that mean that forgiveness lets the person who hurt us off the hook? Well, yes, and no.

When a person has hurt us, either physically, mentally, or emotionally, in a "fair world," we have the right to retaliate, do we not? Truly, unforgiveness is wanting and waiting to see them rightly punished for what they did to us. If they don't receive that punishment, then they seemingly have received mercy. In the meantime, we are holding on to the hurt and to the unforgiveness, because we want them punished! We want justice in the form of them hurting as much as we are.

Choosing to forgive, we let go of that hurt and unforgiveness. We let go of wanting to see them hurt as much as we do. We essentially say, "I release them from my providing or enforcing the punishment they deserve, even if only in my own mind." Like the song says, I let it go.

GRACE

Grace is receiving what we don't deserve. Grace is receiving mercy when we've done something deserving of punishment. When we have hurt others, we deserve punishment. We deserve retaliation, we deserve justice for what we have done, maybe even to be hurt in return. What we don't deserve is mercy or forgiveness. Therefore, when we extend forgiveness to one who doesn't deserve forgiveness, we extend grace and mercy.

Choosing to forgive, we are still saying, "I release them…" but I do so with grace, knowing they don't deserve my forgiveness, yet choosing to extend it anyway. What we need to fully comprehend, though, is why we need to forgive, especially when the hurt is so bad that the wounds are still fresh, or the scars only recently formed.

WHY FORGIVE?

In a "just world," why would we ever forgive someone who hurt us? Why would we let them off the hook of deserved punishment, deserved pain? They hurt us; they deserve to know and feel the pain we went through, may even still be going through. In a just world, retaliation is paramount. And yet… how many are the punishments we ourselves deserve? And if I deserve punishment, then how can I expect forgiveness if I don't extend forgiveness?

FORGIVENESS IS NOT

Forgiveness is not allowing the other person to get away with hurting you. While retaliation, vengeance, and seeing the one who hurt you receive justice all seem to be "right" and "just," extending forgiveness, letting go of my need to be the one administering "justice," results in my being set free.

Forgiveness is not making concessions to the other person, nor is it sweeping the hurt under the rug. And most definitely it is not saying to them, "It's okay." Because it's not okay, but it is forgiven, not for the other person, but for my own freedom.

Forgiveness is not for the other person. A long time ago, I heard, "Not forgiving someone is like ingesting poison and expecting it to hurt the other person." Unforgiveness holds onto the hurt, like consuming a poison; forgiveness is letting go of that poison, which has been hurting only me.

Forgiveness is not giving in to the other person, being magnanimous or generous toward them out of the "goodness of my heart." Again, forgiveness is for me because it sets me free from the prison of pain, poison, and constant focus on the other person.

FORGIVENESS IS

Forgiveness is about you, the one giving, the one forgiving. Forgiveness is letting go of your right to punish, and by doing so, letting go of the poison you've been carrying. Forgiveness is the one who was hurt saying, "I forgive you—period." Forgiveness, letting go, is finding freedom.

Years ago, I met and had the pleasure of working with Beth Hunter, author of the book/workbook, *Forgive and Live*. Working with her and reading her book is where I came to fully grasp that not extending forgiveness placed me into a prison of my own making. I don't like being linked to others through negative, poisonous thoughts and focus.

How can I say it was poisonous? Because I know the effects of that poison—on my body, on my mind, even on my spirit. But here's the truth: while I held onto that unforgiveness, I didn't realize how poisonous it was or how much I was in darkness. I didn't realize how I was in a prison of my own making, with bars or walls, separating me from everyone else.

Only when I let go, only when I had forgiven the hurt and the resultant pain, did I experience freedom. And that freedom was like a light shining into a darkened prison, leading me into a world free from a heavy, heavy burden. I felt light-hearted and like a heavy weight had been lifted from my entire body. My health improved. My heart and mind were no longer fixated on the other person, with dark thoughts and desires of their experiencing pain or justice. My spirit felt free to connect with others, and most importantly, free to once again connect with my God.

FREEDOM TO LIVE

Extending forgiveness helped me to realize that while I'd been holding on to the unforgiveness, I had been slowly dying. It was as if life flooded in, for the first time in years. I found freedom through forgiving, and I found that to live, truly live, I had to extend forgiveness. But did that mean that everyone who'd ever hurt me was forgiven—I wish.

One of the most important things Beth Hunter taught me is: Forgiveness is a Process. The next was: Trust the Process. I smile as I type that, because I found it to be an extended process, and one that needs to be entered into often. I still experience hurts, betrayals, and pain from what others do or say. I still need to remember to choose to forgive. And here's the KEY: Forgiveness is a choice.

CHOOSE TO FORGIVE

In "The Lord's Prayer," where Jesus answered His disciples' request to "teach us how to pray," Jesus said, "Forgive us our trespasses (wrong-doings) as we forgive those who trespass (do wrong) against us." Today, when I pray that prayer, I often add, "I choose to forgive," sometimes saying it multiple times, sometimes adding a name. Why? Because it is my choice to forgive, as it is my choice to hold onto unforgiveness. But I want to live, so I choose to forgive. Yes, I also want to be forgiven, by others and by God, but knowing my living life to its fullest is contingent upon my forgiving, I choose to do so.

My life's catchphrase is, "Love Provides." Corollary to that is, love forgives; love doesn't hold onto wrongs, love doesn't even keep a record of wrongs. Love provides—forgiveness, and through forgiveness, freedom. You can choose to not forgive, but that way leads to a slow, agonizing, and very dark death. Or you can choose to forgive. I choose to forgive to live.

M.A. FULTS

Born into an Army family, and with thirty-nine years serving in and then working for the US Navy, Fults spent many years traveling and living in foreign countries, including four years in Tehran, Iran.

She holds a BFA in Drama Production from the University of Arizona and an MS in Management from the Naval Postgraduate School in Monterey, CA. After retiring for the second time in 2022, Fults continued her lifelong pursuit of learning while embarking on her newfound passion for heart healing, financial advising, and life coaching. She has been blessed with one son.

Charity Awareness: *www.Compassion.com*

MARANDA CARLILE

FORGIVENESS IS CLARITY, NOT ALWAYS CLOSURE

. . . .

DON'T CARRY BITTERNESS, CARRY BOUNDARIES

For a long time, I believed forgiveness required closure.

A conversation.

A shared understanding.

Some acknowledgment that the other person finally saw what I saw, maybe an apology, maybe accountability, maybe remorse.

But life taught me otherwise.

When hard things happen, when life cracks open, it's easy to let that hardship become everything. Pain narrows your focus. Confusion takes up space. Betrayal loops in your mind until it feels all encompassing. You begin to wonder, *How do I get through this? Why did this happen to me? Where do I even start over?*

I have lived there longer than I needed to in many situations.

Because what I eventually realized was this: waiting for apologies, explanations, or understanding kept me tethered to pain that no longer deserved my energy.

So there is a choice.

- You can stay in anger.
- You can stay in hurt.
- You can stay circling the same questions, hoping for a different ending.

Or you can ask a different set of questions.

What can I learn from this?
How can I grow from this?
What is this asking me to become?

Those questions don't erase what happened. They don't minimize the hurt. But they do something powerful, they stop the hard thing from being the only thing.

The pain doesn't disappear, but it no longer defines you. It no longer consumes you.

That is forgiveness.

And life has shown me that forgiveness isn't always about going back and making peace with someone else. It isn't always about understanding the *why* behind what they chose to do.

Sometimes forgiveness is about moving forward and making peace with yourself.

Not forgetting what happened. Not excusing it.

But becoming clearer about where your energy goes. About your intentions. About choosing peace over the endless pursuit of explanations.

That clarity is freedom.

FORGIVENESS DOESN'T ALWAYS LOOK LIKE A CONVERSATION

Sometimes forgiveness looks like leaving with grace.

Leaving a situation. Leaving a relationship. Or choosing to stop placing your energy where it no longer belongs.

Not every ending comes with clarity or conversation. Some arrive quietly, through decisions made without you and assumptions you never agreed to carry. When you wait for closure, you stay connected to something that's no longer choosing you.

I left what I once believed was a partnership with grace, and I accepted when a contract that shaped my clinical foundation was quietly withdrawn. Both taught me the same truth: misplaced trust can be costly, but clarity is priceless. I carried grief for a season, then chose to move forward—leaving bitterness behind.

BLESS AND RELEASE

Forgiveness doesn't require access or explanation. It requires discernment.

- Bless and release.
- Release the need to be understood.
- Release the urge to explain.
- Release what costs you your peace.

FORGIVENESS IS UNLEARNING PERFORMANCE

As I was putting these ideas together, how forgiveness has helped me not only survive, but thrive, I realized something I hadn't fully said out loud before: my worth had always felt tied to performance. I had to show up, get good grades, be a good daughter, a good sister, a good mother, always doing, always proving.

But that's not what it's really about.

Every pause used to feel like failure. Not because it was, but because my nervous system had been trained to equate worth with productivity. Forgiveness began when I chose to re-pattern that belief.

A huge part of forgiveness—real forgiveness—is forgiving yourself for what you thought you had to do to be okay.

Forgiving yourself for how you survived.

Forgiving the version of you that didn't know another way.

Because eventually, you realize that kind of energy isn't sustainable. You cannot live that way forever.

So I stepped back and asked myself: *What do I actually want? What matters most?* And when I really sat with those questions, the answer wasn't complicated. It was my family. My time with them. The simple things. The things that don't require me to prove anything.

FORGIVENESS IS COMING HOME

Another kind of forgiveness arrives quietly, without conflict or explanation.

Over time, you may notice certain friendships change, not because of something said or done, but because the exchange is no longer mutual. You're the one reaching out, showing up, holding space. And eventually, the absence becomes noticeable.

That kind of absence can hurt, not because anyone is at fault, but because it reveals something important about how you love. Some people feel deeply. Some people invest fully. And not everyone meets relationships with the same capacity.

Forgiveness, in these moments, isn't about blame. It's about acceptance. It's recognizing when the energy you've been sending outward needs to come back home.

And when you let it come home, something shifts.

Healing can be effortless. I could make all the money in the world, and it wouldn't be enough, but being with my husband in the hammock in our backyard while the sun filters through the grapevines, with my children nearby, *that* matters.

That's where my body settles. My nervous system softens. That's where I let myself breathe again.

One thing that's key is having something green and natural, grass under your feet, fresh air, the wind on your face. I love going out to the tree swing in my front yard and letting the wind move through me. People underestimate how healing that can be.

Even something small like a garden can do it. When we first got married, my husband built some planter boxes and we planted corn. Watching it grow into food we could eat was moving. The process of nurturing something and watching it grow taught me patience and quiet hope.

Forgiveness can be like that, too. You don't always see what's happening under the surface, but something is happening. Something is growing. Something is coming back.

FORGIVENESS IS WHAT YOU CARRY FORWARD

Looking back, I have boundaries. And boundaries aren't cold. They are what you build when you finally love yourself enough to protect your peace. Forgiveness isn't saying, *"That didn't hurt."* Forgiveness is saying, *"That hurt and I get to choose what I carry forward."*

Because the truth is, your value doesn't diminish just because someone couldn't see your vision. You don't need validation from people who couldn't walk with you where you were going. What feels like failure is often alignment in disguise. Sometimes the ground has to give way beneath you so you can finally learn how to build something of your own.

Maybe your goodbye is still unfolding. Maybe you're standing in that quiet space where something no longer feels right, even if you can't fully explain why. If that's you, hear this, because I needed to hear it too:

- You're not too much. You're just in the wrong room.

- You're not crazy. You're clear and that can unsettle people.

- You're not difficult. You're discerning.
- You're not broken. You're just done shrinking.

If something no longer honors your values, you are allowed to walk away with clarity, with strength, and without apology.

THE KIND OF FORGIVENESS THAT FEELS LIKE HOPE

There's another thing that makes me feel deeply fulfilled: helping someone feel better in my line of work.

Ive had numerous patients share their transformations under our care, but the one that has always stood out. I recently had a patient tell me, through tears, "I've been to so many doctors, and every one of them told me this was just how my life was going to be, that I was getting older and would have to push through it." Then she paused and said, "But I have my life back. You gave me hope again. I feel like I did when I was twenty-five."

That moment stayed with me.

It reminded me that hope is real, and that sometimes forgiveness is simply choosing hope again.
When life is heavy, hope can feel distant. Hardship narrows your vision until pain becomes the only thing you see. But hope returns when you ask yourself different questions:

- "What can I learn from this?"

- "How can I grow from this?"
- "What is this asking me to become?"

That is forgiveness in motion.

For me, forgiveness isn't a sentence you say; it's a life you build.

It's the quiet moment when your body finally exhales. It's choosing peace over proving. It's building boundaries that allow you to breathe, grow, and stay whole.

I don't carry bitterness. I carry boundaries. And that is how I learned to thrive.

BLESS AND RELEASE

Over time, I gave this process a name.

When something no longer aligns with me, when a relationship, an expectation, or a season begins to cost more than it gives, I bless and release. Not in anger. Not in avoidance, but with clarity—to bless is not to pretend it didn't hurt. It is to honor what was, acknowledge what it taught me, and recognize the role it played in shaping who I am becoming.

And to release is not to forget, it is to stop carrying what no longer belongs in the life I am building.

That simple practice became my quiet compass.

It guides how I choose relationships, how I protect my energy, how I decide what comes with me into the next season—and what does not.

Just as I once learned to ask, *What can I learn from this? Who do I want to become?*

I now return to that same posture when life disappoints me, not to bypass the pain, but to keep it from becoming the only thing I see.

Thrival begins when you stop chasing closure and start choosing alignment—when clarity becomes enough, and when you understand that forgiveness isn't a feeling you wait for, it's a decision you make.

So when something no longer aligns, I bless and release.

And in doing so, I make room for peace, for growth, and for the life still unfolding. So pause for a moment.

Ask yourself, where are you still waiting for closure that may never come? And what would shift if clarity were enough?

You might try this today: Name one thing—just one—that no longer aligns. Bless it for what it taught you. And release it from the life you are building next.

MARANDA CARLILE

Maranda Carlile, FNP-BC, is a board-certified Family Nurse Practitioner, TEDx speaker, international presenter, and founder of Astra Health and Wellness. She is Menopause Society Certified and has completed advanced fellowship training through the Academy of Anti-Aging & Regenerative Medicine (A4M). Maranda specializes in helping high-performing women and men rebalance hormones, heal the gut, restore energy, and reclaim their health through a personalized, root-cause approach. She serves as a cohort leader for the BHRT Academy and is widely recognized for her expertise in functional lab interpretation, hormone optimization, and gut health. With over fourteen years of trauma-informed experience as a Sexual Assault Nurse Examiner (SANE), Maranda brings a rare blend of clinical precision and deep empathy to her work. She understands the impact of being dismissed when something feels "off" and believes true healing begins when patients feel seen, heard, and believed.

As a wife and mother of three, Maranda is passionate about helping others feel whole again—physically, mentally, and emotionally.

Author's Website: *www.AstraHealthAndWellness.com*

Charity Awareness: *www.NationalMSSociety.org*

MARIS SEGAL & KEN ASHBY

FORGIVENESS: THE PATH TO FREEDOM

Forgiveness is not a standalone act. It's a relational force that softens judgment, clears emotional weight, and restores our ability to connect and grow. We explored forgiveness in our own lives, not as a passive surrender, but as an active choice—one that deepens empathy, strengthens boundaries, and reclaims the energy we need to move forward. Forgiveness is a consistent thread that weaves into our life and leadership work pillars of Respect for ourselves, and for others, owning our part with Responsibility, choosing new meaning through Reframing, and rising again with Resilience.

Maris: "Hello," I answered, as the old wall-phone rang like a warning bell, slicing through the tension of the Sci-Fi movie my husband and I were watching. It was a Friday night at 10 PM—who could be calling? "Is Richard there?" "Who's calling?" I replied instinctively. A click and a hang-up. Immediately, I felt it—heat coursing through my body. Blood pulsing in places I hadn't noticed before. My instincts weren't just whispering, they were screaming. My heart thundered, and I could feel it crack.

I hit "star 69" (to call back the last number) as if my life depended on it, and a moment later, I heard her voice. I said, "Who is this?" "It's Stephanie," she said—flat, emotionless. I turned to my husband, handed him the phone, and said the words that would change everything: "It's Stephanie for you." He took the phone from me in shock and immediately hung up on her.

That breathless, suspended moment—was the beginning of a long unraveling that I never anticipated. I could feel the unraveling of sixteen years of our friendship, our seven-year beautiful marriage, that had withstood surviving and losing everything in the Northridge, CA earthquake, then his landing a job in NYC. The unravelling of trust, of the future we had envisioned together, and the unravelling of my heartstrings one by one. Without missing a beat, I said, "Do you have something to tell me?" We know that life can change in a split second, and in that moment, it can often feel like the longest year of your life! That pretty much sums up how I felt.

He said it was an internet chat room connection, and he had not yet met her in person, but had been planning to go the next week as part of his upcoming business trip. Hours later, with respect and tears, we agreed that we were worth working on and we would go to couples and individual therapy. He also agreed to hold off on his trip. Whew, I thought, I had a reprieve to get my arms around what was happening.

I immediately left the apartment, never imagining it was over or that we would never share a bed again. Off I went, walking the nine uptown blocks to "our" favorite spot—the same path we had walked hundreds of times. Everything was different! Never having dined there alone, it seemed surreal. He left our apartment that night, and so many realizations flooded into my head. I left for the office that next morning with a whole other perspective on how our weekend would play out and how I could possibly become a divorce statistic!

After months of "how did I miss the signs?", he broke his commitment to "us" again and went to meet her in person. I got angry and felt victimized. "How could he not be true to his word, and how could he not choose me?" And that's pretty much where I lived for the next year! I stayed focused, hiding in my global work. With therapy and a new personal development path, I began to explore my role in the breakdown of our marriage. And I left victimhood behind. (FYI—he married and divorced her a few years later.)

When betrayal enters the room, it doesn't knock. It barges in and rearranges everything. For me, the betrayal wasn't just about infidelity; it was about lost identity and the shattering of promises that had once felt eternal and trusted.

I could never have fathomed forgiveness at such a deep soul-level and beyond the depths of my pain. He never asked for it. And yet, I realized that my anger only meant I was giving him control over me and my emotions. Well, that did not serve me at all! So, one day, in an exercise directed by my therapist, I stood naked and alone in front of my full-length mirror to truly face myself, all of me, vulnerable and raw, and messy. Through my tears, I heard the whisper of a female voice say, "Forgive!" In that moment, I recognized the voice of the universe telling me that I had a choice—stay angry or get even more uncomfortable and forgive him for his actions, and for not having the capacity to change. I remember staring at my own reflection, wondering how someone so full of love and loyalty could feel so hollow. I had given everything. And now, I had no idea what remained of us or of me.

I forgave him, and ultimately, I forgave myself. That forgiveness released me from the weight of my anger and freed my heart for more than I could ever have imagined in my life now, with Ken.

Ken: During an intense leadership development program, I suddenly came down with a UTI—fever, pain, disorientation—the whole mess. As a guy, this was unexpected. My doctor confirmed it was uncommon and prescribed meds, which thankfully brought things back to normal. The experience left me unsettled.

While recovering, I picked up a copy of Louise Hay's *You Can Heal Your Life*. I was curious, not seeking scientific validation, but open to insight. Hay suggested UTIs could stem from "anger with oneself and lack of forgiveness." At first, I thought, "That's not me—I'm not angry." But then something surfaced.

During the pandemic, I panicked, concerned about market instability, so I pulled all our investments into cash. Not long after, the market soared. I'd missed massive gains. And the truth hit: I wasn't just disappointed—I was furious with myself.

What made it worse? I had once been a licensed stockbroker. I knew about the random walk theory—that the market's movements are unpredictable and timing it is nearly impossible. Still, I acted out of fear, and I paid for it. I had betrayed myself and my expertise.

In hindsight, the physical pain mirrored the emotional turmoil I hadn't fully acknowledged. But the real healing didn't come from antibiotics. It came from forgiving myself. Letting go of the self-blame did more for me than the medicine. It taught me that unresolved anger doesn't just live in the mind—it lives in the body. And forgiveness is the release valve.

If you've ever been betrayed, you know the spiral: *I should've known... I should've left... I should've been more...* We have both lived there, blaming ourselves for not seeing what we couldn't have known. But anger, shame, and healing don't coexist. Eventually, we had a choice to make—stop punishing our past self for not knowing what our future self now understands.

Forgiveness—especially of ourselves—is radical. It used to feel like something reserved for saints or sermons, not for broken-hearted humans trying to survive. But survival wasn't enough—we wanted to *heal*. That meant letting go and loosening our grip on the past. When we learned that forgiveness wasn't saying that what happened was okay, it was saying, *I won't let it define me.*

Our painful experiences unknowingly cracked open the door to unexpected freedom. A second chance and a soul-deep connection neither of us could have imagined. Today, after more than twenty years together, we stand in gratitude. We honor what we lived through, what we learned, and what we've chosen to let go.

Now, as relational leadership coaches, we help others rewrite their stories with grace and boundaries. Forgiveness is one of our greatest tools. If you're holding pain, waiting for closure, replaying what you wish you could change—this is your permission to let it go. Not because it didn't matter. But because *you* do. Forgiveness isn't the end of your story. It's the beginning of your next chapter.

Whether you're healing from betrayal, family hurt, or the wounds of your own regrets, forgiveness can't be forced. It must be invited. Here are practices that helped us get there:

- **Seek Support**: Clarity and healing come from communication and walking through the experience with a coach, therapist, and/or clergy.

- **Write a letter** to the person who hurt you (you don't have to send it). Pour everything onto the page, your pain, your anger, your questions. End the letter with an affirmation: *I release this, not for you—but for me.*

- **Burn the Letter:** Bury it. Tear it into pieces at sunset. Whatever feels symbolic to you. Ritual gives your subconscious permission to let go.

- **Look in the mirror** and speak aloud: *I forgive you. You didn't know. You did your best. I release you.* Say it until it no longer feels foreign. Say it until it feels real.
- **Reframe** every time a painful memory surfaces, reframe it with a compassionate lens. Instead of "How could I be so naïve?" try, "I was deeply loving, and that's worth honoring."

- **Remind Yourself:** *That was then, this is now.* Use grounding techniques—breathwork, movement, and affirmations to keep your energy in the present.

MARIS SEGAL & KEN ASHBY

Maris Segal and Ken Ashby are transformational and quantum leaders who consult, coach, and collaborate with executives, entrepreneurs, and rising leaders to bring their professional, personal, and philanthropic vision to life.

Segal Leadership Global (SLG) was launched to meet the shifting needs of leadership with a focus on evolving and transforming human relations skills into powerful tools to drive a people-first culture with bottom-line impact. The SLG Relational Leadership experience is designed to empower leaders at every stage and age of their journey with the mindset, heart-set, and skillset needed to drive vision and positive change within themselves, their teams, and the broader organization. Their book, *The RFactor*, an entertaining story of evolving relationships, sits at the core of their work. In addition, Ken and Maris have been TEDx speakers and featured co-authors in over twenty-five inspiring leadership-centered books.

They were individually recognized by the White House with the Presidential Lifetime Achievement Award for their philanthropic dedication and were awarded internationally with the Gentlemen and Women of Heart Awards. IG @_the_rfactor
Author's Website: *www.SegalLeadershipGlobal.com*

Charity Awareness: *www.UnsilencedVoices.org*

MICHELLE MARIE SHOCKLEY

TRUE FORGIVENESS LIES IN UNDERSTANDING

Growing up, I used to say I had the fear of God in me—and the fear of my mother, but not necessarily in that order. Looking back, I say this with a mix of reverence and regret, and I pray God forgives me for this blasphemous statement.

While many girls, teenagers, and women seemed to enjoy flourishing relationships with their mothers, mine was marked more by tension than tenderness. I was never abused or neglected, but I always carried a quiet fear. My mother, I believe, was overwhelmed by her children. As the youngest and—by today's standards—probably hyperactive, I often acted out to get her attention.

Cleta—named after the cow belonging to her older sister's best friend—was a simple woman, shaped by hardship and self-doubt. She often believed that others looked down on her, and this belief kept her from stepping into community spaces like church. Although she graduated from high school, her grammar was unmistakably Arkansas hillbilly. As a child, I remember her as a fun, caring mom—baking cakes for PTA events and letting my friends come over. Yet during my middle and high school years, something shifted. She became passive-aggressive and sometimes loud, even frightening. It wasn't until later that I came to understand the deep wounds behind her behavior—pain that left a lasting imprint and shaped her voice, her reactions, and her fears. To this day, I still flinch at loud voices and noises.

Was the loudness in her voice due to me reminding her of her past? Was I a walking reminder of her second failed marriage—a daily echo of a difficult past? She was pregnant with me in 1969 while still married to my biological father, Jim, who was serving in Vietnam. Before I turned two, she divorced him and married my stepfather, Rudy—a kind and gentle man who raised me as his own. Still my mother's voice began to change during my middle school years, sharpened by the turmoil caused by my older sister, Sheila. Sheila pushed boundaries, ran with the wrong crowd, fell into addiction, tangled with the law, and struggled with mental health. Our mother gave everything—money, time, and what little peace of mind she had—trying to save her. In retrospect, I believe Mom saw herself in Sheila. Saving her daughter became, symbolically, a way to save herself.

If that had been the extent of the story, it might already have been enough. Somehow, there were deeper wounds still. Sheila gave birth at sixteen, and I recall how oddly fixated our mother was on wanting a granddaughter. "We don't want any boys here," she would repeat. It struck me as strange at the time—why would a first-time grandmother care so much about the gender of her grandchild? I was only ten and didn't give it much thought.

As a joke, I used to tease my mother by saying I wanted an older brother. Of course, it was just a child's fantasy—I was the youngest, and she had had her reproductive organs removed when I was six. No older brother could possibly appear, or so I thought.

When I was around twenty-two, my mother sat down with me and finally shared a long-held secret. Between her first and second marriage, she'd had an affair with a married soldier. She became pregnant and chose to give the baby up for adoption. That baby—my half-brother, Travis—was born in 1962 and raised by a loving family in Louisiana. Suddenly, pieces of our family puzzle fell into place. The blue baby bracelet in her sewing kit, her fixation on having a granddaughter, her bitterness toward men—all of it made sense. That revelation softened something in me. I could see her pain with new eyes.

In my early adolescent years, my stepfather and I trained in Tae Kwon Do together—something my mother disapproved of completely. She had strong biases against foreigners, especially against Asians, perhaps made worse by the fact that my biological father married a Korean woman after their divorce. She didn't support my passion for martial arts, nor was she pleased when I later became engaged to a German man. When

I graduated from Indiana University with a bachelor's degree in German language and culture, her reaction was brutal: "You can take your diploma and wipe your bottom with it." That statement still haunts me today.

After I moved to Germany in 1994, I began hearing more stories from other family members. My eldest sister, Cheryle—fourteen years my senior—told me how Mom used to turn all the clocks forward by an hour just to trick me into going to bed earlier during my hyperactive years. This whimsical fact surprised me, but I found it to be funny. I have no idea how many years she tricked me with this manipulation. That, for me, was pure creativity from a challenged mother.

Other stories were not so funny. I had frequent illnesses as a child—perhaps a subconscious plea for attention. My parents would give me whiskey and honey to soothe my cough. To this day, I can still taste this homemade concoction. Cheryle informed me that mother would give me whiskey and cola in my bottle when I was a toddler. It was to calm me down and make me take a nap. This confession broke my heart. It also explained my aversion to alcohol, my lifelong sugar cravings, and a feeling of unease I could never quite name.

In hindsight, there were many factors that contributed to the strain between us. Physical distance gave me the space to heal. By moving far away, I eventually found the perspective to value my mother. She did the best she could with what she had —her experiences, her fears, and her limitations. She fought fiercely for her children, battled systems she barely understood, and endured pain from those she loved most. Cheryle was the pleaser. Travis grew up in a different home, Sheila was the rebel, and I was the arrogant one who looked down on her. Cleta carried that burden with grace.

When my mother passed away in 2019, something unexpected happened. Two high school friends reached out, sharing how much they admired her. They told stories I had forgotten, reminded me of her generosity and kindness—of how deeply she had impacted them. My simple-minded mother, Cleta, was a fantastic woman to them. While I was out looking for a diamond in the distance, I had missed the gemstone sitting quietly at home.

Though parts of my childhood are still not completely healed, I believe I have forgiven my mother. I have come to understand that she did the best she could with the skills, awareness, and patience she had. The last time I saw her was in 2016. Dementia had taken hold, but she was cheerful, gentle, and kind. The harshness was gone, and my heart filled with love. I really enjoyed talking with her and experiencing this almost naivety in her. We could not speak much after that visit; geography and her illness prevented further communication; I was unable to say goodbye as her condition no longer allowed her to speak on the phone. I do know I apologized to her before her mind slipped away completely.

My journey toward forgiveness was paved by a deeper understanding of who my mother truly was.

I pray she forgave me, too.

MICHELLE MARIE SHOCKLEY

Born in rural Tennessee, Michelle lived in Mississippi and Michigan before her mother and stepfather settled down in Southern Indiana. She lived there until the age of twenty-four, when she moved to Germany in 1994 to marry her college sweetheart. From the marriage, Michelle has two children, Alexa, who lives in America, and Carsten, who lives in Germany.

After twenty-two years of marriage, Michelle separated from her German husband and decided to remain in Germany, where she today runs her own business as an interim manager, trainer, and public speaker. Michelle has been training sport clubs, companies, and executives in Martial Arts, Aerobics, English, and Human Resources topics since the year 2000. She enjoys traveling and reading.

Michelle has a Bachelor of Arts degree from Indiana University in German language and a vocational certification as *"Steuerfachgehilfin"* (tax accountant) in Germany.

Author's Website: *www.MichelleMarie.world*
Charity Awareness: *www.Wir-Fuer-Kinder.net*

DR. MICHELLE MRAS

TO ERR IS HUMAN

Throughout life, we are advised to turn the other cheek, not to hold grudges, and to forgive others because holding onto anger and resentment is like drinking poison while expecting the other person to suffer. For many years of my life, I held grudges, anger, and pain. I drank the poison while those who harmed me walked unscathed. As I grew older and wiser, it became evident that all the negativity I was holding onto was causing more hardship within me. I realized that although forgiving others is praised as a good thing to do, it is far more beneficial to forgive ourselves, offering grace to the person we once were.

"To err is human, to forgive, divine."

I began intentionally walking upon my personal growth journey by accident. Seriously, an automobile accident left me with a traumatic brain injury (TBI). My ability to talk and walk without assistance was taken away. I was in the middle of learning my new normal as a TBI survivor when I was diagnosed with Breast Cancer. There was a series of years where my brain was focused on the physical pain. Once the major brain injury symptoms subsided and the cancer journey seemed to stabilize, it freed mental space to focus on my mindset. My mental shift was not linear nor was it fun. In order to completely heal from the traumatic brain injury and the physical pain of the cancer, I needed to get my mind in a place of peace.

Many of the things holding me back from mental and physical recovery were locked behind a massive door of limitations. Have you ever found yourself in that position? When you want something so badly, but you just can't let yourself do it because you "aren't worthy"? I had so many inner critics that were unleashed because of my traumatic brain injury. It seemed like every time I achieved one small accomplishment, some trauma from my past would arise from within my subconscious. This awakened numerous inner-critic voices in my mind. That massive door of limitations I had kept locked for years opened wide. All the inner critics that shared a luxury penthouse in my mind were set free. My incessant insecurities fed them well. They seemed as if they were going to have free rein in my mind. I couldn't efficiently function in life that way. I decided to make a conscious effort to quiet my inner-critic voices. My soul begged for peace. Without peace, I would not be able to truly heal from my traumas.

Each of my inner critics needed to be addressed individually. Many were based upon painful incidents I never wanted to face again. Nevertheless, I faced them. What I found within these memories is that what I believed would cause nightmares wasn't the actual event. My trauma was based more on facing how I would judge myself for the way I responded in the various situations. I have always considered myself tsmart and quite proud of how my brain works, but there have been times in my past when my ability to respond with my intellect was hindered The awfulness of my experiences caused my subconscious to lock onto those memories with the verbiage, "It was your fault, you should have been smarter."

As I addressed each past incident/battle, my mind came to the conclusion that everything that happened was my fault. Logically, I knew it wasn't, but my mind created a special inner-critic voice just to address my stupidity. To confront these badgering onslaughts, I had to face, evaluate, and pull apart each memory. In order for me to confront and overcome them, I had to own a tiny piece of whatever it was.

I know that it is very controversial for a victim to take ownership of what happened. Please realize, I don't own the "bad things." I decided to own how I responded. I recognize that I did the best I could at the time and with the knowledge and experience I had at that moment. The total loss of control in the experiences that have haunted me caused an overwhelming feeling of helplessness. By creating a small piece of control, I was able to take hold of the chaos. As complex as my explanation sounds, it was freeing for me. I gained peace through owning the only thing I truly had control over—my attitude. I spent most of my life feeling like a victim of the unfortunate things that happened to me. I released the pain and shame when I forgave myself.

Now that I am an older woman, I could easily berate the younger version of me for being foolish. Instead, I embrace the decisions my younger self made in times of crisis. When it comes to my ideas of Survival to Thrival, I believe the way I shifted to thrival mode was to develop the skill to forgive those who hurt me, but more importantly, forgive the person I was at that moment in time. Once the source of my biggest trauma was addressed, it freed up mental processing space for the other traumas to be addressed. One by one, I freed myself from drinking the poison of grudges, anger, and pain. I am free.

If there is something in your past that hurts whenever you are reminded of it, face it. Find someone to talk to. Asking for help is nothing to be ashamed of. If nothing else, seek professional help to get you started through the mental processes. Perhaps you're reading this book as a step toward your healing journey to thrive? I assure you, those big doors to your past that you don't want to open, the ones filled with skeletons, need to be opened. Find that younger version of yourself and let them know it's okay. You survived because of the decisions that were made. Decide to keep moving forward in order to free your younger self from carrying the burden. Forgive yourself for making the decisions you made. You did the best you could at the time.

Forgiveness is the biggest gift you can give yourself. It's not enough to only forgive others. Forgive yourself for the thoughts and actions you made. To forgive yourself frees you to be the best version of you. I spent over forty years of my life simply hiding from my past trauma of being human trafficked.

I remained in survival mode throughout all my young adulthood, marriage, having children, and going through life pretending to be fine.

After making the decision to heal, I discovered getting out of active fight or flight mode and shifting into survival mode felt great. But once I reached that level of healing, my soul craved completeness. It was evident that healing would take time. To learn and apply my tools more quickly, I shared them with others. That is how I became a John C. Maxwell Certified Coach, then stepped into the Inspirational Speaker career. Sharing my journey is part of my healing. Never again shall I be ashamed of the traumas I endured. My stories are not a ploy to receive sympathy or play the victim. My goal in life is to openly share my past pains and journey to becoming the woman I am today.

I am living proof that healing can happen, there are better tomorrows, and sharing stories helps heal the teller and the listener. Sharing these types of life stories is painful and can be triggering for others. I train my clients on how to structure their stories to inspire and raise others to a healthier state of mind. The power of shifting from survival to thrival mode is a gift shared within every interaction I make. It is my strong belief that the more we all heal, the more beautiful the world will be. Together we all rise to thrive. Unapologetically!

DR. MICHELLE MRAS

Dr. Michelle Mras is an award-winning global and TEDx keynote speaker, executive speaking coach, international bestselling author, and co-author of thirty books, including twenty Amazon bestsellers. Michelle is the host of the MentalShift show on *The New Channel (TNC)* in the Philippines, and co-host of the Denim and Pearls podcast. She has speaking parts in several sci-fi movies; check *IMDB.com* for her. Her music EP album can be found on *MichelleMras.com*. Dr. Michelle was nominated for the Most Influential Filipina in the World and is a United Nations Ambassador for Peace.

Dr. Michelle Mras is a survivor of multiple life challenges, including a traumatic brain injury, breast cancer, and human trafficking. Dr. Michelle is a proud military daughter and spouse who has traveled and lived around the world. She uses her vast experience to guide her clients to recognize the innate gifts within them, to stop apologizing for what they are not and step into who they truly are. Dr. Michelle's driving thought is that every day is a gift. Tomorrow is never promised. Every moment is an opportunity to be the best version of you... Unapologetically!

Author's Website: *www.MichelleMras.com*

Charity Awareness: *www.Kenna-Foundation.org*

MR. WHISKEY
BURDENS, BOUNDARIES, UNITY

. . . .

"Whoever would foster love covers over an offense, but whoever repeats the matter separates close friends."
~ Proverbs 17:9 NIV

"Even *he*, I would forgive."

Those were the words that Jesus Christ spoke to me in a dream when I called out asking, "Would you not forgive even the Antichrist if he cried out to you?"

The notion that I was the Antichrist came from severe emotional and verbal abuse at the hands of my alcoholic father, who was religiously and mentally insane. Twisting and weaponizing the Word of God was one of many ways in which he abused our family and me.

He broke my mother's skull open. He sexually, verbally, and emotionally abused her. He continually committed adultery. He emotionally and verbally neglected and abused his children, myself included. He has publicly harassed people. Violently, he has hurt people and killed animals without cause. In a controlling bubble with skewed views of the world, he "raised" us.

My father held the responsibilities of parenting over our heads, and as he has admitted to being, he's a liar and a narcissist. He betrayed everything he raised me to do and be with his vile actions. He has spent his life, according to his own admission, trying to fill a hole in his heart with women, cars, dogs, drugs, and alcohol.

Yet, he never has, nor will he ever find true satisfaction in such things.

"Son, I love vodka more than you. More than my life!"

It hurt to hear that. Truly, it did.

I used to have bone-chilling nightmares about him.

At one point, my father and I were going to fist-fight to the death. Many of you must think that to be a joke or an exaggeratio,n but it was the truth. Not many can actually imagine how violent, aggressive, and dangerous my father is. It was inevitable. He had continuously endangered my family and threatened my then-fiancée. His madness could only be stopped in one poetic way—by his own offspring. Indeed, his one and only son.

Such is the past. I love my father, and I talk to him daily, in fact. Sometimes, multiple times a day! When I truly forgave him, the nightmares (for the most part) stopp,ed and we were able to move forward, rather than continue the frustrating and complicated cycles of the past.

I understood, for the first time, what others meant about a weight being lifted off of you. The peace I felt and the lightness of my body were surreal.

What you've heard, though, is only a small fraction of all the pain my father has caused me and countless others. So, *how*? How did I forgive him? *Why* did I forgive him?

It wasn't easy. Forgiving people never truly is, and every situation is different.

A lot of atheists try to use my strong faith as an excuse for my desire to forgive. They say that my religious beliefs skew reality and that I forgive those who should not be forgiven out of obedience to God rather than my own feelings.

I disagree.

Although the Bible and even some karma-based ideologies emphasize forgiveness, it has nothing to do with religion. Forgiveness is a human choice. We don't owe forgiveness to anyone. However, we've often heard that forgiveness is more for ourselves than for others, and that's true—to an extent.

There are some important distinctions to be made known, though.

Working with addicted individuals is what has really helped shape my mind around forgiveness. Specifically, having a raging alcoholic father has played a huge role in understanding forgiveness better.

Forgiveness, for me, in the past, was basically just a free pass and clean slate. It's not, anymore.

A lot of people like to live by a simple saying and rule: Forgive and Forget.

That's great and all, but it's also not. Forgetting and forgiveness do not require each other to exist. Forgetting can certainly make forgiving a lot easier, but it's dangerous. Therefore, I have a better saying: Forgive and Protect.

This is forgiveness with caution. However, this caution shouldn't come with resentment or a grudge. It should consist of respect, boundaries, and accountability to keep you and others safe, to not compromise morals, and to maintain that relationship and prevent the past from repeating.

Earlier, I mentioned how working with addicts taught me a lot about forgiveness, and this ties heavily into the idea of boundaries and accountability. With any addiction, the loved ones of the addict often forgive in a way that enables the person to continue their addiction and endangers themselves and others. Through working with them and dealing with my own father, I eventually learned how to forgive without doing so.

It's a different feeling when you forgive like that- hence the lightness and relief you feel. There's an invisible weight and tension that you don't even realize is there until it's gone.

It seems awful at first, not giving someone everything they want, especially for those of us who are people-pleasers. However, I learned that being held emotionally hostage is a common circumstance that will further toxic cycles and behaviors—all at your expense! Forgiving isn't permission to keep hurting you or to keep doing something awful. Forgiving doesn't equate to forgetting everything or being naïve. Forgiving should come with an intention of change.

When forgiveness is done properly, there'll be a greater balance in your life. To reference back to the Bible quote in the beginning, forgiveness is a part of love, and love is a part of forgiveness. When used together properly, it can heal grievous emotional and spiritual wounds that are destroying and hindering your life in many ways, both noticeable and unseen. Those who would repeat the matter—bringing it up constantly, never letting it go, or permanently holding it against someone —will just create division and more resentment, which can lead to detrimental consequences. Due to this, I've seen many divided households, friendships, and relationships.

There is a way to forgive, though, where you keep or restore your power, hold the person accountable, and set boundaries to prevent future incidents. That's all we can do, since we can't change the past. Forgiveness is about moving on from the past to live through the present and set up a future, in a way that the past will not repeat itself.

I don't agree with a lot that my father or others have done. Yet, I also know that I'm not the final judge, nor am I anywhere near perfect. I have my morals, for sure, but I can't enforce them onto others. What I can do and do know is that I can forgive them and have a relationship with them, so long as I don't enable their behaviors and protect myself and others. I can't control what they do, but I can control what I support them doing and what I don't. I can control what boundaries I set and what accountability I have.

Through this, I still have a father, and he still has a son, but neither of us compromises morally or hurts the other, despite the grievous past.

Forgiveness is powerful. It's healing. It doesn't mean forgetting. It doesn't mean enabling. It means choosing freedom over grudges and bitterness. It means choosing unity over division. Choosing humanity and life over death. I've seen what holding on can do to a person. I've also seen what letting go can do. If we can still have relationships with the people who hurt us while keeping ourselves safe, the world becomes a lot less lonely and full of a lot more love. I'd rather have peace than pain, even if that means having it with boundaries. Even if that means accountability. It's all balanced.

MR. WHISKEY

Mr. Whiskey, formerly an Electrician's Mate Nuclear Operator, is a U.S. Navy veteran, podcaster, author, speaker, preacher, comedian, and entrepreneur. As the founder of Couple O' Nukes LLC, he is dedicated to helping individuals improve their lives through global networking, information sharing, and community building—both virtually and in person. Through the Couple O' Nukes podcast and his travels around the world, Mr. Whiskey focuses on mentoring young adults, connecting with outcasts, and empowering passionate dreamers. His mission spans suicide prevention, addiction recovery, fitness, health and wellness, military matters, relationships, parenting, career development, financial literacy, and faith.

When not actively working, Mr. Whiskey can often be found outside with his three-pound Chihuahua, running several miles at a time, writing fiction or poetry, designing women's Kaiju-based fashion, or spending quality time with his elderly neighbors. He also dedicates a significant amount of time to studying the Bible, as well as Hebrew and Greek.

Author's Website: *www.CoupleONukes.com*

Charity Awareness: *www.ProjectCallisto.org*

NANCY E. MOORE

THE HARDEST PERSON TO FORGIVE

When am I finally going to lose these fifteen pounds?

When am I going to work out consistently?

When am I finally going to learn piano?

When is my business going to grow?

When am I going to be free of debt?

When am I going back to school?

When? When? When?

These are the questions I've asked myself more often than I care to count. They play on repeat, especially in the morning as I wake up. When I was younger, I made a list of things I was going to accomplish when life seemed wide open and full of wonder. I was going to light the world on fire. I was going to do great things.

Then … life happened. I hit my first bump in the road not long after high school. "It's fine," I told myself. "This just pushes things back a bit. No big deal." But then came another bump. And another. Each time, I pushed the timeline back just a little more. "There is still time," I reassured myself.

But somehow the years kept moving on, and things got in the way. It's not that I wasn't busy; life was full. Work, responsibilities, relationships, the day-to-day demands of being an adult. I kept telling myself there would be time for those other things, the dreams, the goals, the promises I made to myself. Until one day, I looked up and thought, "How did so much time go by?"

As time went on, I found I was not happy. I turned my focus toward something that felt deeply important, healing my relationship with others. Along my journey, I discovered the concept of forgiveness. Not just as an idea, but as a practice. Really forgiving people for the things they had done to me.

I began to read all I could understand about forgiveness. I studied how unforgiveness ties us to one another, ties us to pain, and keeps us stuck. I learned how it burrows into our lives, quietly weighing us down, and how freeing it is to let go. I looked into how forgiveness is looked at spiritually. For example, Christianity says forgive as God has forgiven you; Buddhism says it is the art of letting go of anger and practicing compassion; Islam holds mercy and forgiveness as sacred; and Indigenous traditions show forgiveness as part of communal healing and restoration. The message is that universal forgiveness is essential for our well-being. Forgiveness teaches us not to let the pain of the past own us now.

I took this lesson seriously, I practiced it, and I got good at it. I forgave those who hurt me, disappointed me, and betrayed me. I learned how to release the anger, how to breathe a little freer, how to reclaim my peace. It was great!

However, in all that work I was doing, I completely missed something. Something big. I forgot to learn how to forgive MYSELF.

While I was busy untangling knots of unforgiveness with others, I left the biggest knot, the one inside me, untouched. I hadn't even noticed how much guilt, shame, regret, and disappointment I was quietly carrying. I was proud of how I showed up for others. Proud of how my relationships had grown, but the one relationship I neglected deeply and completely was the one I had with MYSELF.

I was so busy striving, working, creating, and constantly reaching for the next thing that I never paused long enough to check in with myself. I had been holding myself hostage.

If someone had asked me, "Do you like yourself?" I wouldn't have known how to answer. My mind would race to see what they meant, "Do you mean in my work? My personal life? My career?" I would have tried to rationalize it. "Of course, I've forgiven myself. Look at where I am now, how could I be here if I hadn't?" But that wasn't really true.

I had given forgiveness and grace to others, but not to myself. I was setting the bar for myself so high. And every time I missed the bar, the conversations in my head were terrible. Words I would never say to someone else, I would say to myself.

At some point, I started to notice something: I was moving forward in so many ways, but there were areas where I was completely stuck. Projects left unfinished, goals untouched, dreams deferred... again.

I caught myself mid-exercise, explaining why something hadn't gotten done, and suddenly heard it. That voice, the one whispering, "What's wrong with you? Why do you always do this? Why can't you get it together?" The questions began to spiral, "How did I let this happen? How do I fix this without anyone knowing? If I ask for help, will they laugh at me?" I felt like I was drowning in quicksand. The more I struggle with the thoughts, the deeper I sank. I wasn't really hiding anything from anyone else. I was hiding from ME.

So, I decided to change. It started with small, tiny shifts, little reminders, "God made me this way, and God does not make junk." Next, I added, "Everything I need is already around me, I just need to ask for it." Little by little, these truths became my reality. Helping me out of the mess I had created around me. I started to realize just how heavy self-unforgiveness is, and how exhausting it is to carry around shame disguised as motivation. So, I did what I had done before when forgiving others, I started with TODAY. I grabbed a journal and started writing. I just let everything pour out, the disappointment, the frustration, the rage, the sadness, the fear. I prayed, cried, meditated, talked to myself like I was a dear friend and someone I loved, not someone I was trying to punish. It was ugly and real. Some of those pages I will never open again; they are full of pain I do not want to relive, but writing them freed me from them.

Slowly, something shifted. Forgiving myself did not mean pretending I hadn't made mistakes. It didn't mean erasing the missed opportunities or broken promises to myself. It meant understanding that I had done the best I could with what I knew, where I was, and who I was at the time. It meant realizing that expecting perfection, especially in areas I had never been taught or prepared for, was unfair. It meant understanding that asking for help wasn't weakness... it was wisdom.

These days, I still hear that old voice sometimes, the one that says, "What are you thinking?" But now I just smile and reply, "Well... let's see where this takes us." I've learned that forgiving myself is not a one-time event; it's a practice. It's a muscle that gets stronger each time I choose compassion over criticism, grace over guilt, love over shame.

And most importantly, I've learned that the same grace I have so freely given to others.... I deserve to, and so do you!

NANCY E. MOORE

Nancy E. Moore is an Image Strategist and Digital Entrepreneur Coach with over fifteen years of experience transforming personal style into powerful branding across the beauty, television, film, and commercial industries. From working behind the scenes as a makeup artist, educator, and creative director to leading high-profile editorial shoots and ad campaigns, Nancy has mastered the art of visual storytelling and understands how personal image shapes confidence, influence, and opportunity.

Today, she merges her creative flair with digital strategy to guide entrepreneurs in building magnetic, authentic brands that stand out online. As the author of *Style Made Simple: Your Guide to Daily Looks* and the co-founder of a wealth-building company for women, Nancy is passionate about equipping others with the tools to thrive—both in business and in life.

Her signature offering, the Digital Entrepreneur Essentials Package, is a step-by-step framework that helps clients develop a clear and cohesive online presence through brand identity, color analysis, marketing visuals, and strategy—all with a personal touch.

Author's Website: *www.NancyEMoore.com*

Charity Awareness: *www.SurvivalToThrivalSeries.com*

NEETU N. PRABHU

YOU DON'T HAVE TO BLEED ANYMORE

There comes a point when the bleeding isn't physical. It's emotional. Invisible. You're not limping down the street—but you're bleeding through every conversation, every overachievement, every fake smile. And no one sees it because you're so good at covering it up.

THE ONE PERSON I DIDN'T KNOW I HAD TO FORGIVE

I forgave the man who cheated on me. I forgave the man who beat me to a pulp. I forgave the man who strangled me, choked me.

I forgave the man who raped me. I forgave the man who gave me an STD. I even forgave the man who abused me when I was a child.

Was it hard? Yes. But those wounds were obvious.

The one person I didn't expect I needed to forgive? Me.

I had no idea I was still carrying me—my shame, my silence, my "I'm fine." Me, suffering in silence so everyone else would be okay. I was mad that I didn't leave earlier. That I stayed quiet. That I smiled through things I should've screamed about.

But I get it now. I was doing the best I could with what I had. And at some point… I had to stop punishing the girl who didn't know what this woman now knows.

FORGIVENESS ISN'T A MOMENT—IT'S A WAR

People think forgiveness is a decision. A line you cross. One day you wake up, feel generous, and let it all go. Bullsh*t.

Forgiveness is a *practice*. Some days? A moment-to-moment one. A slow unhooking from everything that ever tried to take your power.

It started when I noticed I was avoiding myself. My memories. My truths. All the things I buried so I could keep showing up for everyone else. Until I simply couldn't anymore—I chose not to.

I was bleeding in bits every day and still pretending I was alive. I couldn't even fool *me* anymore. So, I stopped running. I sat with the parts of me I hated. The ones I avoided. The parts I was scared of. Raw. Vulnerable. Naked. It was *really, really rough*.

I sank into feelings I spent years avoiding. Only this time—I willingly allowed it. I came face-to-face with the darkness—not just a remembrance, but a reliving. Super scary. Super yucky.

And when I came back up for air? I wasn't the same.

I was free.

THE PITY PARTY I DIDN'T WANT TO ADMIT I WAS THROWING

I asked myself—more like tortured myself—over and over:

- "Why didn't I leave earlier?"
- "What the hell is wrong with me?"
- "I failed my kids."
- "I've lost my identity."
- "Who even am I anymore?"

It was my own private pity party—and I was the damn headliner. Front and center. Spotlight on shame. I wish I could tell you I snapped out of it. That some angel whispered, "You are worthy," and I floated into freedom. But it wasn't that cute. It was messy. Ugly. Real.

I had to coach myself like my life depended on it—because it did.

YOU FORGIVE BECAUSE YOU DO—& THIS IS A CHOICE YOU CAN MAKE

Not because they apologized. Not because they deserved it. Not because justice came knocking. *(It sure didn't.)*

You forgive because you deserve to sleep again. To laugh without guilt. To be held and kissed without flashbacks. You forgive because you're done cutting yourself on their brokenness. You forgive to cut the cord between your identity and your injury.

You forgive so you don't keep bleeding on people who never hurt you. You forgive to come back to yourself. This forgiveness?

It's the fast expressway to your freedom. And this feeling? It's ecstasy. It's peace. It's pure gold.

THE WEIGHT WAS TRULY MINE

Nobody tells you this: Sometimes, the pain doesn't stop because you won't put it down. Not because you're weak, but because you've carried it so long, it's become part of your posture. You don't even notice it anymore. Until one day, someone hugs you... and you flinch. Or your kid says something small... and you snap. Or you try to rest... but your mind is too loud with regret.

That's when you know: It's not them anymore. It's you. You're still holding what they did. Still defending yourself in imaginary arguments. *(I used to play both sides of the argument. I'd even rest my case. Yuck.)*

Are you still looking for closure in a place you already escaped from? Let it go. Put it down.

You don't need their permission to be free. You just sign your own permission slip this time.

FOR THE WOMAN WHO THINKS FORGIVENESS IS WEAK

I know what you're thinking:

- "But if I forgive him, it's like I'm saying it was okay."
- "But if I forgive myself, I'll stop growing."
- "But what if I get hurt again?"

Here's the truth: Forgiveness isn't weakness. It's strength. It's sovereignty. It's the moment you stop letting someone else narrate your life. It's not saying what happened was okay. It's saying *you're okay now.* You're still here. And you choose to become better, not bitter.

YOU DON'T HAVE TO BLEED ANYMORE

You don't have to fake it anymore. You don't have to smile tears of blood. You don't have to keep pretending you're okay when you're barely holding it together. You've already done that—for years. You kept it moving. Held it all down. Smiled through things you should've screamed about. You didn't crack. You slowly bled. Quietly, in the places no one could see. And you've paid enough.

It's time to speak your truth without flinching. To walk into a room without shame crawling behind you. To become the kind of woman who doesn't look away from her own reflection.

And if you're still waiting for a sign? This is it. Do what you need to do. Cry. Yell. Scream in the shower. Grieve the life you thought you'd have. Say all the things you wish you'd said. Then stand up. And walk out of the story where you're still scattered, shattered, and shedding red.

Because you don't have to bleed anymore. Not today. Not ever again.

Maybe you were broken. Maybe you hit the ground harder than anyone knows. But you get to rebuild now. Not to prove anything. Just to be free. Because honestly? You already are. It's time to stop waiting for rescue. And start living like the rescuer arrived—and it was you.

It's time to get out of this cage. And the good news? You already hold the key. You're the woman who doesn't die in the dark. You're the woman who makes something holy out of hell. You're the woman who walks out of the story that tried to erase her—and writes a new one with her own damn hands.

Not just healed. **Rewritten.**

Not just surviving. **Unshakable.**

Not just free. **Untouchable.**

This isn't your comeback. This is your arrival.

NEETU N. PRABHU

Neetu Prabhu, Founder and CEO of Unity Wealth Strategies, is a distinguished wealth strategist serving ultra-high net worth clients and business owners. She specializes in wealth building, legacy planning, and multigenerational wealth transfers, utilizing tax-free income strategies to revolutionize her clients' financial futures. Neetu is recognized for her fiduciary excellence and ethical service, earning accolades such as the prestigious Million Dollar Round Table Court of the Table award and multiple honors for her impactful decade-long tenure in financial services.

Beyond her professional endeavors, Neetu is passionately committed to empowering single moms and survivors of domestic violence. A philanthropist at heart, she champions financial literacy for women, acting as a guiding force to foster independence and resilience. She is also a multi-time #1 Amazon Bestselling Author and a featured speaker alongside notable figures like Brian Tracy and Erik Swanson.

Author's Website: *www.LinkedIn.com/in/NeetuPrabhu*

Charity Awareness: *www.SurvivalToThrivalSeries.com*

DR. ONIKA SHIRLEY

THE PATH TO FREEDOM THROUGH FORGIVENESS

Forgiveness is often seen as a simple act of letting go, yet it carries profound significance that can change the trajectory of our lives. It is a powerful tool for healing and liberation that many overlook in times of hurt and trauma. At its core, forgiveness is not just about condoning someone's actions or dismissing what they've done to you; it's about freeing yourself from the chains that bind you to past grievances.

This chapter aims to empower you to embrace forgiveness as a means of transformation. Through thoughtful insights and practical steps, you will learn how to forgive others, forgive yourself, and release the weight of past situations and circumstances that hinder your growth. It may seem daunting, but forgiving is a journey that begins within. It is a personal choice that requires courage, introspection, and compassion.

As we embark on this journey together, consider the aspects of your life that still carry the sting of unresolved pain. Perhaps it is a betrayal by a friend, a critical failure, or a long-held grudge that festers and grows. They can feel like heavy stones in your pocket, dragging you down as you wade through life. Now imagine what it would feel like to release those stones. Imagine the sweetness of lightness that comes when you're not burdened by anger, resentment, or regret.

THE WEIGHT WE CARRY

Before we dive deeper into forgiveness, it's crucial to understand the weight we carry when we hold onto grudges. Studies have shown that unresolved anger and resentment can lead to a range of physical and psychological issues, including stress, anxiety, and even chronic illness. By clinging to our grievances, we inadvertently create a cycle of negativity that affects both mind and body. Letting go is not just a metaphor; it's a necessity for holistic well-being.

Begin by acknowledging the hurt. This acknowledgment is not an act of weakness, but rather an embrace of your reality. Recognize the emotions tied to that pain—anger, sadness, frustration. Allow yourself to feel these emotions without judgment. Only when we accept how we feel can we begin to understand the depth of our pain and move toward forgiveness.

THE PROCESS OF FORGIVENESS

Forgiveness is not a single act but a process that unfolds over time. Here are some steps that I have used over the years, and if you're interested and ready to be free, you can incorporate them into your journey:

1. Reflect on What Forgiveness Means to You:

Before you can forgive, take time to understand what forgiveness means in your context. It could involve writing down your thoughts or talking to someone you trust. Ask yourself: What would forgiving mean for my life? How would it change my relationship with the person who hurt me? Understanding your motivations strengthens your resolve to forgive.

2. Empathize with the Offender:

This step can be particularly challenging. It involves trying to see the situation from the other person's perspective, which can humanize them. Consider their background, experiences, and the circumstances surrounding their actions. This doesn't excuse their behavior; instead, it broadens your understanding.

3. Decide to Forgive:

Choose to forgive. This commitment can come with its own challenges, especially when emotions are still raw. You might want to articulate this commitment by writing a letter to the person you are forgiving—expressing how you feel, the impact of their actions, and your decision to move forward.

4. Communicate Your Forgiveness (If Possible):

If appropriate, communicate your forgiveness to the other person. This could be a face-to-face conversation, a message, or even just a personal acknowledgment that you've moved past the issue. However, remember that forgiveness does not always require confrontation or reconciliation, especially if it compromises your well-being.

5. Focus on Yourself:

Remember to turn your attention inward. Engage in self-care practices that nurture your spirit and mental health. This can include meditative practices, journaling, or simply spending time doing what you love.

6. Practice Self-Forgiveness:

Don't forget the importance of forgiving yourself for any perceived failures, mistakes, or regrets. Self-forgiveness is just as crucial as forgiving others. Reflect on how you can learn from your experiences rather than dwell on them. Recognizing that everyone makes mistakes helps alleviate the weight of self-blame.

Matthew 6:14-15 (NIV): "For if you forgive other people when they sin against you, your heavenly Father will also forgive you. But if you do not forgive others their sins, your Father will not forgive your sins."

OPENING THE DOOR TO BEING FORGIVEN

One of the most profound revelations on the path to forgiveness is understanding that forgiving others can create space for your own redemption. When you forgive someone, you open a door to being forgiven yourself. In every relationship, there will be moments where we falter and fail. Embracing the concept of forgiveness extends beyond forgiving others; it invites an opportunity for the people in our lives to extend compassion to us as well.

When we create environments of forgiveness, we foster healthier relationships. It signals that mistakes are human, allowing both parties to grow and learn. This courage to forgive cultivates connection, compassion, and understanding among friends, family, and communities.

THRIVE BEYOND TRAUMA & PAIN

Forgiveness does not mean you forget the pain inflicted upon you, nor does it imply that you reconcile or recreate a friendship. It means you have consciously released the emotional bond that ties you to that grievance. When you forgive, you are no longer held hostage by your past; instead, you are empowered to thrive.

As you continue this path from mere survival to true thrival, it is important to integrate forgiveness into your daily practices. Rather than viewing it as a one-time event, see it as a lifelong journey. It might involve re-evaluating relationships, setting boundaries, or simply practicing kindness toward yourself and others. Each time you choose to forgive, you take a step closer to a life enriched with joy, peace, and freedom.

Ephesians 4:32 (NIV): "Be kind and compassionate to one another, forgiving each other, just as in Christ God forgave you."

THE ONGOING JOURNEY

Incorporating forgiveness into your life is a transformative act of self-love and liberation. As we conclude this chapter, remind yourself that you are not alone on this journey. Countless others are seeking freedom from their burdens and reclaiming their power through forgiveness. Embrace the journey, as it is through the act of forgiveness that we cultivate resilience and discover the depths of our strength.

As you embark on this path, may you find courage in your choices, release the weight of resentment, and cultivate a heart that thrives—not just in the absence of pain, but in the presence of profound peace and connection.

DR. ONIKA L. SHIRLEY

Dr. Onika L. Shirley is the Founder and CEO of Action Speaks Volume, Inc. She is a Procrastination Strategist and Behavior Change Expert renowned for helping individuals build unshakable confidence, overcome procrastination, and transform dreams into reality. A Master Storyteller and International Speaker, Dr. O serves in Global Ministry and is an international bestselling author, multiple award recipient, serial entrepreneur, and global philanthropist who has impacted lives in the USA, Africa, India, and Pakistan.

As a Motivational Speaker and Christian Counselor, Dr. Onika is dedicated to making a positive difference. Her accolades include being recognized as an Exemplary Global Leader and a Woman of Excellence by I Change Nations, receiving the Passion Purpose Peace Award, and the Presidential Lifetime Achievement Award.

With a heart full of purpose, Dr. O continues to walk in service, striving to make a lasting impact on the lives of others.

Author's Website: *www.ActionSpeaksVolumes.com*

Charity Awareness: *www.FeedingAmerica.org*

PAM KURT

EACH CHAPTER HOLDS A GIFT

"Life is like a book. There are good chapters, and there are bad chapters. But when you get to a bad chapter, you don't stop reading the book! If you do...then you never get to find out what happens next!"
~ Brian Falkner

As I write this chapter, I'm humbled and honored to join another collaboration of extraordinary authors and people. We each face our own struggles, but being part of a like-minded, supportive group is more powerful than we often realize.

How do you get to be the best version of yourself?

Everyone has a unique path and story. That's why it's vital to share yours—someone will find hope simply because you persevered. Even when it feels like there's no choice, there always is. Be proud you made it.

I once believed my story would have a happy ending—after the struggle, happiness would come. But life unfolds in many chapters, each with its own challenges and joys. As we grow older, we realize there's always more to live for, more to fight for, and more to appreciate. It's natural to wonder how all these chapters fit together into a fulfilling life.

I've shared my childhood story before: growing up in a rural community, losing my father to a car accident at eight, and adjusting to a new family after my mother remarried. My mother and I struggled to get along, so I left home at eighteen. College was difficult—I lacked money, didn't know how to find help, and had to work my way through. Eventually, a job took me to Washington, D.C., where I met my ex-husband. I thought he was my happy ending.

He was charming and complimentary, and we married—but things soon changed. His controlling nature turned to abuse, and by twenty-five, I was divorced, a single mother, still in college, and financially unstable. Another chapter closed, still searching for the happy ending. I realized there was much more life—and learning—ahead.

After my divorce, I focused on providing for my son, believing hard work would eventually lead to my "best life." I set timelines for myself, imagining milestones as chapters that would mark my arrival at happiness.

I thought I'd become my best self at eighteen, then after marriage and having a child, then after my divorce, and later after graduating from college.

I earned my Associate's, Bachelor's, Master's, and Juris Doctorate—all while raising my son. Looking back, I marvel at how I made it work.

I thought I was finally set. But years passed between graduating, passing the bar, and opening my own practice—all because I struggled to believe in myself.

I worked many jobs to make ends meet for most of my life. One of my "jobs" was a substitute teacher. Once I decided to open my open practice, I didn't let go of the "side jobs"; there was so much doubt. And I said, God, if this is what I am supposed to do, let me know. I remember this prayer as clear as day.

One day, as I was heading to another teaching assignment, I prayed for guidance. I was afraid to let go of my side jobs, unsure if my legal practice would succeed. But the next day, the phones wouldn't stop ringing—there was enough work for everyone. I hired interns and paralegals, declined teaching assignments, and followed the call. Things began to fall into place.

I thought opening my own practice would finally make me the best version of myself. But life changes, goals shift, and being your best self is an ongoing journey.

This January (2026) marks 17 years since I opened my law practice—a journey filled with highs and lows. I grew from a solo practitioner with a few part-time helpers to leading a team of over 15 attorneys across four offices. I believed this achievement meant I'd finally arrived at my best self. But was it enough?

Life shifted again. I remarried a college friend, but his battle with alcoholism brought new challenges. I thought I could focus on becoming my best self once he got sober—but life didn't follow that script, either.

I started looking at the office and my career. I did enjoy helping people, but as lawyers, staff, and clients come and go, I realized I would give so much of myself that there was rarely anything left for me.

I finally recognized my biggest weakness: giving more than I received, caring more about others' well-being than my own. I thought this realization would unlock my best self—but there was still more to learn.

Through more prayer, reflection, and life experience, I realized being my best self is a daily commitment. Each day is an opportunity to practice forgiveness and gratitude, and to discover what my best looks like in this moment.

There's rarely a single finish line where you can declare you've 'made it.' Some challenges do bring a sense of completion, but life itself is precious and deserves to be valued every day. Funny—I used to think only older adults said things like that.

For me, being the best version of myself is a work in progress. As life shifts and new chapters begin, I rely on God's guidance and daily gratitude. With faith and intention, I can always be my best self and create my best life.

So, what makes you happy? What lights you up inside? Your passions may change over the years, and self-reflection can help you uncover new sources of joy. Has your answer changed as your life has evolved?

One way to begin your journey toward your best self is to ask: *If money and time were no object, what would you do?*

As an attorney handling family law, I've asked clients this question for years. It helps them—and me—focus on desired outcomes and find hope for the future. I began using it in my own life, too.

One day, I posed this *question* to a client facing her third divorce at 76. Why not dream big? We all deserve to look forward with hope.

She surprised me: she wanted to be an astronaut. I was taken aback—usually, clients want to go back to school, spend more time with family, or advance their careers. But a 76-year-old aspiring to be an astronaut?

Her answer made me pause. Instead of mapping out a direct path, I asked her why she chose that dream. She said she wanted to watch the stars, feel weightless, and float.

That sparked an idea: I could still help her reach those dreams. She took an astronomy class, bought a telescope, and her grandson took her to Orlando for a NASA simulation. She wasn't technically an astronaut, but she achieved the experiences she truly wanted.

We've all heard it's about the journey—and it truly is. But it starts with setting big goals and daring to dream.

If money and time were no object, what would you do? Who would you become? Pursue those dreams—and trust that on your journey, you'll learn more about yourself than you ever expected. Each step is a new chapter in your personal book.

Sometimes, the journey is more valuable than the goal itself. Sometimes, God sets us on a path where the real reward is something even better than we imagined.

As you begin your personal journey to your best self, take your time. Do what matters to you, and make it count. You deserve happiness and freedom. Surround yourself with a supportive community, and you'll grow into your best self along the way.

My wish for you is that each day, your journey begins and ends with positivity as you write new chapters and move closer to your best self.

DREAM. BELIEVE. ACHIEVE.

Love,

Coach Pam

PAM KURT

Pamela D. Kurt is an attorney, Bestselling Author, speaker, and certified 10X Business Coach dedicated to empowering women to unlock their fullest potential. With a thriving family law practice and a history of leadership roles and board positions, Pam has always been driven by a passion for helping others. Today, she channels that passion into her business, *Best Version of You, LLC*, where she guides women through personal development, spiritual growth, and business success. A prolific author, Pam has co-authored twelve books and contributed to multiple bestselling series, including *The Everyday Women's Guide* and *Becoming an Unstoppable Woman*. Her works, such as *The Successful Woman's Mindset* and *The Path to the Best You*, have topped charts in categories like Women in Business, Self-Help, and Personal Transformation. Her writing journey, which began as an attorney drafting legal documents, has evolved into a powerful platform for sharing stories of resilience, success, and empowerment. Pam has also been featured in prestigious publications like *Enterprise World*, *Tycoon Magazine*, and *Brainz Magazine*, solidifying her voice as a thought leader in women's empowerment. Connect with her at *pam@bestversionyou.com*.

Author's Website: *www.PamKurt.com*

Charity Awareness: *www.ForbesHouse.org*

PATTY SHIH-MEI LEE CAMPBELL

FROM WOUNDS TO WINGS

The difference between surviving to thriving is forgiveness. Have you ever wondered why some people walk around with weights on their shoulders, chips on their shoulders, and sarcasm from their mouths? It's as if they have a bone to pick with you. They don't seem happy. They carry negative energy. Life may have dealt them trauma, frustrating relationships, and unfair treatment. Most of us have been bullied and mistreated at some stage of our lives.

I was bullied as a kid at an all-girls school in Singapore. I remember classmates ripping up my homework and laughing while they did it. I carried the pieces of torn paper to my teacher, tears streaming down my face. I don't remember how my teacher dealt with those girls.

I remember being called "weird" when I first moved to the United States, because I was from another country, with a Singaporean accent, and looked different. I didn't know what "weird" meant.

I remember when my ex-husband left my son and me one day, never to return as a family unit. The wounds were deep. I felt like damaged goods. I felt unwanted and abandoned.

I remember when friends betrayed me, telling me I was in their inner circle, yet they treated me like an outsider. During my many years of depression, hardly anyone reached out. I often felt alone.

I remember when so-called Christians took my money to invest and lost it all. Thousands of dollars gone—just like that.

I remember when contractors swindled me out of thousands of dollars, and realtors and management companies hurt me with unfair treatment in the real estate industry.

I also recall when the school I had supported and was loyal to for years rejected my children's book one day and banned me from reading to the kids, including my own son's class.

We can all recall those moments in time, clear as day, because they happened to us and had a profound impact on us. However, we probably don't remember the times when we have caused harm to others, especially if it was unintentional. Some people are so in denial and unaware of themselves because of their own emotional wounds that they have no clue what they are doing to you.

We are all wounded people, causing wounds to others. We all need forgiveness, and we all need to forgive. When Jesus taught his disciples to pray, he asked God to "forgive our debts, as we forgive our debtors." (Matthew 6:12)

This is an entirely counterintuitive statement. What do you mean by "forgive?" When someone mistreats us, we want justice. We want revenge. We want them to feel the pain that they have inflicted upon us! We want them to suffer the consequences of their choices and bad behavior, and yes, we even want them to go to jail sometimes!

So, why would Jesus say to forgive? Doesn't that give them license to continue sinning and causing harm? Doesn't God see the injustice that was done? Where is the justice? When is the wrong made right? Most of us believe in Karma—what goes around comes around. We believe there's a higher power in the universe, even a deity that judges right from wrong. So, why is there so much injustice on this earth?

Without going into a deep philosophical debate here, let's focus on the forgiveness part. Forgiveness is the key to being set free from bitterness and anger. When we're wounded, we instinctively try to heal the wound, whether physical or emotional. When we get cut, we cover and apply pressure to stop the bleeding. When our feelings get hurt, we put up walls around our hearts to protect ourselves from being hurt again. We are created to preserve our well-being. Even Darwin coined the term "survival of the fittest." Those who can recover quickly and thrive are the ones who will survive and pass their genes on to the next generation, keeping their lineage alive.

When we encounter conflict, we tend to fight or flee. We either find the inner strength to fight off our attacker, or we run away from danger to survive another day. Once wounded, we do everything we can to heal that pain. We go into protective mode. We don't want to experience pain. Those are natural reactions to being wounded. We lick our wounds and take time to heal. However, when we cannot let go of the emotional hurts done to us, we create a wall, and that wall can be built so high over time that we are trapped inside. When we don't deal with our hurt and release it, we harbor pain, anger, and then bitterness. We become jaded and have a tough exterior. We become sarcastic because we joke about the truth that hurts. We stop trusting and keep our guards up, hardening our hearts so people can't hurt us.

I know you're all thinking about the people in your lives right now who may be like that. Perhaps that person may even be you? The million-dollar question, then, is "How do we heal and move forward?" The million-dollar answer is forgiveness. When we consciously choose to forgive the person who hurt us (whether it was years ago or recently), it does not erase the pain inflicted. It does not mean you will forget what happened. It does not mean they shouldn't pay for their accounts. However, forgiveness releases your heart from carrying the pain and prevents you from being trapped in negative thoughts and patterns that further damage you. It releases the power that the perpetrator has over you. You may not have control over what someone does to you to hurt you, but you do have control over how you respond to the hurt and move forward in your life. You can either be frozen in time and stuck in a negative spiral, or you can be released from the traps of unforgiveness and thrive in your life.

See, when Jesus said to forgive your debtors, he wants you to live free from the encumbrances that debt incurs, whether it's yours or someone else's. Jesus wants us to be free of all things that hold us back from thriving. When Jesus was nailed to the cross and dying, He prayed, "Father, forgive them for they do not know what they are doing." (Luke 23:34)

How can he forgive the ones who are killing him? He demonstrated perfect love and sacrificed himself to show us how it's done, even while he was hurting.

What has happened in your life that has damaged you? How are you coping? Do you cope through alcohol and drugs? Do you cope with mental breaks from reality? Do you comfort yourself with food or shopping? Have you forgiven those who have hurt and damaged you? Will you consider forgiving them today? Will you choose to soften your heart today and trust God that He can heal your heart? If you choose to forgive, then say, "I forgive you, and then name the person." Then watch and see if there's a shift in your heart that releases freedom in that area of your life, if it feels like a burden has been lifted off your shoulders.

My prayer for you today is that you take that courageous step to forgive. Sometimes, you have to forgive someone from the past. Sometimes, you have to forgive more than once, especially if the hurt continues to be inflicted. You will have to learn to draw healthy boundaries to protect yourself from further hurt and damage to your soul. It's ok to say no to unreasonable requests. It's ok to limit interactions with a toxic individual. Most of all, it's okay to forgive, because you are the one who will be set free.

PATTY SHIH-MEI LEE CAMPBELL

Patty Shih-Mei Lee Campbell is a bestselling author of several books, including *Make People Matter*, *The Book of Frequency*, and *The Survival to Thrival* series. Her first children's book, *Meilea's Chinese New Year*, was written in 1992 when she was earning her Master's degree in Education. Her passion for educating and reaching people's hearts and minds through her voice continues to burn brightly. She lives in the San Francisco Bay Area with her husband and son and cares for her elderly mother, who now resides with her. Patty is an entrepreneur with several businesses across real estate, finance, and healthcare. She is President of the Rotary Club of Novato Evening (2025-2026) and a member of the Novato Chamber. Patty enjoys serving her community with her time, money, and energy. Her older son got married in 2025 and now lives in Boston with his wife.

Author's Website: *www.AbundanceGroup.us*

Charity Awareness: *www.TurnTable.com*

RITU CHOPRA

FIRE & GRACE: THE INNER SCIENCE OF LETTING GO

Years later, I thought I had forgiven, but the truth was I had just forgotten the hurt that wounded my soul.

Forgiveness is not a weakness. It's not forgetfulness either. It's biology, identity, and emotion, intertwined in a storm that our nervous system doesn't easily release.

Almost everyone has been hurt by someone, a loved one, a friend, or even themselves. Pain replays in our minds like a broken record, looping through the same old ache. Sometimes it's sharp and fresh; sometimes it hums quietly under the surface, disguised as indifference or pride.

WHAT MAKES FORGIVENESS HARD

The sting of betrayal, the ache of words that can't be unsaid, the slow erosion of trust, these experiences etch themselves deep into memory, stronger than most of us are willing to acknowledge. Pain replays like a record stuck on the same track, looping through the body as much as the mind. And yet, we keep listening, as if the repetition might finally deliver understanding.

THE ROOTS OF RESISTANCE

When we're hurt, our brains do what they were built to do: protect us from the memory of the hurt. The scientific facts are that the amygdala, our internal alarm system, tags the event as "unsafe." Every time we recall the memory, the same circuitry lights up as if it's happening again. How many times have we heard that our bodies keep the score, with heart rate quickening, muscles tensing, and hormones surging? We recognize the feelings.

Forgiveness feels threatening because, at a primal level, we equate it with vulnerability. To forgive seems to invite danger back in. It asks the ego to step aside, to release control, to stop rehearsing the story of how we were wronged. That surrender is resisting with every cell of the ego, which is built to define and defend itself with every ounce of its being.

We tend to cling to pain because it validates our experience. It becomes a part of our identity. "I am the one who was betrayed." "I am the one who was left." Without realizing it. We often imbue our wounds with significance, weaving them into the fabric of our identity. In doing so, we mistake the pain for who we are, allowing it to define us rather than merely being something we experience.

FORGIVENESS IS NOT FORGETTING

Forgiveness is often misunderstood as excusing harm or erasing memory. It's neither. Forgiveness doesn't mean reconciliation; it doesn't require the other person to apologize, change, or even be alive.

It's the act of reclaiming your peace from the grip of pain. It's saying:

You no longer get to rent space in my mind or rule the weather of my heart. Reclaiming energy from the suffering cycle is true forgiveness. This is a radical act of liberation.

THE SPIRITUAL PATH OF RELEASE

Across spiritual traditions, forgiveness is seen not as an act of willpower, but as a shift in consciousness.

In Buddhism, it's the letting go of attachment to the story.

In Christianity, it's divine grace flowing through human hearts.

In Hindu philosophy, it's *Kshama,* a virtue of the soul that dissolves the residue of karma.

Spiritually, forgiveness begins when you see pain not as punishment, but as a teacher.

THE THERAPEUTIC WORK OF HEALING

Therapy teaches that forgiveness often requires passing through grief first. You can't skip sorrow, rage, or disappointment. Emotional bypassing, pretending you're "over it" before you are, only deepens the wound.

Step 1: Give it a Name

Write down what happened and how it made you feel. Be raw and specific. This is emotional truth-telling, not judgment.

Step Two: Feel It

Allow the body to express, cry, shout, move, breathe. Let energy move where it freezes. Somatic therapies remind us that emotions are not thoughts; they're sensations that need motion to release.

Step Three: Reframe It

Ask yourself: *What did this experience awaken in me? What part of me grew through the breaking?*

Every hurt that doesn't harden us has the power to deepen us.

Step Four: Forgive Yourself, Too

Often, the hardest person to forgive is the one in the mirror, for staying too long, for not knowing better, for not healing fast enough. But self-forgiveness is the cornerstone of peace. When you hold yourself in compassion, you teach your heart how to soften toward others.

TRANSMUTING PAIN INTO POWER

Energetically, resentment is heavy. It lives in the body as tension, especially in the heart, throat, and gut. Forgiveness shifts vibration. When you release bitterness, your frequency rises; you become lighter, more transparent, more aligned with your higher self.

Science calls it neural rewiring. Spirit calls it transmutation. Either way, the energy shifts, and that's the miracle.

THE FREEDOM BEYOND THE FIRE OF PAIN

Forgiveness is courage. It's choosing peace over pride and the soul's declaration that love is stronger than pain.

Forgiveness doesn't always come with closure. Sometimes, it's just silence. No apology. No validation. Just a quiet knowing that you no longer wish to carry the weight.

That could be the secret: forgiveness doesn't come from giving it away, but from growing into it. The act is not a performance. Freed hearts remember what they were made for: loving, healing, rising.

FORGIVING YOURSELF IS HARDER, TOO

Often, the hardest person to forgive is the one in the mirror. We look at ourselves and replay every misstep, every harsh word we've said, every time we didn't meet our own expectations or someone else's. We carry invisible chains made of regret, guilt, and self-reproach, and we wear them as though they define who we are.

SELF-FORGIVENESS IS THE CORNERSTONE OF PEACE

Acknowledging that we are human, that we have erred, and that we have loved imperfectly, all while recognizing that the soul's essence remains untarnished. To forgive ourselves is to give permission to grow beyond our mistakes, to release the inner critic that insists we must remain trapped in yesterday's sorrow.

The act of self-forgiveness ripples outward.

Self-forgiveness is also a form of energy work. The tight knots of shame and guilt live in our bodies, often lodged in the chest, stomach, and shoulders. They manifest tension, anxiety, or even chronic illness when left unresolved. To forgive ourselves is to allow these knots to loosen, to create space for breath, for movement, for vitality. It is a conscious release of the weight that no longer serves you, a reclamation of the energy that fear and regret once consumed.

Practically, self-forgiveness can be cultivated through reflection, journaling, and ritual. Writing a letter to yourself, speaking words of understanding out loud, or visualizing your younger self embraced and held in light are all powerful ways to begin this work.

And like all forms of forgiveness, it is not instantaneous; it is a process, a steady unwrapping of layers until the heart no longer needs to clutch its own pain as a shield.

THE WEIGHT OF UNFORGIVENESS

Almost everyone has been hurt by someone, a loved one, a friend, or even themselves. Pain replays in our minds like a broken record. What makes forgiveness so hard? Our biology and identity are deeply rooted in our resistance to forgiving, according to neuroscientist Joe Dispenza.

Resentment reinforces neural pathways that keep us stuck in the past. In response, our bodies release stress hormones that keep us angry or victimized. You forgive to free yourself, not the other person.

Fear of being hurt again makes forgiveness risky.

Forgiveness is often described as one of the most challenging emotional tasks we face. Several interconnected reasons contribute to why letting go of resentment or anger is so difficult.

MYTHS OF CONTROL & IDENTITY

One reason we struggle to forgive is the false belief that holding a grudge gives us power. We think that if we forgive, others win. But in reality, unforgiveness chains us to the past. Dispenza teaches that true power comes from letting go - because only then can we step into a new future.

Our ego clings to pain because it becomes part of our story. We say I am the one who was hurt, and that identity feels safe, even if it's painful.

THE SCIENCE OF RELEASE

Research shows that forgiveness reduces cortisol (the stress hormone) and increases serotonin (the happiness chemical). When we forgive, we literally change our biology.

How to Begin Forgiving

- **Acknowledge the Pain**: Don't suppress it; feel it fully, then decide to release it.

- **Reframe the Story**: Instead of, "They hurt me," try, "This experience taught me strength."

- **Practice Gratitude**: Focus on what you gained (resilience, wisdom) rather than what you lost.

- **Meditate on Freedom**: Visualize cutting energetic cords and stepping into a state of peace.

Forgiveness isn't about condoning hurtful actions—it's about reclaiming your power. Are you ready to let go? The choice is yours.

RITU CHOPRA

Ritu Chopra inspires people with her sincerity in coaching and professional leadership experience, which includes managing business and IT operations.

Ritu has solved complex technical challenges in her work with Fortune 500 companies over the past twenty-plus years. Using proven methods and tools, she leverages her management and coaching expertise to bridge IT-business gaps, boost engagement, and empower teams.

As president of Chopra Management Services, Ritu is a creative force, motivational speaker, and certified leadership coach. She is the author of *Art of Life*, *Mastering Life*, *Women Leadership in 21st Century*, and her upcoming title, *Magic in Mindfulness.* As an executive coach, Ritu leads seminars and coaching programs tailored to niche areas, including personal mastery, women in leadership, and mindfulness in daily life.

Ritu brings her passion, humility, and dedication to inspire her clients to engage their heads and hearts in clarity and creation.

Author's Website: *www.RituChopra.com*

Charity Awareness: *www.SurvivalToThrivalSeries.com*

DR. SABRINA PATEL

FOR + GIVE: CHOOSING GRACE WHEN THE STANDARD IS HIGH

Forgiveness is a big one. And—if I'm honest—it's hard. I actually think it's easier for me to forgive other people than it is to forgive myself. Maybe it's a perfectionist thing. Perhaps it's because I hold myself to such high standards. I don't know. I know I can extend grace to others more easily than I can to myself.

In medicine, that shows up a lot. There are cases where the diagnosis isn't precise in the moment, or a plan has to change when new information comes in. The pressure can feel enormous because someone else's life is connected to the decision you make in *that* moment. Even when outcomes are okay, I will still replay it, analyze it, and find ten ways I "should have" done better. Those are the moments where I probably need to give myself grace—and those are the moments where I find that grace hardest to give.

With other people, it's different. I almost instinctively try to step into their perspective and ask, "Where were they coming from?" My perspective is always different from someone else's; maybe they honestly thought about it another way. That lens helps me forgive and move on. It helps me cope. It lets me keep going.

But forgiving myself? That's where I get stuck.

EXPECTATION, PRESSURE, & THE ILLNESS THAT WOKE ME UP

Growing up, my parents didn't put pressure on me. If anything, they made it easy to change paths when life got hard. The pressure was internal—I put it on myself. And for most of my life, that worked. I set the bar high. I met the bar. Then I raised it again.

There was one season, though, when expectation came from outside of me. When I married into a traditional Indian family, it was the first time I felt like there were standards I had to meet that weren't my own. That was hard for me. I can handle my own pressure because it's mine; I set it, I own it. But external expectations felt different. I internalized them. I carried them. And I think that weight—combined with internal stress I wasn't releasing—played a role in getting sick.

After I had my son, I was diagnosed with an autoimmune condition. I didn't have symptoms beforehand, no family history, nothing obvious. I was young. On paper, I looked fine.

But inside, I was operating at a constant high-stress baseline that I had learned to call "normal." When I decided to heal, I realized it wasn't just about meds. Yes, medication helped. But what truly moved the needle was reducing the stress I'd normalized, stepping out of environments that weren't good for me, and letting go of expectations I had been holding like a second skin.

That's where forgiveness started to matter in a new way. I had to forgive myself for not knowing sooner. I had to forgive myself for ignoring my body's signals. I had to forgive myself for living like an unsustainable pace was "fine." And I had to forgive others—lovingly and without resentment—so I could step away, reset, and choose differently.

THE HARDEST PERSON TO FORGIVE

If I list the people I haven't forgiven, I can't think of anyone. Truly. I forgive easily because it helps me move forward. But if you ask whether I've forgiven *myself* for the times I wasn't perfect, or for the days I was tired and still tried to be everything for everyone, or for the moments a decision could have been better, my honest answer is: I'm not sure I have. I tend to "keep it moving," work harder, and raise the standard again.

That's the tricky thing about high standards. They can call you higher—or they can become a measuring stick you use to punish yourself. And I don't want that for me. I don't want that for my patients. So here's the reframe I'm learning:

Forgiveness isn't an excuse; it's an exit.

An exit from shame loops. An exit from perfectionism that masquerades as safety. An exit from environments that keep you dysregulated. Forgiveness is a door that lets you leave what isn't serving you and step into something that will.

And yes, it's still hard.

THE "FOR + GIVE" SCALPEL

Sometimes we get hung up on the word *forgiveness*. So I like to take a scalpel to it, separate it into **four,** and **give**.

- **For others, I give grace**. I put myself in their position and try to understand. That doesn't mean I excuse harm. It means I refuse to hold on to it so tightly that it hardens in me. Letting go makes me more weightless. It frees up energy for healing.

- **For myself, I give patience**. That's the part I'm still practicing. I can acknowledge pressure without making it my identity. I can remember that, as a physician, a mother, a partner, and a human, none of those roles requires perfection to be meaningful.

When I think of forgiveness as *for + give*, it becomes a practice of generosity. Generosity toward someone else's humanity *and* toward my own.

WHEN THOSE YOU LOVE DON'T ACCEPT HELP

There's another angle to forgiveness that I face in medicine and in my personal life: **what to do when someone I love resists the help I know could serve them.** It is hard to watch someone decline advice you're trained to give, especially when you can see the path forward. In those moments, I forgive the gap between what I know and what they are ready to receive. I forgive the timeline not matching my urgency. And I set my standard: I will stay compassionate, transparent, and honest—but I will not carry their choice as if it were my failure.

That boundary *is* forgiveness. It's forgiveness for them (no resentment about their pace) and forgiveness for me (no self-condemnation about outcomes I can't control).

FROM SURVIVAL TO THRIVAL: HOW FORGIVENESS MOVES THE NEEDLE

Survival is white-knuckling your way through pressure, perfectionism, expectations, and outcomes you can't control. Thrival is loosening your grip with grace. It's noticing where you are not at ease and choosing to step away when you can. It's letting energy guide you before you crash. It's telling the truth: *I am doing my best. I will keep learning. And I will not punish myself for being human.*

That mindset shift didn't come from theory. It came from my own healing process—learning that my body needed less internalized stress and more honest boundaries. It came from leaving spaces that looked "fine" on the outside but weren't safe for my nervous system. It came from believing that forgiveness is not for the other person only—it's for me. To move. To breathe. To become lighter.

STANDARDS OF EXCELLENCE—WITHOUT THE SELF-PUNISHMENT

I still believe in high standards. I'm a physician; I know what best practices look like. In clinic, I'll always be direct: take the medication as prescribed, prioritize sleep, move your body, eat in a way that supports your hormones and inflammation pathways, manage stress, do the labs, and follow up. But excellence is not the same as perfection. Excellence is consistent attention to what's within your control. Perfection is trying to control everything—including what isn't yours to carry.

So I write my own standard of excellence like this:

* I prepare thoroughly.

* I act with integrity.

* I communicate clearly and compassionately.

* I learn from new data.

* I adjust when something isn't working.

And when I fall short in a moment, I don't abandon the standard. I **forgive**, recommit, and move forward.

JAMAICA, COURAGE, & THE LONG VIEW

Some lessons only make sense when you look back across years. Leaving Jamaica at seventeen taught me courage: the quiet, persistent kind that shows up again and again, even when you're scared. It taught me how to rebuild, how to ask for help, and how to keep choosing growth over comfort. Those early decisions were my first practice in forgiving myself for being new at something, for feeling "other," for learning as I went. That same courage is what I still carry into medicine, motherhood, and healing today.

SELF-FORGIVENESS IN REAL TIME

Here's what self-forgiveness looks like for me right now:

- **When I replay a tough case,** I review it once with a learning lens, not a punishment lens. I extract the lessons. Then I close the file in my mind and refuse to reopen it at 2 a.m.

- **When my body says, "This isn't safe,"** I believe it. I don't explain it away. I step back from environments and expectations that dysregulate me.

- **When someone I love resists help,** I stay clear and kind— and I don't treat their no as my failure.

- **When perfectionism shows up:** I notice it and choose excellence instead. Excellence is kinder and more sustainable.

- **When I feel behind,** I remember that healing has its own timeline and that grace is part of the treatment plan.

None of this is effortless. But effort isn't the enemy. *Self-punishment* is.

A GENTLE PRACTICE YOU CAN TRY

If forgiveness feels abstract, try this simple practice:

1. **Name the weight.** What are you carrying that isn't yours? Whose expectation? Which old story?

2. **Cut the word.** Write "forgive" as **for + give**. Under "for," list the people and situations you're carrying resentment toward—including yourself. Under "give," list what you will give each one: grace, a boundary, an apology, patience, and release.

3. **Choose one micro-act.** What is one small, loving action that reflects this choice today? A conversation, a walk, a breath, a pause before you say yes.

4. **Close the loop.** Before bed, say, "I forgive you" to your own name out loud. It might feel awkward. Do it anyway.

You don't need to feel forgiving to *practice* forgiveness. The practice itself softens the feeling over time.

WHAT I KNOW NOW

I used to think forgiveness was mostly about the other person. Now I know it's a treatment I give myself. It's how I become more weightless. It's how I reclaim energy for healing. It's how I move from survival—gripping and striving—into thrival, where standards of excellence coexist with kindness, and where courage keeps opening doors.

I still hold myself to a high bar. I still believe in doing the work. I still expect a lot from myself. But now I anchor those expectations in grace. I let forgiveness be the exit from shame, the boundary with pressure that isn't mine, and the invitation to try again with softness.

I'm not perfect at it. I probably never will be. But I'm practicing. And every time I choose *to give* for others, and for myself, I become a little lighter, a little braver, and a lot freer.

DR. SABRINA PATEL

Dr. Sabrina Patel is a board-certified family medicine physician and the founder of Zia Health, a concierge functional medicine and wellness clinic based in Ormond Beach, Florida. With advanced training in hormone optimization, root-cause medicine, and functional wellness, Dr. Patel helps patients restore balance, reclaim energy, and align with their healthiest selves.

After facing personal health struggles postpartum and being diagnosed with an autoimmune condition, she pivoted from conventional protocols to integrative approaches that transformed her life—and now her patients' lives too. Born and raised in Kingston, Jamaica, Dr. Patel brings a unique cultural lens to healing, blending evidence-based science with compassion and intuition. She is a devoted wife and mother of two young boys, with a love for baking, the arts, and travel. Through her work, she empowers others to reconnect with their bodies, rediscover their vitality, and live in alignment with their purpose.

Author's Website: *www.SabrinaPatel.com*

Charity Awareness: *www.SurvivalToThrivalSeries.com*

SAMARA BETH

LETTING GO, RISING HIGHER: THE POWER OF FORGIVENESS

Forgiveness is the bridge between what hurt us and what can heal us. It's not always loud. In fact, most forgiveness happens quietly, in moments no one sees, like when you unclench your jaw, loosen your grip on the past, or stop rehearsing that one painful conversation in your head.

I never thought I had a "forgiveness story." I wasn't angry. I wasn't bitter. I didn't have a dramatic courtroom moment where I told someone who wronged me, "I forgive you."

But life has a funny way of offering you plenty of chances to forgive, sometimes the same person more than once. Sometimes yourself.

And sometimes, the person you need to forgive... is the one you loved the longest.

My marriage spanned twenty-two years. We traveled, moved frequently, built a family, navigated military deployments and hotel-living, laughed, cried, fought, and tried. I didn't get married thinking I'd be a single mom rebuilding her life while helping her kids adjust to a new normal.

Divorce wasn't in the plan. But neither was betrayal. Neither was the long, slow erosion of trust. Neither was watching someone become a stranger right in front of me while trying to keep life together for everyone else.

I wasn't just grieving the end of a marriage. I was grieving the loss of the life I thought we were building. The one I sacrificed for. The one I forgave within, again and again, until I finally realized, forgiveness doesn't mean staying. It means releasing. And sometimes, that release must include the version of yourself who accepted far less than you deserved.

People assume forgiveness is something you offer when someone apologizes. But I learned that most of the people who hurt you will never say, "I'm sorry," at least not in the way you need to hear it. In fact, I don't recall anyone saying, "I'm sorry" to me.

Forgiveness, I've come to believe, is a self-rescue mission.

When the dust settled after the divorce, I didn't feel free. I felt hollow. Numb. Angry at myself for not leaving sooner. Furious for staying silent. Heartbroken that my children would grow up split between two homes. Humiliated that I, the fixer, the connector, the do-it-all mom, couldn't fix my own marriage.

I wanted to fast-forward to healed. A healed mind, body, and soul. But healing doesn't come from rushing—it comes from reckoning.

So, I got real with myself. I journaled. I cried in the shower. I went to trauma therapy. I hired coaches. I prayed. I meditated. I forgave family. I forgave friends. I forgave me. I forgave the God I felt abandoned by. I forgave the version of myself who had to hold it all together for so long.

Forgiveness doesn't mean you forget what happened. It means you stop letting it hijack your future.

It's saying, "That chapter hurt, but it's not my whole story."

It's saying, "I can love the memories and still choose peace over pain."

It's saying, "I deserve more, and I forgive myself for not believing that sooner."

Forgiveness took root in me when I realized I was carrying too many heavy things, like resentment, regret, and remorse. There wasn't room for possibility until I put some of it down.

But let me be honest… sometimes it still creeps in.

Like when I'm balancing work and motherhood solo for the hundredth day in a row.

Or when I see him parenting differently than I would.

Or when I remember that I buried our child with him, built businesses with him, moved cross-country and overseas and through borders, more times than I can count... and now I have to co-parent with a man I no longer know.

That's when I must forgive all over again. Not for him. But for me. For our kids.

Because my peace is sacred. Because my joy is too expensive to rent out to resentment. Because my daughter is watching me model what love and boundaries look like.

Because my son needs a mom who teaches him that forgiveness doesn't mean weakness, it means wisdom.

Forgiveness isn't about pretending everything's okay. It's about choosing what deserves your energy. It's about closing the door without slamming it. It's about choosing healing over harboring.

Forgiveness also showed up in the smaller spaces of life, like with friends and family who didn't show up when my son, or my dad, or my marriage died.

With clients who ghosted after long proposals. With mentors

who disappointed me. With people who said they'd help and never did. With myself, for pushing too hard, expecting perfection, being too available, or waiting too long to say what needed to be said.

I had to learn that forgiveness isn't approval; it's release. It's not letting someone off the hook. It's taking the hook out of your own heart. Even if it's my dad, who never found the time to take a promised father-daughter trip or take me fishing as an adult.

There's a kind of quiet courage in forgiving people who don't know they hurt you. And there's a loud, holy kind of strength in forgiving yourself.

Because let's be real, self-forgiveness might be the hardest of all.

I had to forgive myself for:

- Not building boundaries sooner.
- Chasing validation from people who couldn't love me back.
- Saying "yes" when I should have said "no."
- Losing myself in motherhood.
- Quitting when I was afraid, and staying when I should have walked away.

Forgiveness gave me my voice back.

And when I got it back, I used it on stages, on interviews, in books, in coaching calls, and in whispers to my kids when they are sleeping.

Today, I teach my clients how to build brands, books, and businesses, but behind every brand breakthrough is someone who needs to forgive themselves first. For waiting. For hiding. For not believing they were enough. For falling, for failing, for fearing.

Forgiveness, for me, is not a one-time moment. It's a practice. A commitment. A way of walking in the world where I don't hold onto anything that doesn't serve my future.

And if you're in the middle of a storm, like a breakup, a betrayal, a big mistake, I want to offer you a hand. Not to pull you out, but to remind you that you're not alone in it. You don't have to stay stuck in the story someone else wrote for you. You get to write your own next story and your own ending.

Here are five ways I coach my clients, and myself, through the art of forgiveness:

1. Forgive fast, heal slow.

You don't need to wait to start the process. You just need to be willing. The healing will catch up.

2. Write the letter, even if you never send it.

Get the words out of your body and onto paper. Anger likes to fester in silence.

3. Say it out loud: "I forgive you."

Even if you're alone. Even if it's into your pillow. Naming it starts the release.

4. Practice radical compassion.

You don't have to excuse behavior to understand it. Hurt people hurt people. Healed people heal people. Choose to be the latter.

5. Redefine your power.

You are not what happened to you. You are what you do next. You are the writer now.

Today, I stand as Badass Bamboo, not because I never bent, but because I've learned how to rise softer. Stronger. Wiser.

I don't carry old pain into new seasons. I don't let the past dim my possibility. I don't let resentment take up space in my purpose. I release. I rise. I forgive.

You can too.

If no one has told you today: You are worthy of peace. You are allowed to change the story. You are allowed to forgive and still have boundaries. You are allowed to grow.

Let's do it together.

Let's WIN your brand.

Let's WIN your healing.

Let's WIN your life.

Be Badass Bamboo.

SAMARA BETH

Samara Beth is a keynote speaker, 10X Certified Business Coach, national award-winning event producer, and bestselling author with a career spanning over thirty years across North America. As the founder and CEO of Samara Beth & Co., she empowers entrepreneurs to W.I.N. their brand by creating powerful and memorable events, experiences, retreats, and stages. By increasing their revenue, visibility, and brand impact, Samara Beth & Co's W.I.N. Pillars—Willpower to overcome challenges, Innovation to think creatively, and Networking to build powerful communities—have helped countless businesses grow successfully. Samara's journey is one of resilience, adaptability, and transformation, leading to her nickname "Lil' Bamboo." She has built multiple businesses, cultivated thriving communities, and navigated personal and professional challenges with unwavering determination. Known for her contagious energy and light, Samara has inspired thousands through her speaking engagements, courses, retreats, and books, helping individuals turn obstacles into opportunities. Recognized as a "Volunteer of the Year" and a recipient of the "Humanitarian Award," she continues to uplift others, leaving a lasting impact wherever she goes.

Author's Website: www.SamaraBeth.com
Charity Awareness: *www.AFMDA.org*

STEPH SHINABERY

LAY DOWN THE ARMOR: HOW I PRACTICE FORGIVENESS IN MY BODY

Forgiveness once felt like a distant moral commandment. Now it lives in my body: energy reorganizes, breath returns, jaw softens, ribs expand. It's not forgetting or excusing—it's my nervous system realizing it can finally stop bracing.

Anesthesia taught me to read signals—tiny shifts before big changes. When we're scared, we hold; when we trust, we release. I put people to sleep and wake them up. Forgiveness is how I wake myself up, too.

THE MOMENT I STOPPED WAITING FOR AN APOLOGY

Not long ago, I planned an in-person event—something I'd dreamed about for years. I invited a collaborator whose presence felt like the right counterbalance. Life happened; he didn't show. No call. No explanation. The old loop spun up fast: *You can't do this alone. People will ask. You'll fail, and it'll be public.* My chest tightened; my shoulders lifted toward my ears like they had an opinion.

Here's what I didn't do: I didn't chase an apology. I didn't start justifying, blaming, or bargaining. I let the fear talk—and then I let my breath talk louder. I asked *Steph, what's the next loving step?* Book the room. Order the materials. Invite two trusted friends. Show up.

I showed up with my nerves chattering. Courage doesn't erase fear; it redirects energy. Instead of holding a grudge, I kept myself. I sent silent gratitude for what he was navigating and released him from the role I'd assigned. I forgave—not because it was okay, but because I wouldn't let it run my event or my body. Choosing presence over story has become my theme.

Forgiveness starts as a decision in my body: I stop armoring against this.

WHAT FORGIVENESS FEELS LIKE (IN REAL TIME)

Whether in anesthesia, coaching, or Temple Somatics, I see the same pattern: threat causes us to tighten, guard, and stop the flow of energy.

During a craniosacral session, the practitioner's gentle presence let my jaw unclench and my breath widen. I forgave the hurry, shoulds, and perfectionism I'd been holding. Presence is medicine.

When I facilitate somatic work, I picture three rings: Source (always-okay), Soul (play, connection), Body (the animal storing alarms). Forgiveness helps the body trust the source again. We allow release—sometimes by shaking, humming, or lying quietly until the system believes: *You're safe. Let go.*

THE UNFINISHED APOLOGY I OWED MYSELF

Before anesthesia, I followed the road of *shoulds, ticking boxes* while quietly dimming. In my forties, I quit, took on debt, and went to anesthesia school. It was terrifying, but I moved one brave inch at a time. That choice rebuilt me—and surfaced resentment at myself for waiting so long.

I forgave my younger self for not choosing sooner: Of course, you stayed. You did *your best with what you had. Today, we choose again.* This freed up energy for my future instead of relitigating my past.

MICRO-FORGIVENESS
(TRAFFIC, DETOURS, & TINY RESETS)

Forgiveness isn't always dramatic. Sometimes it's a Tuesday traffic jam. I used to fume; now I practice micro-forgiveness: *I release my argument with reality, detour, play music, and let curiosity replace stress. That's energetic leadership—where my attention goes*, energy follows.

Forgiveness ≠ Reconciliation (Boundaries Belong)

Love is a stance. Sometimes it stays, sometimes it says "enough." Forgiveness isn't reconnection. I can bless you and still hold a boundary. My clearest boundaries come *after* forgiveness—then I decide from presence, not pain.

At my solo event, people wondered where my collaborator was. I chose to be present with myself. The room relaxed; so did I. Forgiveness cleared the static for courage to do its work.

THE BODY DOESN'T LIE
(HOW I NOTICE IT'S TIME TO FORGIVE)

My body signals when I need forgiveness work:

- **Jaw**: clenched or aching after I "win" a mental argument with someone who isn't in the room.

- **Breath**: trapped high in my chest when I think about a name, a place, or a missed chance.

- **Posture**: shoulders forward, heart guarded, like I'm bracing for a blow that already landed.

When I notice those, I do this five-minute protocol:

1. **Name the charge out loud:** "My chest is tight and I'm replaying the story."

2. **Orient to support:** feel the chair under my sit bones, widen my back.

3. **Drop a genuine gratitude** in the room I'm in—something small and specific.

4. **Ask one loving question**: "What am I still carrying that isn't mine?"

5. **Let something move**: shake, sigh, hum, or cry for two minutes. Then choose a kinder next step.

It's simple and it works. It brings me back to the present— where change happens.

THE FORGIVENESS I DIDN'T EXPECT: LETTING JOY BACK IN

After a painful breakup, I dove into somatic work. In the Smoky Mountains, I joined others in hands-on healing— breath, movement, sound—helping release what bodies held. The joy and relief I witnessed told me I'd found something worth sharing.

What surprised me was the joy. Forgiveness opened space for play. We keep joy out when we guard old wounds. Forgiving doesn't deny what happened; it denies it the right to run our future.

HOW GRATITUDE MAKES FORGIVENESS EASIER

Gratitude finds me when I'm lost—I can't be grateful and resentful at once. A sticky note—"I'm grateful we work together"—reset a tough shift. Gratitude shifts my chemistry before circumstances, metabolizing resentment and making forgiveness possible.

THE STORY I TELL MY CLIENTS (& MYSELF)

In coaching, we name Gift, Purpose, and Path—our true north. When they align, mornings change; life fits your energy. Naming creates coherence, and forgiveness restores it when life scrambles you.

Forgiving isn't letting someone off the hook; it's freeing your own nervous system to reclaim energy for what matters.

PRACTICE: FIELD GUIDE TO FORGIVING IN THE WILD

Use this the next time a text stings, a plan collapses, or a voice in your head says, *Not enough:*

1. **Ground, then decide.** Bare feet on the floor. Hand on sternum. Three box-breath cycles. Please don't email or explain from a spike; it's expensive.

2. **Tell the truth.** "I felt hurt when you didn't show," or "I'm disappointed this changed." No dramatics, no minimizing. Truth regulates.

3. **Bless and boundarize.** "I wish you well" (blessing) + "I'm moving forward with X" (boundary).

4. **Move one brave inch.** Book the room. Write one email. Put your feet in the grass. Pray.

5. **Close your loop.** Two minutes on the floor: one hand heart, one hand belly. Hum until your jaw loosens. Let your body experience safety again.

Repeat tomorrow. Healing is practice.

FORGIVENESS IN COMMUNITY

I used to worry more about public failure than private peace. In that event, I ran solo, and I felt the community's eyes on me. I also felt their hearts. People don't actually need us to be flawless; they need us to be present. When I named what was true, thanked them for trusting the work, and delivered what I promised, the room met me. Courage cleared the static; forgiveness kept the channel open.

Forgiveness isn't just personal hygiene; it's community care. When I stop rehearsing old scenes, I can show up for others— their stories, genius, and breakthroughs. Energy I once spent guarding becomes energy I can give.

A FINAL WORD TO THE PART
OF YOU THAT'S TIRED

If you're exhausted from carrying it, you're not weak—you're wise. Your body wants a new strategy. Try: *I forgive myself for not knowing sooner. I forgive them for being human. I choose what's next.*

Forgiveness isn't a one-time ceremony; it's a daily stance. Some days I nail it; some days I start again. When I forget, I return. Return is the most compassionate verb I know.

If you need a reason to try again, use mine: I want to wake up excited to be myself—like Dalí, wondering what prodigious thing I'll do today. Forgiveness makes room for that kind of morning.

Write This Down: *Forgiveness lets my body drop its armor so my soul can play.*

Lay down the armor; your life is waiting on the other side of soft.

STEPH SHINABERY

Steph Shinabery is The World's Best Possibility Coach, a Nurse Anesthesiologist, Artist, Speaker, and the Founder of Genius Code Academy.

After spending much of her life in a career that lacked the inspiration and fulfillment she knew was available to her, she began a journey to answer the question: "What is it I truly desire?"

Her journey led to the creation of the Genius Identity Code™, a process for unlocking your gift, purpose, and path, and helping people see, believe, and execute their unique genius to achieve miraculous outcomes.

Steph works with creative experts, entrepreneurs, and coaches to help them embrace their authenticity and create a life that gets them excited to jump out of bed every day!

You can find her talk, "Wake Up Your Genius Machine," on Amazon Prime Video's *Speak Up: Empower Your Ideas, Season 4*.

Author's Website: *www.StephShinabery.com*

Charity Awareness: *www.SurvivalToThrivalSeries.com*

TYLER WATSON

FORGIVENESS ISN'T WHAT YOU SAY, IT'S WHO YOU BECOME

Most people think forgiveness is something you say. "I forgive them." "I've moved on." "It's fine now."

But if saying it is all it takes, why do so many people still avoid the ones they claim to have forgiven? Why do they get tense at the thought of seeing them again? Why do they flinch at their name, their face, their memory?

Here's the truth: If any part of you, your body, your emotions, your thoughts, reacts negatively to someone you've "forgiven," you haven't truly forgiven them. Forgiveness isn't just a decision. It's a full-body integration. Your cells hold memory. Your organs hold emotion. Your nervous system stores trauma.

And unless all parts of you are released, aligned, and free… It's not forgiveness. It's suppression.

THE ILLUSION OF LOGICAL FORGIVENESS

You can't outthink pain. You can't override trauma with statements. You can't force healing through logic. People often say, "I've forgiven them," but they're still carrying the weight. They still avoid conversations. They still protect their heart. They still fear repeating the past. That's not forgiveness. That's coping.

True forgiveness is an identity change. It's when your body no longer braces. It's when your soul no longer flinches. It's when you're no longer trying to be better than the person who hurt you.

MY JOURNEY: FORGIVING MYSELF, MY PATTERNS, & MY PARENTS

I've had to walk this path many times. I've had to forgive myself deeply, fully, for things I never thought I'd say aloud. Addictive patterns with pornography. Moments I let my wife down.

Goals I set and didn't follow through on. Lies I told myself about what I was capable of. Shame I carried about not being enough. Each time, I wanted to just move on. But my body wouldn't let me.

The guilt showed up in my actions. The shame shaped how I showed up in relationships. The regret leaked into my business, my leadership, my dreams. I had to go deeper. I had to learn that true forgiveness doesn't mean you deny what happened, it means you no longer carry the frequency of who you were when it did.

And the most painful forgiveness? Forgiving my parents. My mom went through seven divorces.

My dad went through three. I watched my family fall apart again and again. And part of me believed it was my job to fix it. To save them. That belief made me sacrifice my joy. It made me take on more than was mine. It made me try to earn peace through pain.

And when I finally forgave them not just logically, but with every cell in my body, I felt something I hadn't felt in years: Freedom. Forgiveness didn't mean I had to agree with their choices. It didn't mean I had to carry their wounds. It meant I could respect them without replicating them. I could love them without losing myself. That's the power of true forgiveness.

THE STORY THAT CHANGES MY LIFE

One of the most powerful moments of forgiveness I've ever read came from the book *Left to Tell* by Immaculée Ilibagiza. During the Rwandan genocide, her entire family was slaughtered. Not by soldiers. By her neighbors and former friends.

Years later, after the violence had subsided, she was given a chance to face the man who murdered her family.

Accompanied by the jailer, she walked up to this man who had caused her so much pain. And then... She looked the man in the eyes and simply said: "I forgive you."

The jailer was furious. He wanted her to scream. To demand justice. To retaliate. But Immaculée chose something higher. She chose mercy. Forgiveness trumps justice. Because justice balances the scales. But forgiveness frees the soul.

EVERY TRIGGER IS A TRANSFORMATION WAITING TO HAPPEN

Here's something I've learned again and again: Every single trigger, especially the ones caused by other people, is a transformation waiting to happen. If you have someone in your life who's hard to forgive, don't just see them as a problem to manage. See them as a gift.

I know that may sound extreme, especially if the wound runs deep. But I've found that the people who have caused us the most pain are often the very mirrors revealing what we need to shift to become capable of where we are going.

Who you want to become, what you're called to create, and the life you're stepping into, it requires a version of you who no longer gets thrown off course by old pain. If someone still triggers you, that's a sign. It's not shame, it's an invitation. A spotlight on the part of you that's ready for an upgrade.

What if forgiveness wasn't just about peace with the past, but preparation for your future? What if instead of anger, you gave gratitude? Not because you liked what happened, but because it revealed the weakness in your armor, the very weakness you're now being invited to strengthen. The way you respond to your deepest pain becomes the blueprint for your greatest transformation.

Forgiveness isn't just a moral high road. It's a power move. It's you saying, "I don't need them to change for me to rise." And when you take the trigger, transmute the pain, and align every part of you back to truth. You don't just forgive. You evolve. And nothing, not even the past, can hold you back anymore.

FORGIVENESS IS THE GATEWAY TO THRIVING

If you're still in survival mode, still hustling to prove, still aching to be enough, still replaying what they did to you... it's time to stop coping and start healing.

Forgiveness isn't about pretending it didn't happen. It's not about letting someone off the hook. It's about unhooking yourself from the pattern. All true forgiveness leads to transformation. It upgrades your frequency. It restores your identity. It makes you better.

And it's not just for others. It's for you. It's for every dream that's waiting on the other side of your pain. It's for every relationship that deserves the real you. It's for the version of you that no longer reacts, but responds with power, peace, and purpose.

Try This: The Forgiveness Frequency Check-In

Ask yourself:

- When I think of this person (or myself), do I feel tightness or release?

- If they walked in the room, would I feel peace or pressure?

- Is part of me still trying to prove something to them?

- Do I feel responsible for their emotions, reactions, or outcomes?

If any part of you answers "yes," that's where your forgiveness work begins.

One of my missions in life is to help people change in minutes instead of years. Just because something has happened and it feels real doesn't mean it has to stay. The same transformation is a choice.

Instead of harboring pain or suffering, allow yourself to break free and become the best version of you. With the right tools, it is possible to transform and truly forgive faster than you thought possible.

Thank you for who you are for reading this, and if you do want to go through a process to help you shift, be sure to check out the link in the bio. Don't let other people stop you from your transformation. Learn to forgive others at a cellular level and allow it to transform your identity and truly become unstoppable.

TYLER WATSON

Tyler Watson is a coach, speaker, and mentor specializing in turning survival-mode strivers into powerful creators. After escaping the cycle of depression, financial struggle, and striving for worthiness, Tyler dedicated his life to helping others break free.

Through his Cellular Alignment Technique and personal mentoring, Tyler has helped thousands accelerate their breakthroughs, generate quantum leaps in income, relationships, and confidence—and most importantly, choose from truth instead of fear. Tyler's mission is simple: to help you remember your divine ability to create without limits and thrive with full choice.

Start your journey from striving to thriving with Tyler's free gift here: https://www.alignmenteffect.com/more

Author's Website: *www.AlignmentEffect.com*

Charity Awareness: *www.SurvivalToThrivalSeries.com*

VICKI PARKER

THE FIRST FORGIVENESS: RECLAIMING YOURSELF

Forgiveness is often seen as something we give to others, but I've learned it starts much closer to home—with ourselves. Before we can release the pain or unmet expectations weighing on our hearts, we must first turn inward and offer grace to ourselves, the one who has carried the longest burden.

This chapter comes from my journey of learning that forgiveness isn't a single moment or one-time decision. It's a process—a gentle untying of old stories and beliefs that no longer serve us. Through my father's absence, supporting foster children, and the choices I've made, I came to see forgiveness isn't about condoning or forgetting. It's about reclaiming freedom, restoring alignment, and creating space for possibility.

As you read, I invite you to bring curiosity and compassion. Notice where you've withheld forgiveness from yourself. Consider how your choices—your "yeses" and "nos"—have shaped your path. Every step, misstep, and triumph is part of the journey from survival to thrival.

Pause where you feel called. Journal or meditate if it helps. I hope these pages support your journey to free your heart and step into the life that opens when forgiveness leads the way.

Forgiveness is not a destination—it's a gift we give ourselves so we can thrive.

THE QUIET RELEASE: FORGIVENESS, IDENTITY, & THE COURAGE TO COME HOME

I always thought I would be a wife and a mother.

In my younger years, I imagined a good husband, a lively home, and at least three children—maybe even a baseball team of boys. That life never arrived as I expected. Instead, I chased security through movement: building businesses, training leaders, boarding planes, and justifying my pace as purpose. I told myself I was making a difference, helping others provide for their families.

When I left Hyatt Hotels to study improv in Chicago, I had no idea how magnetic the road would become. After my first traveling training gig, I was hooked. Cities, airports, upgrades, and late-night dinners in unfamiliar places became part of my identity. Travel didn't just support my life; it became my life.

People would ask what I did in Chicago.

"I play," I'd say. "I work on the road."

And I meant it. I had season tickets to the theater, ballet, symphony, and more. Culture fed me. Art nourished me. Connection sustained me.

What thrilled me most about the road wasn't the glamour—it was the people. I'd fly in for a friend's show or drive hours for a hug, a meal, or a rooftop evening. I loved the freedom, the movement, the connection.

Most people burn out on travel. I never did.

What I didn't know then is that sometimes movement keeps us from being still long enough to forgive.

I've supported Royal Family Kids Camp for years—a summer camp for children in foster care. These children arrive carrying stories no child should bear. The mission is simple: to show them unconditional love, intentional structure, and the steady presence of trusted adults, even if only for a week.

This past summer, I was assigned one child instead of the typical two.

A ten-year-old girl, whom we will call Bethany.

When she stepped off the bus, she ran toward me as if we were old friends. I didn't recognize her at first. Later, I learned the truth: Bethany had once been my camper before. She had since been adopted. Her name had been changed.

She had been Lauren.

When children are adopted, their names often change to create a new identity—one unburdened by the past. It's an act of hope. Her body remembered me before my mind did, and her trust came quickly—faster than either of us expected.

By night one, she was glued to me. On day two, she began testing. By day three, she pulled back. And by day four, the lies came pouring out.

Items from our communal table went missing. Word games. Toys. Craft supplies. Later, we found Bethany quietly playing with them in front of the other girls. Then we discovered the bag ~ filled with far more than we realized had disappeared. Even our small first-aid kit was in there. My personal mini flashlight, too.

Her behavior triggered me in ways I didn't expect. I held her accountable. I reminded her that the younger girls looked up to her. I invited her into leadership. I asked her to be an example of what godliness looks like.

But beneath the surface, something deeper was happening.

Her hoarding wasn't rebellion.

It was *survival.*

Children in foster care often leave with only what they can carry. Possessions and stability aren't promised. Holding on meant safety; letting go meant loss.

And suddenly, I saw myself.

When I was twelve, my parents separated. I never entered foster care or suffered abuse, but in three years, our family of seven became two. The life I knew vanished. Resources and security changed. As the only girl among five siblings, I learned to hold things tightly—emotionally and materially.

Scarcity doesn't always come from poverty.

Sometimes it comes from a sudden absence.

As the week went on, Bethany pulled away—just as she had before. It's a familiar pattern at camp: by day two, children realize our love can't extend beyond the week. To protect themselves, they sever the attachment before it's taken from them.

On the final day, I spoke with her privately.

I told her God placed her where she was for a reason, that her new mom wasn't temporary, and that this relationship was meant to last. I acknowledged she was pushing me away and invited her to let her mother in fully.

I don't know what was rooted in her heart that day.

But I know what it uprooted in mine.

In 2018, as my father neared the end of his life, he asked if I could forgive him for leaving.

"I already have," I told him.

That wasn't true.

I didn't want him to carry my pain, so I spared him. But in doing so, I betrayed myself. I hadn't forgiven him—or *myself*.

Through Bethany, years later, God showed me the truth I avoided for decades:

I hadn't forgiven myself—for chasing the dream, for choosing the road, for building a life without marriage or children, for believing my father's leaving meant I was unworthy of being chosen.

And here's the deeper truth: I love my life and who I've become, and I also grieve the life that never unfolded.

Both truths can coexist.

Forgiveness isn't about erasing the past—it's about untying the identity we built around it.

I forgive my father for leaving. And now, finally, I forgive myself for the stories I carried, the survival strategies that outlived their purpose, and the choices that shaped my life as it is.

I am not a victim of those choices; I am their author.

A MOMENT OF GENTLE REFLECTION

Take a breath. Let your shoulders soften.

Now, allow yourself to be honest:

What choices have you made that led your life to look different from what you once imagined?

Where have you judged yourself instead of forgiving yourself?

What narrative about your worth have you unknowingly carried?

Now consider this:

If you fully forgave yourself here... what might become possible

- What would soften?
- What might open?
- What part of your heart could finally exhale?

THE SUBCONSCIOUS MIND

Much of our self-sabotage does not live in our conscious choices ~ it lives in the stories we tucked away for protection long ago.

Dr. Joseph Murphy wrote in *The Power of Your Subconscious Mind*:

> *"As you sow in your subconscious mind, so shall you reap in your body and environment."*

Forgiveness is not just spiritual—it's neurological, emotional, and cellular. When we forgive, we rewrite the scripts that quietly govern our decisions, release what drives us, and reclaim authorship of our future.

Unforgiven beliefs will always seek to protect us.

Healed beliefs allow us to thrive.

I once believed forgiveness was something I extended outward.

Now I know I must also extend this inward.

Bethany taught me that hoarding isn't about things—it's about safety. My subconscious showed me that my singleness wasn't about circumstances; it was about a story I'd never fully understood.

Forgiveness does not undo the past. It frees the future.

And in that freedom, a new kind of endurance begins to form.

Because once you forgive yourself... You no longer fight yourself.

And that is where perseverance is born.

A PRAYER FOR RELEASE

Dear God,

Thank you for the memories that reveal what I'm ready to heal.

Thank you for the courage to release what once protected me but no longer serves me.

Teach me how to forgive not only those who hurt me, but also the versions of myself who did what they could with what they knew.

Help me lay down the identities built in survival and rise into the truth of who You created me to be.
May forgiveness open the door to endurance, and endurance shape the life I now choose with intention.

Amen.

VICKI PARKER

Vicki Parker is a women's empowerment and wellness coach, innkeeper, entrepreneur, and connector of souls. With deep reverence for family and conscious living, she supports women in remembering who they are, reclaiming confidence, and cultivating authentic relationships.

Vicki is a certified NLP practitioner, licensed BANK Trainer and Coach, creator of the Unstoppable Confidence 5-Day Challenge, and an experienced speaker on emotional intelligence, feminine leadership, and frequency-based living. Known by her family as the "spark plug," she travels with intention, presence, and gratitude. She currently resides in the Cuyahoga Valley National Park, where she tends to both souls and spaces with care at The Inn at Brandywine Falls.

Author's Website: *www.VickiParkerUnlimited.com*

Charity Awareness: *www.MDA.org*

YURI CHOI

FORGIVENESS: THE ALCHEMY OF COMPASSION

About a decade ago, I found myself sitting cross-legged in a quiet Buddhist class in town. I was curious, but not fully convinced I *needed* to be there to learn something new. A friend had invited me to a session on kindness and compassion, and although I'd been exploring my spiritual path for years, part of me thought, *I've probably already learned this.* I had my yoga practice. I meditated. I journaled. I considered myself a pretty compassionate person.

So, I walked in thinking, *This will be sweet... affirming... maybe even boring.* I had no idea that by the end of that hour, something in me would shift forever. Not through some dramatic moment, but through a simple question that cracked me open in the most unexpected way. It dismantled long-held assumptions and forever changed the way I understand both forgiveness and compassion.

The teacher began with a quiet yet piercing truth: "Kindness and compassion are easy when life is soft. The true practice begins when the world feels unfair, violent, or deeply unjust." Then he asked a question that drew stillness into the room, "Can you extend compassion to everyone, equally?"

It was 2017. A terrorist had driven his car into a crowd in London. The collective grief was raw and tangible. I, too, felt the pain and the outrage. Then came a question that made the air shift. "Can you have compassion for the terrorist?"

The discomfort in the room was immediate. Some exchanged uneasy glances. Finally, one woman voiced what many were thinking: "You can't be serious." But he was. With calm conviction, the teacher invited us to expand our spiritual awareness—not in a way that condoned harm, but in a way that challenged the limits of our compassion. He asked us to explore what it means to hold compassion not just where it is easy, but where it feels impossible. Naturally, there was resistance. Why offer compassion to someone who caused harm? Would that not dishonor the victims? Would it not betray justice?

The teacher, steady and composed, offered a different lens. "I am not asking you to excuse the action," he said. "I am asking you to consider that people who cause pain are often the most disconnected from themselves. And if your compassion only extends to those you believe deserve it, is it truly compassion —or is it another form of control?" His words landed with weight and clarity. *It is easy to believe we are compassionate until life places us in moments where compassion feels nearly impossible.*

And I know this deep down: Spiritual maturity is not about comfort and just feeling *better*. It is about learning to hold complexity and seeing the world with greater depth. So, his question haunted me—in the best way. It is easy to identify the person who has been hurt as the victim. And yes, from a human perspective, that is true. And though through a spiritual lens, something more layered often appears. Those who harm others are often the ones most wounded themselves. *Hurt people hurt people.*

To carry that much pain and project it outward through cruelty requires a profound inner disconnection. Violence does not emerge from a whole and peaceful soul. It is the expression of pain that has gone unseen, unhealed, and unspoken for too long. This is not about minimizing the damage. Rather, it is about widening the lens and recognizing the root beneath the symptom.

Since that day of this profound realization, I have practiced a small, private ritual. Whenever I feel hurt, betrayed, or deeply triggered, I pause and ask myself: *What kind of pain might they be carrying to act this way?* I do not ask to excuse them. I ask to free myself. This question is often the doorway into forgiveness - not as a performance, and not as perfection, but as a conscious and sacred choice.

Forgiveness is not the same as forgetting. It is not about becoming silent, dismissing boundaries, or pretending things are fine. Forgiveness is not a weakness. It is power reclaimed. It is the sacred act of transmutation: bitterness into wisdom, rage into discernment, pain into purpose. To forgive someone is to take your power back. It is a declaration: You no longer get to shape how I love, how I feel, or how I move through the world.

Forgiveness is the shift from reacting to pain to creating peace. Unforgiveness is not just a thought; it lives in the body. It settles into our muscles, tightens our breath, and shows up in the way we speak, love, and protect ourselves. We believe we have buried it, but unprocessed energy does not vanish. It lingers, waiting for us to meet it with compassion so it can finally be released. That release is the true gift of forgiveness. It is not something we offer to others as much as it is something we offer ourselves. It is the softening that happens in a space where once there was tension. It is the transformation of contraction into expansion.

We live in a world that often celebrates outrage. Anger is labeled as strong. Bitterness is seen as justified. We rehearse the stories of how we were wronged, imagining what justice should have looked like. But peace does not arrive through punishment. And no apology—no matter how sincere—can create the freedom that only your willingness to let go can provide.

Forgiveness is not about them. It is about you. It is the quiet decision to no longer carry what weighs you down. It is a spiritual rebellion, a heart-led revolution, and a choice to embody peace in a world that often prefers pain. Is it a possibility that we are all here to remember who we truly are? Some remember through being hurt. Others, through the act of hurting. Most of us, through a complex combination of both in this beautiful journey of life. The true transformation begins when we choose not to let the pain close our hearts. When we stop waiting for others to free us and begin to free ourselves.

Forgiveness does not mean the past is erased. It means you no longer allow it to shape your future. It is not a spiritual trophy or a public performance. It is quiet. It is personal. It is deeply honest. Forgiveness is not the end of the story. It is the beginning of a new one. It offers our energetic field a blank slate, free from the weight of old imprints, heaviness, and emotional residue. It allows us to return to being carefree creators of our own lives. Forgiveness is not about forgetting. It's about remembering who you truly are, and choosing, moment by moment, to live from that knowing.

What if we chose freedom again and again, until peace became the rhythm we walk with, the frequency we breathe in? You don't need perfect words. You don't need closure. You don't even need them to make it right. All you need is a single moment of willingness, like a crack in the armor, a soft opening in the heart. What if that is enough for you to shift into what truly feels light in your body? Because it is through that opening that your soul begins to exhale.

Each time you choose forgiveness, you reclaim the energy that was scattered in pain, and you transmute it. *You become the alchemist.* You take what was heavy and turn it into light. You can turn what was sharp into soft, integrated wisdom. You can turn what was bound into liberation. And that is your soul's deepest longing: to be free, whole, and to be the energy of love. And this is who you really are.

Reflection Prompts

1. Who am I still carrying in my heart that I have not fully forgiven?

Is there a person, memory, or moment I am still energetically tied to? Have I withheld truth from myself, or avoided feeling something all the way through? I do not need to fix it. I simply need to witness it.

2. What pain might they have been holding?

Without excusing their actions, what might have shaped their behavior? What love, safety, or truth were they never given? What unmet need may have influenced their choices?

3. Where in my life am I still withholding forgiveness from myself?

Is there a version of me that acted out of fear or confusion? What would it feel like to meet that version with gentleness and say, "I love you anyway"?

YURI CHOI

Yuri is the Founder and creator of Yuri Choi Coaching. Choi is a performance coach for entrepreneurs and high achievers. She helps them create and stay in a powerful, abundant, unstoppable mindset to achieve their goals by helping them gain clarity and understanding, leverage their emotional states, and create empowering habits and language patterns.

She is a speaker, writer, creator, connector, YouTuber, and the author of *Creating Your Own Happiness.* Choi is passionate about spreading the messages about meditation, the power of intention, and creating a powerful mindset to live a fulfilling life. She is also a Habitude Warrior Conference Speaker and emcee, and she is a designated guest coach for Psych2Go, the largest online mental health magazine and YouTube Channel.

Her mission in the world is to inspire people to live leading with L.O.V.E. (which stands for: laughter, oneness, vulnerability, and ease) and to ignite people's souls to live in a world of infinite creative possibilities and abundance.

Author's Website: *www.YuriChoiCoaching.com*

Charity Awareness: *www.SurvivalToThrivalSeries.com*

FORGIVENESS

HABITUDE WARRIOR & INTEGRITY PUBLISHING EDITORIAL TEAM

Habitude Warrior International and Integrity Publishing International take great pride in our editorial team, who put their heart, sweat, and tears into each and every project and national bestseller! Thank you, team!

JON KOVACH JR.
Team Manager

Jon Kovach Jr. strives to assist every author and every team member in the process of self-development for ultimate success.

PAT MINTON
VP of Operations

Pat Minton has been with the Habitude Warrior International team for over 20 years getting her start with Brian Tracy & Erik Swanson.

JILLIAN KOVACH
Editorial Manager

Jillian is a vital team member of Habitude Warrior & Integrity Publishing, bringing her expertise in managing our Editorial Department.

To inquire about joining our team please send us an email to *team@HabitudeWarrior.com!*

FORGIVENESS